Logic, Argumentation & Reasoning

Interdisciplinary Perspectives from the Humanities and Social Sciences

Volume 21

Logic, Argumentation & Reasoning (LAR) explores links between the Humanities and Social Sciences, with theories (including decision and action theory) drawn from the cognitive sciences, economics, sociology, law, logic, and the philosophy of science.

Its main ambitions are to develop a theoretical framework that will encourage and enable interaction between disciplines, and to integrate the Humanities and Social Sciences around their main contributions to public life, using informed debate, lucid decision-making, and action based on reflection.

- Argumentation models and studies
- Communication, language and techniques of argumentation
- Reception of arguments, persuasion and the impact of power
- Diachronic transformations of argumentative practices

LAR is developed in partnership with the Maison Européenne des Sciences de l'Homme et de la Société (MESHS) at Nord - Pas de Calais and the UMR-STL: 8163 (CNRS).

Proposals should include :

- A short synopsis of the work, or the introduction chapter
- The proposed Table of Contents
- The CV of the lead author(s)
- If available: one sample chapter

We aim to make a first decision within 1 month of submission. In case of a positive first decision, the work will be provisionally contracted—the final decision about publication will depend upon the result of an anonymous peer review of the complete manuscript.

The complete work is usually peer-reviewed within 3 months of submission.

LAR discourages the submission of manuscripts containing reprints of previously published material, and/or manuscripts that are less than 150 pages / 85,000 words.

For inquiries and proposal submissions, authors may contact the editor-in-chief, Shahid Rahman at: shahid.rahman@univ-lille.fr, or the managing editor, Juan Redmond, at: juan.redmond@uv.cl

More information about this series at http://www.springer.com/series/11547

Larry Benjamin Miller

Islamic Disputation Theory

The Uses & Rules of Argument in Medieval Islam

Springer

Larry Benjamin Miller
Queens, NY, USA

ISSN 2214-9120 ISSN 2214-9139 (electronic)
Logic, Argumentation & Reasoning
ISBN 978-3-030-45011-3 ISBN 978-3-030-45012-0 (eBook)
https://doi.org/10.1007/978-3-030-45012-0

This Springer imprint is published by the registered company Springer Nature Switzerland AG
The registered company address is: Gewerbestrasse 11, 6330 Cham, Switzerland

To
Lulu and David
κοινὰ γὰρ τὰ τῶν φιλῶν
and
Rudolph Mach
οὐ γὰρ ἐμὸς ὁ λόγος

Foreword

Readers who, in the current volume, are first learning of this work and its author may be surprised to hear Larry Benjamin Miller's doctoral dissertation pronounced one of the more important contributions to Islamic Studies from the latter half of the twentieth century. This itself is a symptom of the considerable disciplinary void occasioned by its *not* being published—as it most certainly ought to have been—close after its acceptance in October 1984 by the Department of Near Eastern Studies at Princeton University. That is to say, *Islamic Disputation Theory* is a field-founding study of an essential discipline in Islamicate Intellectual History: the theory and practice of dialectic, as developed under such rubrics as *jadal, khilāf, munāẓara*, and the *ādāb al-baḥth*. But absent the publication of Miller's pioneering dissertation, its field of study has—until quite recently—lain dormant. It was therefore of considerable moment to learn that—after languishing for 35 years as an unindexed, typewritten photocopy—*Islamic Disputation Theory* was finally to be published; it was of considerable delight to be invited to write its preface.

Why is this such a seminal work? The reasons are many, and stem from the importance of the field which Miller explores as well as the qualities and insights of his exploration. Though a handful of respected Islamicists had scouted certain shallows and bays of the vast ocean of Islamicate dialectical theory and practice,[1] Miller was the first to sound its depths and sketch its coastlines in systematic fashion. His broad survey (though it was, and remains, impossible to be fully comprehensive),

[1] See Josef van Ess, "Disputationspraxis in der Islamischen Theologie. Eine Vorläufige Skizze," *Revue des Études Islamiques* 44 (1976): 23–60; *idem* "The Logical Structure of Islamic Theology," in *Logic in Classical Islamic Culture*, ed. G. von Grunebaum (Wiesbaden: Otto Harrassowitz, 1970): 21–50; George Makdisi, *The Rise of Colleges: Institutions of Learning in Islam and the West* (Edinburgh: Edinburgh University Press, 1981); *idem* "Dialectic and Disputation. The relation between the Texts of Qirqisani and Ibn ʿAqil," in P. Salmon (ed.): *Mélanges d'islamologie. Volume dédié à la mémoire de Armand Abel*, (Leiden: 1974–78), vol. I, pp. 201–206; Wolfhart Heinrichs, "Ǧadal bei aṭ-Ṭūfī, eine Interpretation seiner Beispielsammlung," in *Zeitschrift der Deutschen Morgenländischen Gesellschaft*, Supplement III, 1. (Wiesbaden: 1977), pp. 463–473; and G. Vajda, "Etudes sur Qirqisānī V: Les règles de la controverse dialectique," in *Revue des Etudes Juives* 122 (1963): pp. 7–74.

coupled with his logical analyses, revealed a series of rich and evolving genres of dialogical argument, directing us towards what, in the end, has proven to be a large and influential body of theory traditions cultivated in hundreds of treatises, commentaries, supercommentaries, and glosses.

As is now evident, dialectics is both an essential field and a powerful dynamic in premodern Islamicate intellectual history. Thousands of copies of disputation-theory manuscripts in collections the world over attest to this, as do hundreds of Muslim scholars—by speech and act—in their argumentative works, bio-bibliographies, and histories. Moreover, the elaboration of dialectical theory was both an interdisciplinary and transdisciplinary pursuit; currents of dialectical teachings and practices energized the argumentative domains of law, theology, philosophy, and grammar, permeating their boundaries and invigorating other disciplines besides.

As noted, the full purview of Islamicate dialectics may be too vast to entertain a truly comprehensive study; and as a field of study it is also too much in its infancy—although, since Miller's dissertation, a few scholars have made contributions of broad scope.[2] But even the most truncated historical overview of relevant literature, as follows, suggests the complex development and surprising radius of Islamicate dialectical theory.

From the beginning, we may observe an evolution from "proto-systems" of dialectical teachings and practices into "full-system" theory treatises, shaped by both the intradisciplinary objectives and interdisciplinary strategies of polymath dialecticians. The transition from pre- to early Islam witnessed a plurality of disputation practices infused with new Islamic axioms. A proto-system with regular disputation formulae is evident in the earliest extant works of religious scholarship, with an already sophisticated dialectic exemplified by such as Jaʿfar al-Ṣādiq (d. 148/765), Abū Ḥanīfa (d. 150/767) and companions, al-Shāfiʿī (d. 204/820), and others; law, theology, and grammar were forged in regular disputation.

Refutational treatises and *ikhtilāf* (disagreement) literature proliferated, and the transition from proto-system teachings to full-system theories is evident in the composition of *jadal* works by such as al-Jāḥiẓ (d. 255/868 or 9), Ibn Saḥnūn (d. 256/870), Ibn al-Rāwandī (d. 245/860 or 298/910), Ibn Surayj (d. 306/918), al-Tirmidhī (d. 279/892), Thaʿlab al-Naḥwī (d. 291/903), and others. By the end of the fourth/tenth century, full-system juristic dialectic had emerged in *jadal* treatises by such students of Ibn Surayj as al-Qaffāl al-Shāshī (d. 336/948 or 365/976) and in *uṣūl* and *khilāf* works by such as al-Karkhī (d. 340/952), al-Jaṣṣāṣ (d. 370/981), Abū al-Layth al-Samarqandī (d. 373/983), and others. At the same time, the systematization of dialectic in theological contexts continued—largely in reaction to Ibn

[2] See, in particular, Abdessamad Belhaj, *Argumentation et Dialectique en Islam: Formes et Séquences de la Munāẓara* (Louvain: Presses Universitaires de Louvain, 2010); Amir Dziri, *Die Ars Disputationis in der islamischen Scholastik: Grundzüge der muslimischen Argumentations- und Beweislehre* (Freiburg, Br.: Kalām, 2015); and chap. 2 of Khaled El-Rouayheb, *Islamic Intellectual History in the Seventeenth Century: Scholarly Currents in the Ottoman Empire and the Maghreb* (New York: Cambridge University Press, 2015).

al-Rāwandī[3]—with al-Balkhī (d. 319/931), al-Qirqisānī (d. after 325/937), al-Ashʿarī (d. 324/935), al-Māturīdī (d. btwn. 332–6/943–7), al-Qāḍī ʿAbd al-Jabbār (d. 415/1025), and others.

From philosophical circles, early encounters with Aristotelian dialectic were possibly enhanced through the logic of Ibn al-Muqaffaʿ (d. ca. 139/756) and a known early translation of the *Topics* by Nestorian Patriarch Timothy I (d. 207/823). Translations and commentaries on the *Topics* and/or *Sophistical Elenchi* were produced in the circle of al-Kindī (d. ca. 252/866), and by such as Isḥāq b. Ḥunayn (d. 298/910-11), Abū ʿUthmān al-Dimashqī (d. after 302/914), Abū Bishr Mattā b. Yūnus (d. 328/940), Yaḥyā b. ʿAdī (d. 363/974), and others, culminating in the expansions on these works by Abū Naṣr al-Fārābī (d. 339/950) and Ibn Sīnā (d. 428/1037). Entwined with rhetoric, a belletristic *jadal* theory was developed by Ibn Wahb al-Kātib (fl. ca. 335/946), while *jadal* theory for historiographical contexts is found in the work of Abū Zayd al-Maqdisī (fl. ca. 355/966).

The fifth/eleventh through seventh/thirteenth centuries saw a number of important developments. First, full-system juristic *jadal* evolved, reaching a high stage of remarkably detailed and comprehensive works by al-Shīrāzī (d. 476/1083), al-Bājī (d. 474/1081), Ibn ʿAqīl (d. 513/1119), al-Khaṭīb al-Baghdādī (d. 463/1071), al-Juwaynī (d. 478/1085), al-Ghazālī (d. 505/1111), and others. And in the juristic *ʿilm al-khilāf*, a pair of sub-genres emerged, with *Ṭarīqa* works by al-Marwazī (d. 461/1069), Raḍī al-Dīn al-Nīsābūrī (d. 544/1149), Fakhr al-Dīn al-Rāzī (d. 606/1209), Rukn al-Dīn al-ʿAmīdī (d. 615/1218), Sayf al-Dīn al-Āmidī (d. 631/1233), and others;, and *Taʿlīqa* works by al-Qāḍī Abū Yaʿlā (d. 458/1066), al-Qāḍī Abū Muḥammad al-Nasafī (d. 533/1138), Abū Manṣūr al-Barawī (d. 567/1172), and others. Other *khilāf* works were authored, as well, including a didactic poem by Abū Ḥafṣ ʿUmar al-Nasafī (d. 537/1142) which attracted no less than 17 commentaries. And it is in this period we see the root of a new, streamlined method of *jadal/khilāf* which—flowing from al-Nīsābūrī's *Ṭarīqa* to al-ʿAmīdī's *Ṭarīqa*, and thence to Burhān al-Dīn al-Nasafī's (d. 687/1288) *Fuṣūl*—was eventually universalized by Shams al-Dīn al-Samarqandī (d. 722/1322) as the new genre of the *ādāb al-baḥth*.

Elsewhere, full-system grammar *jadal* progressed; *ikhtilāf* literature not only flourished in law, but appeared in theology and even astronomy; and the influence of juristic *khilāf* method was evident even in medical disputation theory. Importantly, in the seventh/thirteenth century, juristic *jadal* evolved yet further, as exemplified by the works of al-Āmidī (d. 631/1233), Ibn al-Jawzī (d. 656/1258), Najm al-Dīn al-Ṭūfī (d. 716/1316), and others, receiving significant stimulation with the impressive commentary tradition on Ibn al-Ḥājib's *Mukhtaṣar* (eventually numbering over 90 commentaries and 40 supercommentaries and glosses).

Finally, several commentaries on the aforementioned *Fuṣūl* of Burhān al-Dīn al-Nasafī were composed, including one by his student Shams al-Dīn al-Samarqandī. And it was al-Samarqandī (as Miller first showed us) who adapted al-Nasafī's

[3] As Miller shows us at the start of his chapter on Theological Dialectic.

jadal/khilāf into his universalist dialectical theory works, the most famous being his *Risāla fī Ādāb al-Baḥth*. The *Risāla* was eventually to attract over 50 commentaries, supercommentaries, glosses, and superglosses, right into modern times. More importantly, it encouraged additional primary works with their own commentary traditions, often authored by eminent figures of post-classical Islamic intellectual history.

Thus, a new era in dialectic had begun by the eighth/fourteenth century. ʿAḍud al-Dīn al-Ījī's (d. 756/1355) single-folio *ādāb al-baḥth* treatise eventually attracted some 45 commentaries and glosses. An *ādāb al-baḥth* work attributed to al-Jurjānī (d. 816/1413) also attracted a handful—one is still taught today in the Dars-i Niẓāmī curriculum. And by the end of the tenth/sixteenth century, there had appeared at least eight more primary works, by such as Ṭāshkubrī Zādah (d. 968/1560), with over a dozen commentaries and glosses, and Muḥammad al-Birkawī (Birgevi; d. 981/1573), with around seven. Not only did commentaries on al-Samarqandī and al-Ījī flourish, but several spawned their own gloss and super-commentary traditions; for example, al-Shirwānī al-Rūmī's (fl. ca. 840/1436) commentary on the former garnered over 22 glosses with over a dozen super-glosses, while al-Tabrīzī al-Ḥanafī's commentary on the latter garnered ten glosses—one of which generated another ten super-glosses. Juristic *jadal* also continued to evolve in the works of Tāj al-Dīn al-Subkī (d. 771/1370), al-Zarkashī (d. 794/1392), and others. Writings on Ibn al-Ḥājib's *Mukhtaṣar* exploded with over 70 commentaries, many by luminaries—one by al-Ījī eventually attracting 20 glosses, including by such well-known figures as Saʿd al-Dīn al-Taftāzānī (d. 793/1390).

The eleventh/seventeenth through thirteenth/ninteenth centuries brought over 20 more primary *ādāb al-baḥth* works by such as Ḥusayn al-Adanavī (fl. 1070–90/1660–80), with a self-commentary having eight glosses, and Sājaqlī Zādah (d. 1145 or 50/1732 or 37), with nine commentaries, and a spate of didactic poems with commentaries. In the same period writings on the treatises of al-Samarqandī, al-Ījī, al-Birkawī, Ṭāshkubrī Zādah, and others continued to be produced. Certain Ottoman scholars—e.g., al-Sīvāsī (fl. 1109/1698), al-Tīrāwī (d. 1123/1711), and al-Ḥifnī (d. 1176/1763)—wrote commentaries and glosses on more than one primary work, while also contributing their own primary *ādāb al-baḥth* treatises. Finally, in the fourteenth/twenieth century, alongside commentaries on older treatises, over seven new primary *ādāb* works were composed. Some, like the *Ādāb al-Baḥth wa'l-Munāẓara* of Muḥammad al-Amīn al-Shinqīṭī (d. 1393/1973) remain quite popular.

Again, even a much-abridged chronological overview like the above exposes a rich set of evolving traditions with a broad scope of disciplinary applications. Moreover, being such a refined and ultimately rational body of discourse (it is, after all, about putting logic into dialogical practice), the whole of it—spanning well over a millennium—constitutes a major event in the history of thought. And for those who know anything about it, it was Larry Miller, in his *Islamic Disputation Theory*, who sank the first truly significant foundation stone for its study.

Significantly, Miller's dissertation delivered more than a survey and detailed analysis (important in its own right) of a significant portion of the above-mentioned authors and works. *Islamic Disputation Theory* is itself theory-forging—both directly, by presenting a new developmental theory, and indirectly, by exerting a new pressure on intellectual historians, through the application of new lenses and instruments, to recognize and accurately portray the argumentative glue holding entire disciplines together (and, importantly, weaving them seamlessly to each other): dialectic. More refined and accurate accountings of various trajectories in Islamicate intellectual history have been and can be made, subsequent to and drawing upon Miller's work. This is greatly facilitated by his study of what constitutes the real rational lexicon and argumentative grammar of Muslim intellectuals across five critical centuries and multiple disciplines.

In similar fashion, *Islamic Disputation Theory* is also paradigm-forging. Miller provides not only Islamicate dialectic's first historical trajectory for subsequent scholars to refine and build upon, but models of dialectical genre-categories, replete with logical analyses exposing the intertwining of variant but related trends in Islamicate argument theory. This is a handy resource for scholars at all levels who are approaching this imposing body of thought, and its equally imposing literary record, for the first time—or for the hundredth. I say "for the hundredth" because I have myself probably referred back to Miller over a hundred times; and each time I do, I rediscover some fresh insight he had revealed back in the early 1980s. This is certainly not a book that can be digested in one sitting; it must be kept at hand for repeated reference.

Likewise, *Islamic Disputation Theory* is method-forging. Miller practices an efficient technique for exploring difficult technical genres of logic and argumentation theory, sorting and defining distinct genres and trends through contentual and argumentative analysis. In so doing, he also accomplishes the invaluable service of procurement—of making available—bringing to light and summarizing important contributions from numerous difficult to obtain, yet vitally important, sources, several of which remain only in manuscript to this day.

Finally, *Islamic Disputation Theory* is lexicon-forging. Miller gathers together, translates, and brings to light for the first time the technical lexicon—and to an appreciable extent, the technical idiom—of a much-studied premodern discipline, a core *madrasa* topic. Once learned from Miller, these terms and manners of expression appear suddenly to the initiate like well-emblazoned markers stamped all throughout the rational literature of Islam. The terms, concepts, and idioms revealed and translated by Miller constitute the key to huge swathes of what could only otherwise be obscure and difficult argumentative material, in hundreds of important volumes. After reading Miller's dissertation, one returns to one's discipline (especially if it is within law, theology, or philosophy) with a new sight. The marks of dialectic are truly wherever argument is to be found in Islamicate intellectual history, i.e., everywhere.

Simply put, *Islamic Disputation Theory* should have been published 35 years ago, and it is a real shame that it was not. It ought to have been the foundation stone for a new, vital field for Islamic studies. Courses in Islamicate dialectics—with *Islamic Disputation Theory* as a primary reading—ought to have been taught across Islamic Studies institutions from the late 1980s through to this day, and by now there ought to be dozens of monographs and hundreds of articles in this vast field. In other words, Islamic Studies has suffered in the absence of this volume. Happily, however, it can now reach the wider audience it has long deserved, and the field can roll forward with new vigor.

Institute of Islamic Studies, McGill University Walter Edward Young
Montreal, QC, Canada
November 16, 2019

Preface

This book is a slightly revised version of my Princeton University dissertation which I completed in the spring of 1984 and submitted to the Department of Near Eastern Studies. Many of the works that I consulted were only available to me in the manuscript libraries in Europe and the Middle East. Many have since been edited and published. I have not been able to keep up with developments in Islamic studies and did not attempt to consult the printed editions of these manuscripts or more recent scholarship. I made a few changes to the final chapter and added some references that I had written in the margins of my copy of my dissertation.

I am hopeful that this revised edition will spark the interest of intellectual historians, medievalists, classicists, and philosophers.

I am also grateful to Dr. Walter Young for writing a foreword to this book to put it in a larger context.

The fact that this work is even being published at all is due to the efforts and encouragement of two people: my wife, Lulu (Elizabeth) Brotherton, and my lamented friend, David M. Eisenberg. It is to them and my revered teacher, Rudolph Mach, that I dedicate this slightly revised version of my dissertation.

Queens, NY, USA
May 29, 2020

Larry Benjamin Miller

Acknowledgments

This work could not have been written were it not for the financial support of the following institutions: The United States Information Agency, the American Research Center in Egypt, the German Academic Exchange Service (DAAD), and the Princeton Program in Near Eastern Studies.

The following scholars aided me by providing me with manuscripts and typescripts: Dr. J. Aguadé, Ms. C. Crofts, Mr. D. Eisenberg, Dr. M. Galston, Prof. D. Gimaret, Prof. R. Mach, Dr. J. Michot, and Dr. E. Ormsby and Dr. W. Young.

Various colleagues and friends offered advice and criticism during the composition of this work: Mr. D. Eisenberg, Prof. A. Hamori, Prof. R. Mottahedeh, Prof. C. Normore, Dr. E. Ormsby, Dr. R. al-Sayed, and Dr. T. Seidensticker.

To all of the above and to my teachers in Princeton and Tübingen (Dickson, Gaube, Halm, Hamori, Marks, Mottahedeh, Ullmann, and Voigt), I wish to express my gratitude.

My revered teacher, Rudolf Mach, suggested to me that I undertake a study of *al-Risāla al-Samarqandīya fī ādāb al-baḥth* and its commentaries in conjunction with Aristotle's *Topics*. His untimely death deprived me of a learned adviser and dear friend.

I am therefore extremely grateful to Professor Josef van Ess who kindly consented to fill in this great void by agreeing to advise this dissertation and to Professor Andras Hamori for taking on the role of my advisor at Princeton University.

Contents

1 **Introduction** 1

2 **Theological Dialectic (*Jadal*)** 3
Jadal, Speculation, and Truth 5
Question and Answer (The Four Questions) 8
Muʿāraḍa 17
The Signs of Defeat 20
The Rules of Jadal (***Adab al-Jadal***) 24
Conclusion 26

3 **Dialectic and Arabic Philosophy** 29
What Is Dialectic? 29
Dialectical Questions — Form and Content 36
The Rules of Debate 41
The Participants in the Debate 43
Jadal in Theology and Philosophy: An Overview 44

4 **Dialectic (Jadal) in Jurisprudence** 47
The Early Period 47
Question and Answer (The Four Questions) 49
Questions One and Two 50
Question Three: What Is Your Evidence? 52
Question Four: The Mode of Signification 57
Question Five: Objection 57
Muṭālaba (Request) 58
Iʿtirāḍ (Objection) 59
Muʿāraḍa (Counter-Objection) 59
Mumānaʿa, Manʿ 61
Fasād al-waḍʿ (False Construction) 62
'Adam al-ta'thīr (Ineffective *Ratio Legis*) 63
Qalb or *Ishtirāk fī al-dalāla* (*methodos kata peritropēn*) 65
Naqḍ or *munāqaḍa* (Inconsistency) 67

al-Qaul bi-mūjib al-ʿilla (Limited Acceptance) . . . 68
Farq (Distinction) . . . 69
Muʿāraḍa (Counter-Objection) . . . 70
The Order of the Objections . . . 71
The Signs of Defeat . . . 74
The Adab al-Jadal . . . 75
The "Middle" Period of Juristic Dialectics . . . 75
al-ʿAmīdī's *Irshād* . . . 78
al-Barawī's *Muqtaraḥ fī l-Muṣṭalaḥ* . . . 85
Three Other Texts . . . 89
The Final Period of Juristic Dialectics . . . 94
The Muqaddima of al-Nasafī . . . 95

5 The Ādāb Al-Baḥth . . . 103
al-Qusṭās . . . 105
The Introduction . . . 105
Section One: Definitions . . . 108
The Second Section . . . 115
al-Risāla . . . 120
On Definitions . . . 120
The Questions/Problems (*masā'il*) . . . 123

Conclusion . . . 125

Selected Bibliography . . . 127

Name Index . . . 135

Subject Index . . . 139

Chapter 1
Introduction

We are going to attempt to chart the evolution of Islamic dialectical theory (*jadal*) for a period of roughly four-hundred years. In this space there emerged three major genres of theoretical literature – theological, juristic, and general.[1]

The first writings that we have are theological. Similarities in form and content of these writings have allowed us to identify five chapters that were part of practically every theoretical work on the subject. The most important chapters were the two dealing with question and answer, and objection. We have assumed that the structure and contents of these works derive from a virtually unknown work by a famous theologian, Ibn al-Rīwandī. While trying to present a systematic account of theological dialectic, we, also, try to explain its theoretical implications. To this end, we have looked for parallels in philosophical and polemical literature written in Greek, and also included a chapter on how the Arab Aristotelians understood *jadal*.

The Islamic jurists took over the theological teaching on dialectics and applied it to jurisprudence. This can be seen in the way that they substitute their examples for theological ones. Perhaps more telling is their attempt to determine what is the proper order in which to bring the various objections; for, they inherited the precept of the theologians that questioning has a definite order.

Another indication of their dependence on theological dialectic is the emergence of the concept of praiseworthy and blameworthy dialectics (*jadal*). In the middle or late tenth century, we find authors who first mention this distinction and cite verses

[1]The division is suggested by Ibn Khaldūn in his *Muqaddima*, ed. M. Quatremère, 3 vols. (Paris: Institut Imperial de France, 1858), vol. 3, p. 23, line -7 ff.; pp. 24, line -6 ff. This has been translated by F. Rosenthal, *The Muqaddimah* (New York: Pantheon, 1958), pp. 30–34. The genres of dialectic have been discussed by A. Turki in two of his books: *Polémiques entre Ibn Hazm et Bagi sur les principes de la loi musulmane. Essai sur le littéralisme zahirite et la finalité malikite.* (Algiers: Société Nationale d'Édition et de Diffusion, 1976), pp. 32 ff.; and in his edition of al-Bājī, *al-Minhāj fī tartīb al-ḥijāj* (Paris: G.P. Maisonneuve et Larose, 1978), pp. 9 f.

L. B. Miller, *Islamic Disputation Theory*, Logic, Argumentation & Reasoning 21,
https://doi.org/10.1007/978-3-030-45012-0_1

from the Qur'ān in support of it.[2] However, when we look to the commentators, we find that they do not mention this distinction. Indeed, the first commentator to do so was a famous dialectician, Fakhr al-Dīn al-Rāzī.[3] By the eleventh century, however, the two greatest traditionists of the Islamic world, Ibn ʿAbd al-Barr and al-Khaṭīb al-Baghdādī, both mention it.[4]

In the stage after its initial assimilation, the teaching on dialectics either assimilated the rules of theological dialectics or dropped them. At times, however, chapters from the early period occur in later works. The major new influence on works of this period is that exercised by logic. Logical modes of thinking and devices are now introduced into books on juristic dialectics. In its final stages, according to the available texts, the old teaching was totally reformulated into general rules of procedure in a *juristic* debate.

It was out of this final stage that a new teaching emerged, a general teaching on disputation—the *ādāb al-baḥth*. It represents a synthesis of all that came before it.

For better or for worse, we have based this work almost entirely on primary sources, and not on reports from native bio-bibliographical sources. Thus, it is basically a literary study. For our purposes, it does not matter so much whether Ibn al-Rīwandī or anyone else was the first person to write on a given genre. Rather, of utmost importance has been the relationship between the genres and their common characteristics.

In our texts, it is sometimes difficult to say whether the author was a theologian or jurist for often he wrote on both subjects. We have, therefore, assumed that all our authors wrote according to the strictures and technical conventions of their subject-matter.

Concern with theoretical literature has caused us to neglect examples from other genres. It is hoped, however, that this study will facilitate the understanding of other related texts; for, the theoretical works that we are investigating undoubtedly served as models to be followed in composing reports of debates or even in presenting rational argumentation on a given subject.

---

[2] Isḥāq b. Ibrāhīm al-Kātib, *al-Burhān fī wujūh al-bayān*, ed. A. Maṭlūb and Kh. Ḥadīthī (Baghdad: Jāmiʿat Baghdād, 1967), p. 222, line 8 ff. al-Bājī, *Minhāj*, p. 8, line 6 ff. al-Juwaynī, *al-Kāfiya fī al-jadal*, ed. F. Ḥusain Maḥmūd (Cairo: Maṭbaʿat ʿIsā Ḥalabī, 1979), p. 22, line 10 ff. The main verses cited are Qur'ān 16/125; 29/46; 11/32; 4/109; 2/197; 43/58. It is probably that the close association of *jadal* with Islamic theology had made the jurists wary of it, especially in light of the experience of the *Miḥna*. Cf. G. Makdisi, *The Rise of Colleges* (Edinburgh: Edinburgh University Press, 1981), p. 108.

[3] Fakhr al-Dīn al-Rāzī, *Mafātīḥ al-ghaib*, 32 vols. (Cairo: al-Maṭbaʿa al-Bahīya al-Miṣrīya, 1934–62), vol. 5, p. 165, line 14 ff.; p. 167, line 14 ff. on Qur'ān 2/197.

[4] Ibn ʿAbd al-Barr, *Jāmiʿ bayān al-ʿilm wa-faḍlihī*, ed. ʿA. ʿUthmān, 2d ed., 2 vols., (Medina: al-Maktaba al-Salafīya, 1968), vol. 2, pp. 113 ff. al-Khaṭīb al-Baghdādī, *Kitāb al-faqīh wal-mutafaqqih*, ed. M. al-Anṣārī, 2nd ed., 2 vols. (Beirut: Dār al-Kutub al-ʿIlmīya, 1981), vol. 1, p. 230, line 8 ff.

Chapter 2
Theological Dialectic (*Jadal*)

Around the end of the ninth century, Ibn al-Rīwandī wrote a book entitled *Adab al-jadal*. About a generation or so later, Abū l-Qāsim al-Balkhī, known as al-Kaʿbī, also wrote a book on *jadal* in which he purported to correct errors that Ibn al-Rīwandī made in his work. This work was in turn refuted by al-Ashʿarī, the great theologian, who took up Ibn al-Rīwandī's cause against al-Kaʿbī's criticisms. So too another great theologian, al-Māturīdī defended Ibn al-Rīwandī.[1] But of the works just mentioned, none survives.

Fortunately, we have other sources at our disposal that allow us to reconstruct at least part of this earlier teaching. al-Qirqisānī, a Karaite Jew (d. after 937), has devoted a section of his *fiqh*-book to *jadal*, where he quotes a Muslim authority on the subject who may be Ibn al-Rīwandī.[2] About this time, an obscure Muʿtazilite,

[1] For information on the above works, see J. van Ess, "Disputationspraxis in der islamischen Theologie. Eine vorläufige Skizze," *Revue des Études Islamiques* 44 (1976): 31–2. I. Baghdatli, *Hadīyat al-ʿĀrifīn*, ed. R. Bilge and I. Inal, 2 vols. (Istanbul: Maarif Matbaasi, 1951–55), vol. 2, p. 36, line -2. For information on Ibn al-Rīwandī, see A. al-Aʿasam, *History of Ibn al-Rīwandī the Heretic* (Beirut: Dār al-Āfāq al-Jadīda, 1975), and his *Ibn al-Rīwandī in the Modern Arabic References* (Beirut: Dār al-Āfāq al-Jadīda, 1978–9), 2 vols. For information on the other authors, cf. F. Sezgin, *Geschichte des arabischen Schrifttums* 8 vols. at present (Leiden: E. J. Brill, 1967-), vol. 1. For al-Kaʿbī, pp. 622–3; for al-Ashʿarī, pp. 602–6; for Ibn al-Rīwandī, pp. 620–1.

[2] *K. al-Anwār wa-l Marāqib*, ed. L. Nemoy (New York: Alexander Kohut Memorial Foundation, 1939–43). Vajda and van Ess argue for this while Makdisi believes that he copied from Abū ʿIsā al-Rummānī (d. 994). But since al-Rummānī seems to have lived much later, it would appear that the former hypothesis is better. See G. Vajda, "Études sur Qirqisānī V," *Revue des Études Juives* 122 (1963): 9. Van Ess, "Disputationspraxis," pp. 31–2, G. Makdisi, "Dialectic and Disputation: The relation between the texts of Qirqisānī and Ibn ʿAqīl," *Mélanges d'Islamologie, Volume dédié à la mémoire de Armand Abel par ses collègues, ses élèves et ses amis*, ed. P. Salmon (Leiden:E. J. Brill, 1974): 201–6.

L. B. Miller, *Islamic Disputation Theory*, Logic, Argumentation & Reasoning 21,
https://doi.org/10.1007/978-3-030-45012-0_2

al-Maqdisī, included a chapter on *jadal* in his universal history.[3] So, too, his Shiʿite contemporary Abū l-Ḥusain Isḥāq b. Ibrāhīm al-Kātib, henceforth al-Kātib, discusses *jadal* in his book on the various types of explanation.[4] Ibn Ḥazm, the great Ẓāhirite jurist, also mentions it in his book on logic.[5] Finally, a manuscript has recently been brought to light in which Ibn Fūrak details al-Ashʿarī's teaching on the "*adab al-jadal*."[6]

It is on the basis of these writings that we are going to reconstruct the *jadal* works of the early tenth century. The thrust of our analysis will be to consider both the content and intention of the early works. To this end, we have found it useful to contrast this teaching with that of the philosopher al-Fārābī (d. 950). al-Fārābī is, indeed, no neutral observer. He is rumored to have composed a refutation of Ibn al-Rīwandī's book on *jadal*.[7] In the course of reconstructing the early works, we hope to shed more light on the grounds for this disagreement.

The sources that we just mentioned vary somewhat in respect to their content. However, there are five themes that are treated by practically every one of them: (1) the relation of *jadal* to speculation (*naẓar*); (2) question and answer; (3) counter-objection (*muʿāraḍa*); (4) the signs of defeat; and (5) the rules of conduct (see Table 2.1). In what follows, I shall discuss each theme in the order in which, I suppose, it appeared in the earliest treatment dating back to Ibn al-Rīwandī.

Numbers indicate order in which the themes appear in each author:

1. the relation of *jadal* to speculation (*naẓar*)
2. question and answer
3. counter-objection (*muʿāraḍa*)
4. the signs of defeat
5. the rules of conduct

---

[3] Muṭahhar b. Ṭāhir al-Maqdisī, *Kitāb al-bad' wal-ta'rīkh*, ed. and trans. C. Huart, 6 vols., (Paris: Ernest Leroux Editeur, 1899–1919), vol. 1, p. 18 ff. On him cf. Sezgin, *GAS* 1, p. 337.

[4] Isḥāq b. Ibrāhīm al-Kātib, *K. al-burhān fī wujūh al-bayān*, ed. A. Maṭlūb and Kh. al-Ḥadīthī (Baghdad: Jāmiʿat Baghdād, 1967), pp. 222 ff. It is translated by Vajda in "Études," pp. 54 ff.

[5] ʿAlī Ibn Ḥazm, *Kitāb al-taqrīb li-ḥadd al-manṭiq wal-madkhal ilaihī*, ed. I. ʿAbbās (Beirut: Dār al-ʿIbād, 1959), p. 182 ff. In my edition pages 179 and 189 have been reversed.

[6] Ibn Fūrak, "Mujarrad maqālāt al-shaikh Abī Ḥasan al-Ashʿarī, fol.141b: 14ff., MS.253 (tauḥīd), Maktabat Shaikh al-Islām ʿĀrif Ḥikmat, Medina. See, Sezgin, *GAS* 1, p. 611. For a detailed description of the text, see D. Gimaret, "Un document fondamental pour l'histoire de l'Ashʿarisme," (unpublished paper delivered at Orientalist Conference, Japan, 1983). Professor Gimaret is planning to publish an edition of the entire text.

[7] For the evidence, see van Ess, "*Disputationspraxis*," p. 31, note 4.

Table 2.1 Chapters of the *Adab al-jadal?*

Author	(1)	(2)	(3)	(4)	*(5)*
al-Qirqisānī	–	1	2	3	4
al-Maqdisī	1	2	3	4	–
al-Kātib	1	2	3	5	4
Ibn Ḥazm	1	2	–	3	4
Ibn Fūrak	1	2	3	4	5
al-Khaṭīb al-Baghdādī	1	2	3	4	5
Ibn al-Rīwandī	1?	2?	3?	4?	5?

Al-Khaṭīb al-Baghdādī, *Kitāb al-faqīh wal-mutafaqqih*, ed. I. al-Anṣārī, 2nd ed., 2 vols. (Beirut: Dār al-Kutub al-ʿIlmīya, 1980), 1:229 ff. ff. In this part, I am using his work and Ibn Ḥazm's to establish what the structure of the chapters of Ibn al-Rīwandī's work might have been.

Jadal, Speculation, and Truth

For the Islamic theologians, *jadal* (dialectics) is a valid method for attaining truth. It is a method used by God in disputing with the Jews, and a method which God taught (*addaba..bihī*) his prophet.[8] At times, it is synonymous with speculation, *naẓar*, and is, therefore, a duty, incumbent upon every Muslim or something highly recommended.[9] That type of *jadal* which deals with "ramifications of religion" (*furūʿ al-dīn*) as when a jurisconsult (*mujtahid*) gives a legal opinion (*fatwā*) is recommended; but that type which deals with the principles of religion (*aṣl*) such as the "non-eternity" of the world, the proof of the Creator's existence, and defending the truth against doubters is a duty incumbent upon every Muslim.[10] al-Ashʿarī reportedly said:

> *Jadal* and speculation are synonymous in the sense that the dialectician (*mujādil*) and speculator (*munāẓir*) and thinker (*mufakkir*) all use that which intellection (*fikra*) leads to; but they differ in that *jadal* is only possible when there are two people (involved) while speculation could result from one person since it could be intellection, consideration, reflection, or demonstration (*istidlāl*).... (According to one interpretation of *jadal*) when the speculator debates dialectically, his aim is to establish something hard and fast (*iḥkām*), and his method is to turn his opponent away from his (present) opinion to another one....(While according

[8] Ibn Fūrak, "Mujarrad," fol.142a: 20. al-Kātib, *al-Burhān*, p. 225, line 5 ff.; p. 235, line 2 ff. al-Maqdisī, *al-Bad'*, p. 50, line 5 ff. This was evidently a *topos* of the early interconfessional debate literature. Cf. G. Bardy (ed. and trans.) "Les trophées de Damas: controverse judéo-chrétienne du VIIe siècle," *Patrologia Orientalis* 15,2 (1920) p. 192, line 10. B. Voss, *Der Dialog in der frühchristlichen Literatur* (Munich: W. Fink, 1970), pp. 47, 50, 195. Van Ess, "Disputationspraxis," p. 45 ff.

[9] Ibn Fūrak, "Mujarrad," fol.142a: 17.

[10] Ibid., fol.142b: 10–12; 142a: 5–11; 142a: 18–19. The problem of whether the world is eternal or not is Aristotle's classic example of a dialectical problem. *Top.*104 b8. Vajda and van Ess have pointed out several instances in which theological *jadal* may have borrowed from Aristotle's teaching on dialectic. However, they conclude that there has been no direct borrowing. Vajda, "Études," 8 ff. Van Ess, "Disputationspraxis," p. 52–3. We agree with this position.

to another interpretation, it is that) the speculator grapples with his opponent (*muṣāriʿ*) and seeks to vanquish him.[11]

So, too, al-Kātib contrasts investigation (*baḥth*) with *jadal* since the investigator tries to base his premises "on premises that are more evident and more certain in his opinion" while in dialectic one bases the premises on what the opponent agrees to, even though this may not be evident to the intellect (*ʿaql*).[12] In the former one seeks proof, in the latter the opponent's assent.[13] Although both al-Ashʿarī's and al-Kātib's statements would tend to give Islamic *jadal* an Aristotelian flavor, we should keep in mind that *jadal* is in the service of the truth. al-Ashʿarī identifies it with "the command to do what is right and to forbid what is wrong (*al-amr bil-maʿrūf wal-nahy ʿan al-munkar*)," one of the slogans of the early Muʿtazila.[14] All the authors whom we have mentioned stipulate that *jadal* must be in search of the truth.[15]

Of course, if *jadal* is to lead to truth, it must have a strong epistemological foundation. al-Maqdisī discusses this epistemological basis in his chapter on *jadal*, where he attacks "the sophists whom Aristotle called heretics:"

> They denied all acts of knowledge, in principle, claiming that neither the acts of knowledge nor their objects had any basis in reality. They even went on to deny (1) what is perceived by the senses, (2) what is intellected and known *a priori*, (3) what is derived through demonstration (*istidlāl*). All these things, they claimed, were a matter of fancy and imagination (*ḥisbān, khailūla*)[16] just as when one dreams.

So, many people refrained from disputing with them.[17] Whoever did had a difficult task since they denied knowledge derived from the senses and *a priori* knowledge that needs no proof. Since the latter is the basis of the sciences, if someone sought to prove them, it would lead him to an infinite regress.[18]

The subject of al-Maqdisī's discourse is a familiar one to the student of Aristotle. In his *Posterior Analytics*, he mentions a group of people who deny the possibility

---

[11] Ibn Fūrak, "Mujarrad," fol.142b: 16 ff. Cf. al-Baghdādī, *al-Faqīh*, vol. 1, p. 229, line −4 ff.

[12] al-Kātib, *al-Burhān*, p. 224, line -1 ff. Cf. Ibn Ḥazm, *al-Taqrīb*, p. 182, line 9. Van Ess, "The Logical Structure of Islamic Theology," *Logic in Classical Islamic Culture*, ed. G. von Grunebaum (Wiesbaden: Harrasowitz, 1970), p. 25.

[13] al-Kātib, *al-Burhān*, p. 225, lines 3–4.

[14] Ibn Fūrak, "Mujarrad," fol.154b: 1–2. Cf. al-Juwaynī, *al-Kāfiya fī al-jadal*, ed. F. Ḥusain Maḥmūd (Cairo: Maṭbaʿat ʿIsā Ḥalabī, 1979), p. 529, lines 4–5. This testimony adds support to van Ess's thesis that this slogan played an important role in justifying the theological missionaries who held disputations in order to convert the non-believers. Van Ess, "Disputationspraxis," pp. 50–1.

[15] See above note 9. Cf. Ibn Ḥazm, *al-Taqrīb*, p. 185, line 20 ff. al-Baghdādī, *al-Faqīh*, vol. 1, p.230, lines 1–6; vol. 2, p. 25, line -1 ff.

[16] Could this distinction ultimately derive from Aristotle *De Anima* 433b29 where he distinguishes between two types of *phantasia*: *aisthētikē* and *logistikē*?

[17] al-Māturīdī, *Kitāb al-Tauḥīd*, ed. F. Kholeif (Beirut: Dar el-Machreq, 1970), p. 7, lines 7–8, says that "It is agreed that one should not argue with those who reject evidence of the senses (*ʿiyān*, lit. seeing)." He calls these people *munkir* or *mukābir*. On the latter term, cf. the signs of defeat below.

[18] al-Maqdisī, *al-Bad'*, p. 48, line 4 ff; trans. 44, line 2 ff. Cf. text 20, line -2 ff; 32, line 2 ff; trans. 17, line 17 ff. and 19, line 24 ff.

of knowledge, since there is no demonstrative knowledge of the first principles, upon which all other proofs are based:

> If then (1) there is no way to the knowledge of the first principles, then (2) there is absolutely no way for us to know the things that are *from* them. Indeed, there is no way to know anything properly speaking (*ʿalā al-ḥaqīqa*) unless, by God, in the manner of a hypothesis, and that is only so should they too exist.[19]

In this passage Aristotle mentions the very objections that al-Maqdisī brought as the last two claims of the sophists. al-Qirqisānī and al-Ashʿarī also maintain that knowledge must derive from indemonstrable premises.[20] Thus, al-Ashʿarī notes:

> The "way" (*sabīl*) of the objects of sense and knowledge is *necessary* when dealing with matters of the intellect, just as the "way" that things heard (*al-masmūʿāt*) and explicitly expressed (in writing) (*al-manṣūṣāt*) is when dealing with matters of the Law; inasmuch as they are the roots (*uṣūl*) and sources (*ummahāt*) (of all our knowledge). We reduce everything to them and when we reach them, our quest draws to a close (*intahā al-muṭālaba*), and it is improper for the questioner to ask "why is that?"[21]

al-Ashʿarī repeats the claim that knowledge of the senses and intellect must not always be subject to proof and adds the category of objects of religious knowledge to that category. Although Aristotle does not mention religious knowledge in his *Posterior Analytics*, he does mention knowledge of the senses. He stresses the importance of sense perception in providing the particulars that are used in induction to attain a knowledge of the first principles of the various sciences. To deny evidence of the senses, he notes, would also be to deny the possibility of knowledge absolutely.[22] Thus, all three claims of the sophists are discussed in the

---

[19] Aristotle *APo.* 72b13-15 in Arabic translation from A. Badawi, *Manṭiq Arisṭū*, 3 vols. (Beirut: Dār al-Qalam, 1980), vol. 2, p. 338, lines 3–5. Cf. *APo.* 75b5 ff. Cf. M. Ibn al-Muqaffaʿ, *al-Manṭiq*, ed. M. Dānishpazhūh (Tehran: Anjuman-i Shāhanshāhi-i Falsafah-iīrān, 1357), p. 67, line 9 ff.: "Some people contentiously objected (*shaghaba*) against what Aristotle said that…nothing is known except by syllogism (*ṣanīʿa*)." Cf. Yaʿqūb b. Isḥāq al-Kindī, *Rasāʾil*, ed. M. Abū Rīda, 2 vols. (Cairo: Dār al-Fikr al-ʿArabī, 1950–3), vol. 2, p. 302, bottom.

[20] al-Qirqisānī, *al-Anwār*, p. 70, line 4 ff. He reports the argument of al-Maqdisī's sophists and rejects it since we know *naẓar* and *qiyās* per se. *Qiyās* is the "reducing of a thing to its equal (*radduhū ilā naẓīrihī*)," and is in accord with necessary knowledge. Later (92, line 2 ff.) he notes that *qiyās* is based upon *uṣūl* that are not the result of *qiyās*. "Thus there is no infinite regress. This argument is similar to the one used with respect to acts of knowledge and intellectual analogy (i.e., syllogism) which are based on acts of knowledge derived from the senses." In commenting on Aristotle, Ammonius notes, "One cannot bring syllogisms about either the *noēta* or the objects of sense; instead they are about the things that are neither the one nor the other (*ta mesa*). For the *theologian* is not able to prove the *noēta* through syllogisms, but he uses *analogy* and this is reasonable. For syllogisms prove from the cause to the effects and from the more general to the more particular. But the *noēta* are more universal and prior to everything else….Similarly we do not prove by syllogism the objects of sense—e.g., that milk is white, since we know them per se. *In Aristotelis Analyticorum Priorum Librum I Commentarium*, ed. M. Wallies (Berlin: G. Reimer, 1899) *Commentaria in Aristotelem Graeca,* vol. 4, pt. 6, p. 25, line 12 ff.

[21] Ibn Fūrak, "Mujarrad," fol.139a: 15–17.

[22] Aristotle *APo.* 99b35 ff. Cf. A. Long, "Aristotle and the History of Greek Scepticism," *Studies in Aristotle*, ed. D. O'Meara (Washington, D.C.: Catholic University of America Press, 1981): 79–106.

Posterior Analytics. Truth-oriented *jadal* is related to the epistemology of Aristotle's *Posterior Analytics*.

It should be added that although the search for truth is a search for theoretical knowledge, it is still connected with the search for defending and "proving" the truth of Islam. This is doubtless connected with the probable *Sitz im Leben* of the practice of disputation in debates among the various religious communities about the true religion. Thus often enough, opinion or debate position is equivalent to "religion". "If they grant this, then they deny their religion".[23]

Question and Answer (The Four Questions)

For our authors, *jadal* is synonymous with question and answer.[24] The ultimate test as to whether something is proper to *jadal* is whether it falls into one of these two categories. Our authors identify four questions or rather question-types that are to be used in disputation. In what follows we shall begin by considering al-Maqdisī's account of the four questions and then turn to al-Qirqisānī's account.

al-Maqdisī begins his discussion of the four questions of dialectic by again associating *jadal* with speculation[25]:

The scholars who paved the way of speculation (*naẓar*) and disputation (*jadal*) for the theoreticians (*nuẓẓār*) set down a boundary for (determining) the one who went beyond or fell short of them. It made clear who deviated, who behaved peevishly (*taʿassuf*),[26] he whose opinion was faulty, as well as the faults of his evidence (*baiyina*). They laid down four sorts of questions, none of which is subject to truth or falsehood since they are inquiring (*istikhbār*)[27] into:

1. What the opinion is (*mā'īyat al-madhhab*).[28]
2. The evidence (*dalīl*) for it.[29]

---

[23] E.g. al-Bāqillānī, *Tamhīd*, ed. McCarthy, p. 63, line 18.

[24] E.g., al-Kātib, *al-Burhān*, p. 225, line 16 ff.

[25] al-Maqdisī even titles this section "Discussion of the stages of speculation (*marātib al-naẓar*) and its rules (*ḥudūdihī*)," in *al-Bad'* p. 50, line 11.

[26] Ibid., 50, line 13. This word is used in the Arabic translation of Aristotle to translate Greek *duskolainein* at *Top*. 160b3. In Badawi, *Aristū*, vol. 3, p.750, line 1.

[27] Cf. Ibn Fūrak, "Mujarrad," fol.143a: 3 ff., "He said the meaning and essence of questioning (*al-su'āl*) are asking for information (*istikhbār*)." Ibn Fūrak notes that this definition only applies to "dialectical questioning" since "questioning" has a much broader meaning. (It could mean "to beg.") Cf. Abū Hilāl al-ʿAskarī, *al-Furūq fī al-lugha*, 2nd ed.(Beirut: Dār al-Āfāq al-Jadīda, 1977), p. 28, line -8 ff. al-Juwaynī, *al-Kāfiya*, p. 70, line l.

[28] Cf. Ibn Fūrak, "Mujarrad," fol.143a: 12–13: "the first question is about the opinion. It is asking 'What do you say about that?'"

[29] Ibid., fol.143a: 12-3: *an yuṭāliba bil-dalāla ʿalayhī*.

3. The cause (*al-ʿilla*) or the "manner [*wajh*] of the cause".[30,31,32]
4. The Verification of the Cause (*taṣḥīḥ al-ʿilla*).[33]

The last question is the final distinction of speculation (*nihāyat fuṣūl al-naẓar*)[34] and the establishment of the correctness of the thesis (*daʿwā*) or its falsehood.[35]

Let us consider the final three questions. al-Maqdisī has previously explained what he means by *dalīl*:

> It is whatever points out the *quaesitum*...whatever it may be from among the things (*maʿānī*) by which we obtain the object of evidence (*madlūl*). This evidence can be used to show that "x" is the case, as well as to show that "x" is not the case.[36]

For al-Maqdisī, the rising of the sun would be evidence for the statement "it is day," as well as evidence against the statement "it is night." The cause (*ʿilla*) on the other hand is the "necessary reason (*al-sabab al-mūjib*)"or, more literally, the reason that necessitates that "x" is so. al-Maqdisī distinguishes two types of causes, religious-juristic (*sharʿīya*) and intellectual:

> Intellectual cause is that which *per se* necessitates and exists simultaneously with the effect: for example, an act of motion and the moving object ....But religious-juristic cause is that which is newly applied to a thing that has existed prior to this cause, and has had another cause previous to this new one. The new cause changes the thing's juristic status (*ḥukm*).[37]

---

[30] Ibid., fol.143a: -1: *al-muṭālaba bi-wajh al-dalāla*. Cf. Abu ʿAli ʿUmar al-Shakuni, *ʿUyūn al-munāẓarāt,* ed. S. Ghurab (Tunis: 1976), p. 25, #26.

[31] Al-Bāqillānī in his *Tamhīd* illustrates this question when he argues against certain Muslims who maintain that events are influenced by the heavens in that God made them signify [dalāla] what would come about in the world during their various conjunctions. "This is nonsense [khabaṭ wa-takhlīṭ]. For if the sign [dalīl] is connected with the signified [madlūl] then the manner that it is connected [*wajh al-taʿalluq*] must be well known, as for instance in the way that the art of writing is connected with the writer and that the person who produces a piece of writing be [at that time] knowledgeable. Or as novel events signify what is unprecedented... and miracles the veracity of their authors and all such things where the manner of the connection between sign and signified is known." This is not the case in astrology. Ed. McCarthy, p. 57–58. Cf. p. 209–210 [*hādhihi ḥīra wa-qillat dīn wa-īthār lil-takhlīṭ*].

[32] The reference to the "manner of the connection" of the sign to the signified refers to this third "question" and is frequently found in reports of debate or even theological arguments of the kalam style. Thus the Qāḍī ʿAbd al-Jabbār argues that Scriptural injunctions [khiṭāb] signify that God is Omnipotent and All-Knowing, even though "the manner of its signifying [wajh dalālatihī] is based on God's being .... *Al-Mughnī*, vol. XVII, p. 8.

[33] Ibid., fol.144a: 6 ff.: "*ijrā' al-ʿilla ... taṣḥīḥuhā....*"

[34] Or perhaps the last "chapter" or sort of question used in speculation.

[35] al-Maqdisī, *al-Bad'*, p. 50, line 11 ff.; trans. 46, line 9 ff.

[36] Ibid., 30, line 12 ff.; trans. 27, line 12 ff. Cf. Ibn Fūrak, "Mujarrad," fol.138b: 17 ff.: "He said that the meaning of *dalīl* and *dāll* was like that of *ʿalīm* and *ʿālim* in that the former derives from *dalāla* and just as *ʿālim* derives from *ʿilm*, so too does *ʿalīm* (derive from it). He said that *dalāla* is a sign (*ʿalāma*) whereby the signifier (*al-dāll*) indicates the *significatum* (*madlūl*). This sign can be an indication (*ishāra*), effect (*athar*), or a legal qualification that necessitates another (*ḥukm muqtaḍā*)."

[37] al-Maqdisī, *al-Bad'*, p. 31, line 14 ff.; trans. 28, line 18 ff. Cf. van Ess's discussion of this passage in "Logical Structure," p. 36.

The "intellectual cause" is what Aristotle called the efficient cause. Not surprisingly, the discussions that occur seem to concern the juristic-religious cause exclusively. The evidence and "cause" are closely related. al-Maqdisī differentiates between the two:

> Evidence is what leads to and points out a thing, while cause is what necessitates it and brings it into being. One obtains the thing (sought) through evidence, not through the cause, since the cause must also be obtained and (first) becomes known through the evidence. There may be varying evidence to prove that "x" exists and this evidence may cease to exist. But causes cannot vary; when the cause ceases to exist, so too must the effect.[38]

Al-Maqdisī uses terminology reminiscent of Aristotelian logic but the circle of his ideas is a popular type of theological reasoning from the known to the unknown, or from the phenomenal to the non-phenomenal, or simply analogical reasoning (*qiyās*).[39] As we shall see, however, it is connected with Stoic logic.

In this method, a person demonstrates that two things are to be treated as equal because they share a certain "quality" (*ṣifa*) due to a certain (*ʿilla*) cause.[40] In order for this cause to be valid, it must always be accompanied by this "quality." There were certain stock examples: an act of building (*binā'*) requires a builder (*bānin*), an act of writing requires a writer.[41] It was for this sort of reasoning that al-Kaʿbī criticized Ibn al-Rīwandī:

> (Another chapter concerning the *kalām* about arguing (*istishhād*) from the known to the unknown and it contains what al-Ashʿarī mentioned in refuting al-Balkhī [i.e., al-Kaʿbī] in respect to the objections that he brought against Ibn al-Rīwandī in which he claimed to correct the errors that Ibn al-Rīwandī made in his *Adab al-jadal*. This is what he said about it.):
>
> Ibn al-Rīwandī said in his *Adab al-jadal*: "If a moving-thing moves *due to* an act of motion (*lil-ḥaraka*), then it is necessary to judge that every moving-thing moves *by* an act of motion (*bi-ḥaraka*)."

---

[38] al-Maqdisī, *al-Bad'*, p. 35, line 11 ff.; trans. 32, line1 ff. al-Maqdisī's reasoning here is reminiscent of Aristotle's distinction between proof and cause in *APo*. 89 b21 ff.

[39] al-Maqdisī, *al-Bad'*, p. 34, line 1 ff., 36, lines 10–11. Cf. Ibn Fūrak, "Mujarrad," fol.139a: 5 ff. al-Ashʿarī calls this process *istishhād*. al-Fārābī discusses this procedure and identifies it with induction (*istiqrā'*) and applying the cause to the effect (*ijrā' ḥukm al-ʿilla fī al-maʿlūlāt* a method used by "our contemporaries." This method he says is of no use in establishing the judgment (*ḥukm*) although it is of use in destroying it. The method is not suited to jurisprudence since there such a strict procedure is deleterious. al-Fārābī, "Kitāb al- qiyās al-ṣaghīr," ed. M. Türker, Ankara Üniversitesi Dil ve Tarih Cografya Fakültesi Dergisi 16 (1958) pp. 269 ff.; cf. p.282, line 11 ff. and 286, line 7 ff. Aristotle *APr*. Book II.24.

[40] Al-Maqdisī, *al-Bad'*, p. 34, line 1 ff.; trans. 30, line 24 ff. Ibn Fūrak, "Mujarrad," fol.140a: 8 ff. al-Ashʿarī gives several examples of this, one of which is that it "… is when a thing that is known (*fī al-shāhid*) has some attribute (*ṣifa*) due to some cause and that there exists no sign (*dalīl*) that a "thing given this attribute" (*mauṣūf*) "in the unknown" has it for any other reason that this very cause; then, it must necessarily be judged that everything "in the unknown" that has this attribute has it on account of that cause."

[41] Al-Maqdisī, *al-Bad'* 28, lines 13–14; Ibn Fūrak, "Mujarrad," fol. 139b: 10–16.

> Al-Balkhī criticized Ibn al-Rīwandī for this statement. He said: "Were this necessary with respect to the moving-thing and the act of motion, then this would also apply to the one who knows (about this motion) and his act of knowledge. But (this is not the case since) the moving-thing is known to be moving by one thing (*bi-amrin*) and is known to have an act of motion by another. This is like the knower who is known to be knowing (*'ālim*) by one indication (*dalīl*) and *then* is known to have an act of knowledge *after* that by means of another indication…."
>
> Our Shaikh Abū l-Ḥasan (al-Ash'arī) spoke about this. He criticized what al-Balkhī said and verified what Ibn al-Rīwandī said….[42]

In the above passage, Ibn al-Rīwandī uses the method of analogical reasoning to assert that every moving thing has an act of motion. This sort of generalization was known as applying the cause to its effects,[43] al-Maqdisī's fourth question, for, al-Maqdisī understands his fourth question, the verification of the cause, as making sure that the cause is commensurable:

> When there is a discrepancy in its correspondence to the effect, it can no longer be considered to be the cause. For instance, when we suppose that a substance (*'ain*) or religious prescription (*ḥukm*) exists for some reason, then if this substance or prescription should continue to exist when the "cause" ceases to exist, or the "cause" continue to exist when the substance or prescription cease, (it cannot be considered the cause). The rules that govern the soundness (*ṣiḥḥa*) of a cause are the same as those for definitions (*ḥadd*). In fact most people call "cause" definition and this is not far-fetched.[44]

al-Maqdisī makes a very strong claim for his causes: that they are commensurate and convertible with their effects.[45] But this was a typical claim of the theologians of this period.[46]

This method of reasoning by the use of signs shows remarkable similarity to that used by the Epicureans. The emphasis on the "manner of connection" in the third question is reminiscent of the emphasis on the connection of consequence (*akolouthia*) held between a sign and its significatum.[47]

Al-Qirqisānī gives a slightly different account of the four questions, one which is more in line with al-Ash'arī's terminology, and perhaps, with Ibn al-Rīwandī's:

---

[42] Ibid., fol.151a: 18 ff. This passage is the only direct quotation from Ibn al-Rīwandī's work. It is difficult to know exactly where this argument appeared in his work. It would seem possible that he had a chapter on arguing from the *shāhid* to the *ghā'ib*. One thing, however, is clear: the issues treated in the book were theological. Cf. 'Abd al-Qāhir al-Baghdādī, *Uṣūl al-Dīn* (Istanbul: Maṭba'at al-Daula, 1928), p. 30, line 9 ff.; p. 36, line -1 ff. R. Frank, *Beings and their Attributes* (Albany: State University of New York Press, 1978), pp. 12–13.

[43] Ibn Fūrak, "Mujarrad," fol.140a: 7 (*ṭard al-'illa fi al-ma'lūl*). Cf. above note 37.

[44] Al-Maqdisī, *al-Bad'*, p. 32, line 1 ff.

[45] Ibid., 29, line -1 ff.

[46] Van Ess, "Logical Structure," pp. 37–9.

[47] Cf. M.F. Burnyeat, "The origins of non-deductive inference", in *Science and Speculation*, ed. J. Barnes, J. Brunschwig, M. Burnyeat, M. Schofield (Cambridge: Cambridge University Press, 1982) p. 212–7 and note 58 referring to M. Frede, *Die Stoische Logik* (Gőttingen, 1974) note 49, pp. 81–2.

There are four types of question. Question is a kind of inquiry (*istikhbār*)...the questions are:

1. The whatness of the opinion (*mā'īyat al-madhhab*) since you ask first, "What is your opinion about such and such?"
2. The whatness of the proof (*burhān*), since you say, after the first question, "...What is your proof?"

The first two questions are only seeking information: Q should not contaminate them by bringing objections (*ṭaʿn*) against R's opinion or by explaining the falsity of R's belief[48]; however, in the last two types of question, objections and (claims of) falsity occur:

3. Request for the mode in which the proof signifies the opinion (*muṭālaba bi-wajh dalālat al-burhān ʿalā al-madhhab*).
4. Asking R to apply his cause to the various individual effects (*akhdh al-mūjib bi-ijrā' ʿillatihī fī maʿlūlātihā*.[49]

Al-Qirqisānī's account is important not only for its terminological difference with al-Maqdisī's but because it also mentions an important distinction—objection only occurs during the last two questions. This in effect divides the debate into two parts: one in which Q is seeking information from R, and a second in which Q does his best to refute R's opinion.[50]

Al-Qirqisānī also informs us as to why the four questions must be asked in precisely the order in which he presents them. Citing his source, he says:

> The evidence (*dalīl*)[51] that this order (*tartīb*) is correct, is that you do not ask for proof of an opinion until you know what it is or you ask about it. As for the proof that you ask R to show the commensurability of the cause with its individual effects *only* after asking for the proof's mode of signification, is that you only get to it after having first conceded R's claim that the evidence (*dalīl*) indicates his thesis; for, it is only pursuit of a ramification of the opinion and its alleged cause. But you only pursue a ramification after you have granted the

[48] *ʿaqaduhū* must be in the sense of *iʿtaqadahū*. Vajda translates "la faussete de sa construction," in "Études," p. 14, lines 7–8. But see Ibn Fūrak, "Mujarrad," fol. 143 a: 15, "ka-naḥwi man ʿurifa min iʿtiqādihī wa-madhhabihī."

[49] Al-Qirqisānī, *al-Anwār*, p. 471, line 6 ff. Vajda, "Études," pp. 13–4. For the lst question, Vajda refers to Aristotle *Topics* 110a29 ff. and *APr*. 40b17,55. However, there may be a Stoic influence. Van Ess has pointed out the relation between Stoic reasoning from signs ("Logical Structure," pp. 26–9, 33–4). Here we are reminded of the criterion of connectedness, *sunartēsis*, that stipulates that x cannot be a sign for y if y, the signified, exists without it. See Philodemus, *On Signs*, ed. P. and E. de Lacy (Naples, 1978) in Philodemus: *On Methods of Inference*, (Naples: Bibliopolis, 1978), Vol. I, 1–19, p. 156, and 210. The de Lacys also refer to Galen XVIII B 640, 643–5. Cf. al-Qirqisānī, *al-Anwār*, p. 358, line 10 ff. *Doubt and Dogmatism*, ed. M. Schofield, M. Burnyeat, and J. Barnes (Oxford: Clarendon Press, 1980), index s.v. *sunartēsis*.

[50] On this division, see below on juristic dialectic.

[51] The Arabic word "dalīl" is notoriously difficult to translate, because it is used here as evidence, indication, sign or proof.

> ramification under discussion (*al-mufarra*ʿ).[52] That is to say, you do not ask the opponent about the ramifications of his opinion or cause except after having granted them (tacitly). If you had not granted them, you would have objected to what he had claimed about them and would have asked for proof of their validity. This shows that if you ask your opponent to apply his causes to their respective cases (*mawāḍi*ʿ) before you demand the mode of signification, you grant his claim that they establish his opinion, and you ask him to apply his opinion to a case which is similar to it in sharing the same cause.[53] In granting something as a cause without first asking for a proof, you in effect neglect a necessary question[54] and go on to the next question, either through negligence, or in order to out-trick your opponent, or on account of your lack of ability and ignorance.[55] The proof is that you say to R, "I concede that your cause necessitates this opinion, but it also necessitates that you apply it to something that comes more quickly to mind than your original opinion, in the manner in which it signifies the latter's validity. Therefore, either show how the two cases are both true or both false, and otherwise explain how they differ (*fa-afriq baynahumā*)."[56]

That al-Qirqisānī's source was Ibn al-Rīwandī is suggested by the similarity between his reasoning and that of al-Ashʿarī on the problem of skipping from the third to fourth question.[57] Indeed, that our sources report virtually the same questions in the same order[58] indicates that there was method behind their order, and that this order and the questions themselves derive from a single source.

We have alluded to the difference between theological and philosophical dialectic. For the non-philosophers, the aim of "attaining the truth" outweighs the aim of the philosophers to "defend any position or thesis without contradicting oneself."[59]

For al-Kātib, as we have seen, one must try to get the opponent to accept one's proof by getting him to agree to its premises. But the entire operation of getting the opponent to agree is secondary to the primary intention of attaining the truth. For our authors, the questions of dialectic are questions that seek knowledge, epistemic, and not logical questions, although the latter may be of use in debate.

---

[52] The Arabic words literally mean branches or branch out of and therefore are translated as "ramification" rather than consequence(s).

[53] al-Qirqisānī, *al-Anwār*, p. 472, line 7 read: *al-mushārika lahū fīhā*. Cf. al-Maqdisī, *al-Bad'*, p. 34, line 1. The reference is to analogical reasoning.

[54] al-Qirqisānī, *al-Anwār*, p. 472, line 8 read: *taqaʿu bi-tilka mas'alatun lāzimatun*.

[55] Ibn Fūrak, "Mujarrad," fol.145b: -1 ff.: "He may ask him to apply it. This can occur as a sort of trick or on account of Q's inability to dispute P's cause, or his ignorance, or because he treats him lightly, or in order to annex to his cause some opinion that does not hold, or in order to force R, in the process, to reject evidence of the senses or intellect." The above point may have been part of Ibn al-Rīwandī's treatment.

[56] al-Qirqisānī, *al-Anwār*, p. 471, line 16 ff. Vajda, "Études," pp. 14–5.

[57] Cf. above note 50 and compare the language of his four questions with that of al-Ashʿarī in notes 28–31 above.

[58] Al-Kātib does not list the questions but he does mention them. Cf. *al-Burhān*, p. 225, line -2 (*mā al-madhhab*); p. 227, line 8 ff. (*ṭard al-ʿilla*); p. 226, line 3 ff. (*ṭalab al-ʿilla*).

[59] Ibid., p. 235, lines 5–8; al-Kātib criticizes Ibn al-Rīwandī for arguing both sides of the question. But this criticism may be directed against his books in which he put plausible arguments in the mouths of opponents of Islam (in order to refute them?). Cf. J. van Ess, "Ibn al-Rīwandī or the making of an image," *al-Abḥāth* 27 (1978): 5 ff.

This distinction is brought out rather nicely by al-Qirqisānī. He appends to his account of the four questions of disputation (*jadal*) the following report:

> The logicians (*aṣḥāb al-manṭiq*) have an opinion about questioning that the dialecticians (*jadalīyūn*) do not mention. But we should mention it, since it is necessary, of great benefit in questioning and since it also prevents much trouble in debate. They said there are two types of questions: restrictive (*ḥajr*) and non-restrictive (*tafwīḍ*).[60]

But who are these logicians and where do they get this teaching from? The answer is rather curious for those people who suppose that the study of Arabic logic begins with al-Kindī or al-Fārābī or the translations of the late ninth and early tenth centuries; for, the source of this teaching is Aristotle's *De Interpretatione* according to the "translation" of Ibn al-Muqaffaʿ! There we encounter the following statement:

> He said: It is fitting that we should know that there are two sorts of questions. One of them is called restrictive (*mas'alat al-ḥajr*) and the other non-restrictive (*mas'alat al-tafwīḍ*). The restrictive question is one in which the answer to it is a part of it. For example, if someone asks, "Was it so, or not so?" then the proper reply would be to answer, "It was really so" or "It was not really so." For, indeed, what he said in response was a part of the questioner's question. This type of question is called restrictive since the questioner proposes *two or more things*, as if it were that one of them must be the case, and he prevents (*yaḥjuru ʿalā*) the respondent from going beyond these (i.e., the various possible answers proposed in the question) to some other answer (not mentioned in the question).

For example, one asks, "How is John?" and the respondent replies by saying, "So and so." There occurs nothing in this response that was a part of the question.[61] The translator then goes on to explain how one should respond to imperfectly formulated restrictive questions. In Aristotle, the distinction between the two kinds of questions is a distinction between dialectical and scientific ("what is?") questions. The distinction that we have in the old translation is one that derives from the Greek rhetoricians, who, using this passage as their basis, distinguished between *erōtēma* and *pusma*. *Erōtēma* is a question to which one can reply "yes" or "no," while *pusma* is an [open-ended] question that requires a long reply.[62] The distinction is also known to and used by John of Damascus.[63] He mentions the *erōtēmatikos* question that differs from the *pusmatikos* in that the former has a short answer, while the latter requires a long and time-consuming answer. A recently edited anonymous commentary on Aristotle's *De Interpretatione* comments on this passage:

---

[60] al-Qirqisānī, *al-Anwār*, p. 472, line 13 ff. Vajda, "Études," p. 16; at 16, line 7 read *ḥajr* for *ḥasm*. The distinction is also mentioned in Ibn Fūrak, "Mujarrad," fol. 143b: 2ff. There it occurs after discussion of the "third question." There is a curious parallel for this term in Alexander of Aphrodisias, *In Aristotelis Topicorum libros octo commentaria*, ed. M. Wallies, "CAG" vol. 2, pt. 2 (Berlin: G. Reimer, 1891), p. 540, line 10: *ou gar apokleiei (!) hē proeirēmenē erōtēsis tēn toiautēn apokrisin*.

[61] Ibn al-Muqaffaʿ, *al-Manṭiq*, p. 51, line 5 ff. Aristotle *De Int*. 20b26–7.

[62] See the references in H. Lausberg, *Handbuch der literarischen Rhetorik* 2 vols. (Munich: M. Hueber, 1960), vol. 1, pp. 380–1.

[63] John of Damascus, *Die Schriften des Joannes von Damaskus*, ed. B. Kotter, 4 vols. (Berlin: de Gruyter, 1969-) vol. 1, pp. 134, lines 6–8; 172, lines 22–5 and Kotter's references.

> He wishes to distinguish how a dialectical question *dialektikē erōtēsis*) differs from a question of information (*pusmatikē*). To the former, one answers yes or no or nods assent or disagreement, while in the latter case, one needs more arguments (*logoi*) and cannot use the previously mentioned responses. An example of the latter would be "Who and from whence are you among men?"[64]

The anonymous commentary preserves the distinction between dialectical and non-dialectical questions. al-Fārābī also commented upon this passage. He clearly preserves and articulates the distinction that Aristotle made. He knows that there is a choice question (*mas'alat takhyīr*) used in dialectic, where one must choose between contradictory *alternatives*, and that this sort of question differs from the question "what a thing is," since the latter is a question used in logic or science and not in dialectic. "The person who uses non-restrictive questions in dialectic is either seeking instruction, or to deceive (*mughālaṭa*) or simply does not understand what dialectic is."[65] Ammonius treats this question in the same manner as al-Fārābī.[66] He distinguishes between the questions of dialectic that are contradictory alternatives (i.e., precisely two choices, "x" or "not-x") where one must select one part (*morion*) of the contrary alteration (*antiphaseōs*) in reply, and the "what is question" where the questioner is seeking either instruction or guidance.[67]

---

[64] *An Anonymous Commentary on Aristotle's De Interpretatione* ed. L. Taran (Meisenheim am Glan: A. Hain, 1978) p. 90, line 5 ff.

[65] Al-Fārābī, *Sharḥ li-kitāb Arisṭū fī al-ʿibāra*, ed. W. Kutsch and S. Marrow (Beirut: Imprimerie Catholique, 1960), p. 147, line 11. Cf. F. Zimmermann, *al-Fārābī's Commentary and Short Treatise on Aristotle's De Interpretatione* (Oxford: Oxford University Press, 1981), p. 142. Cf. above note 50.

[66] Of course, this only means that al-Fārābī probably follows Ammonius's interpretaion.

[67] Ammonius, *In Aristotelis De interpretatione commentarius*, ed. A. Busse (Berlin: G. Reimer, 1897), in "CAG," vol. 4, pt. 5, p. 203, line 12; cf. 199, line 19 ff. Cf. Alexander of Aphrodisias, *Topicorum commentaria*, to *Top*. 101b23. In his commentary on the *Topics* al-Fārābī remarks, "Rhetorical and sophistical questions and objections are erroneously used in dialectic. Similarly, many people err in using epistemic questions in dialectical conversation although they are unaware of this…." al-Fārābī, fol.217a ff. MS.231 TE41, Bratislava, unpublished typescript of M. Galston. Aristotle, Ammonius, and al-Fārābī all speak of contradictory alterations. But the translator speaks of "two or more choices." This mistake in translation left room for opponents of Aristotle's logic to formulate their attack. The attack focuses upon the fourteenth chapter of Aristotle's *De Int.* where Aristotle claims that the contradictory of any given statement is more contrary than the affirmation of the opposite of the original statement. That is to say the statement "John is just" is more contrary to the contradictory statement "John is not just" than it is to its proper contrary "John is unjust" where "unjust" is affirmatively predicated of John. This doctrine was subject to controversy among the philosophers; the theological attack has other grounds and far-reaching implications. On this attack, cf. Zimmermann, *al-Fārābī*, p. lxxxvi, cxxv. Van Ess, *Frühe Muʿtazilitische Häresiographie, Zwei Werke des Nāshi' al-Akbar* (Beirut: F. Steiner, 1971), text 118, line 2 to 119, line 6. where at 118, line 12 read *bi-ghairi juz'aihī*. Cf. Ibn Fūrak, "Mujarrad," fol.143b: 9–11: Q can posit a restrictive question in which R cannot answer by affirming a "part" of what he mentioned in his question. This is as when Q asks about someone who is neither sitting nor standing, "Is he standing or sitting?" and the only answer would be to say "He is neither standing nor sitting…."

al-Qirqisānī offers the questions of the "logicians" as an alternative to the "four questions." But if one considers the four questions in light of the logicians' questions, one sees that they belong to the *pusmatic* type—they seek information. So too, the emphasis on the order in which the questions should be asked points to their belonging to the category of "scientific" questions.[68] These last two facts suggest that if we are to look for the origins of the teaching of the four questions, we should look to writings on science and scientific inquiry.

In his *Posterior Analytics* Aristotle mentions four questions of scientific inquiry:

> There are four things that we seek. One of them is (1) that it exists and the other is (2) why; (3) if it is, (4) what is it....Since we ask first, "Does it exist?"...and if we know that it exists, we then ask "For what reason (*sabab*)?"
> When we ask, "Why is it (*lima huwa*)?" or, "What is it (*mā huwa*)?" we are looking for the middle term .... Therefore, it is necessary in all our inquiries to seek the middle term and what it is; for the middle is the *cause* (*ʿilla*).[69]

According to Greek commentators, Aristotle's questions are really two sets of questions, one referring to complex *quaesita* and the other to simple ones. In the former one seeks the cause, in the latter the definition.[70] Turning back to the "four questions," we note that the first question concerns establishing the opinion's existence or essence, while the other three concern proving its cause. al-Kātib remarks that *jadal* essentially concerns the cause (*ʿilla*).[71] Now of course this evidence is by no means conclusive. However, in view of our authors' agreement with Aristotle about the sources of our knowledge, their concern with truth and not refutation, and given the widespread knowledge of this passage from Aristotle's writings,[72] one must at least allow that there is some sort of connection.

In searching for the truth, through *jadal*, the theologians did not always walk the straight line of Aristotelian logic. This of course damned them in the eyes of the Arabic philosophers on two counts: firstly, that they applied the method of science to dialectical matters, and secondly they were inconsistent in applying the method; thus, bringing about a confusion over the distinction between the methods of dialectic and science.[73] This point is illustrated by a "trick question" that al-Qirqisānī and al-Ashʿarī report, and that undoubtedly was contained in Ibn al-Rīwandī's book:

---

[68] Cf. the previous note and our chapter on philosophical dialectic below.

[69] Aristotle *APo*. 89b23 ff. Badawi, *Arisṭū*, vol. 2, p. 427 ff.

[70] Badawi, *Arisṭu*, p. 427, notes 1–3, 6. John Philoponus, *In Aristotelis Analytica Posteriora commentaria*, ed. M. Wallies, "CAG" vol. 13, pt. 3 (Berlin: G. Reimer, 1909), p. 336,line 4 ff. Themistius, *Themistii quae fertur in Analyticorum priorum librum I paraphrasis*, ed. M. Wallies, "CAG," vol. 5, pt. 1 (Berlin: G. Reimer, 1900), p. 42, line 4 ff.

[71] Al-Kātib, *al-Burhān*, p. 225, line 15. Al-Māturīdī notes that disputation, *munāẓara*, concerns the essence (*mā'īya,hastīya*) of a thing, in his *Tauḥīd*, p. 7, lines 7–8.

[72] For a detailed discussion see A. Altmann and S. Stern, *Isaac Israeli, A Neoplatonic Philosopher of the Early Tenth Century* (Oxford: Oxford University Press, 1958), pp. 10 ff.

[73] Cf. Abū Ḥaiyān al-Tauḥīdī, *al-Muqābasāt*, ed. T. Ḥusain (Baghdad: Maṭbaʿat al-Irshād, 1970), pp. 203 ff.: I asked Abū Sulaymān (the logician), "What is the difference between the methods of the theologians and that of the philosophers?" He replied, "It is evident to every discriminating

> Have you ever considered something true and later found that it was false? If so, what makes you so sure that you are not in such a position now?[74]

al-Qirqisānī, al-Ashʿarī and al-Kaʿbī all report one answer: that this objection can be used against Q and so it has no effect.[75] Al-Qirqisānī also reports another answer: that if I do change my opinion it is only due to some objection to my evidence.[76] For al-Fārābī, however, this is no trick question. Rather it is a question that aims at determining whether R really knows that his claim is true or whether it is merely a belief. He mentions the answers that al-Qirqisānī gives, saying that they are unsatisfactory "owing to their lack of familiarity with the methods of demonstration."[77] The claim that this question can be used against Q is "a lie and absurd."[78] If Q knows that his beliefs are beliefs, then they are not destroyed by this question. Furthermore, if Q possesses certain knowledge, then no question whatsoever can destroy it.[79]

Muʿāraḍa

With the development of systematic *jadal* based on the four questions, there arose a new problem—how to deal with the old techniques of disputation? How did they fit into the new system? If *jadal* is essentially question and answer, then do techniques such as counter-objection (*muʿāraḍa*) and distinction (*farq, faṣl*) fit in? The problem of what belongs to *jadal* proper is discussed by al-Qirqisānī in his treatment:

> Chapter fifty-nine: on the sorts (of speech) used in theological discussion (*kalām*). Most of the theologians are of the opinion that there are four sorts: question; answer; objection; and distinction. Some of them claim, however, that there are six sorts: the four we just mentioned and two others—foundation (*ta'ṣīl*) and ramification (*tafrīʿ*).[80]

---

person of sound mind, understanding, and education that their method is based upon measuring one expression against another (i.e., *qiyās*) through the testimony of their "intellect" or without it at all. They rely upon *jadal* and what first comes to the senses, or what observation judges, or whatever notions combined with fancy and imagination occur to them.... All this is connected with fallacious reasoning (*mughālaṭa*) and repelling and silencing the opponent with whatever happens to be at hand...." Cf. 205, line 13 ff. al-Fārābī, *Risāla fī al-ʿaql*, ed. M. Bouyges (Beirut: Imprimerie Catholique, 1936), p. 11, line 16 ff. Cf. above to note 17.

[74] Al-Qirqisānī, *al-Anwār*, p. 487, line 12 ff. cf. 68, line 9 ff. Vajda, "Études," p. 40.

[75] See preceding note. Ibn Fūrak, "Mujarrad," fol.149b: 11 ff. ʿAbd al-Jabbār, *al-Naẓar wal-maʿārif*, ed. I. Madkour, *al-Mughnī fī abwāb al-tauhīd wal-ʿadl*, vol. 12 (Cairo: Wizārat al-Thaqāfa wal-Irshād al-ʿĀmma, 1964?), p. 202, line 21 ff. Cf. al-Maqdisī, *al-Bad'*, p. 52, lines 5–6. N. Rescher, *Dialectics* (Albany: State University of New York Press, 1977), pp. 84 ff.

[76] Al-Qirqisānī, *al-Anwār*, p. 487, lines 15–17.

[77] Al-Fārābī, *Kitāb al-Khaṭāba*, ed. Langhade and Grignaschi (Beirut: Dar el-Machreq, 1971), pp. 45 to 51, line 12.

[78] Ibid., p. 45, line 9.

[79] Ibid., p. 47, line 3.

[80] Al-Qirqisānī, p. 470, line 14 ff. Vajda, "Études," p. 13.

While all our early sources report that there is no disagreement about the role of question and answer in dialectic, when it came to counter-objection, there was controversy: a group of theologians denies the use of counter-objection. They argue that it is neither question nor answer.[81] The proponents of counter-objection maintained it was a question and argued by example:

Q: Do you believe in Muhammad?
R: Yes.
Q: What is your evidence (*dalīl*)?
R: The agreement (*iṭbāq*) of the Muslims, that one should believe in him.
Q: Do you believe in Jesus, then?
R: No.
Q: If you only believe in Muhammad due to the agreement of the Muslims that one should believe in him, then you should further believe in Jesus since the Muslims agree that one should believe in him.[82]

The last remark made by Q is plainly not a question, although it could easily be turned into one. Its author, al-Ashʿarī or Ibn al-Rīwandī, argues, however, that it is a question:

> The way that counter-objection is connected with questioning (*su'āl*) is that if Q brings as a counter- objection that P should believe in Jesus (*idhā ʿāraḍahū*) then this is asking for a reply (*istikhbār*) that he say this.

It is called counter-objection because it is a question that occurs subsequent to a (directly) preceding claim. Every counter-objection is a question but not vice versa.[83]

Neither al-Qirqisānī nor al-Ashʿarī give definitions of *muʿāraḍa*, perhaps because Ibn al-Rīwandī did not or because the phenomenon was so clear so as not to need an explanation. al-Maqdisī does give a definition: "It is setting down (two things as) equal and comparing them to each other."[84] Applying this definition to al-Ashʿarī's example, we see that Q has forced R to set on equal footing his belief in Jesus and

---

[81] Ibn Fūrak, "Mujarrad," fol.146A: 6–7. Cf. al-Qirqisānī, *al-Anwār*, p. 475, line 7 ff. Vajda, "Études," p. 20. al-Kātib, *al-Burhān*, p. 229, line 3. al-Maqdisī, *al-Bad'*, p. 32, lines 13–4. (These last two sources are also given by Vajda in note 2 above, p. 20. For another discussion of this phenomenon, see van Ess, "Disputationspraxis," pp. 42–4.

[82] Ibn Fūrak, "Mujarrad", fol.146a: 13–16. al-Qirqisānī, *al-Anwār*, p. 475, line 9 ff., where the example is made more Jewish—believing in Moses and Aaron.

[83] Ibn Fūrak, "Mujarrad," fol.146a: 16–18. This passage also clears up the meaning of al-Maqdisī, *al-Bad'*, p. 32, line −2 ff: The person who has been subjected to *muʿāraḍa* must either reply or admit his inconsistency (read *munāqaḍatihī*); should he abstain from replying to the *muʿāraḍa* then R could abstain from answering any question since Q seeks information (read (*mustakhbir*) and the person subjected to *muʿāraḍa* must give information (*al-muʿāraḍ mukhbir).* Goldziher suggested reading *mustajīb, mujīb* in "Bemerkungen zu Huart's Ausgabe des *K. al-bad' wal-ta'rīch* von al-Balchī," *Zeitschrift der Deutschen Morgenländischen Gesellschaft* 54 (1900): 400.

[84] Al-Maqdisī, *al-Bad'*, p. 32, lines 11–12 reading *wa-maʿnā al-muʿāraḍ (wa) al-muqābala ʿalā al-siwā wal-mumāthala*. If the "wa" is not dropped then the last word does not fit in. Further, in the beginning he seems to promise to define *muʿāraḍa* (p. 8, line -3 ff.). Cf. al-Qirqisānī, *al-Anwār*, p. 476, line 11: *al-taswīya*.

Muhammad. Although the example and definition are clear, the explanation that *muʿāraḍa* is a type of question is clearly wanting. The establishment of counter-objection as a firm part of dialectics was only accomplished much later.

Our authors give many different examples of this phenomena; however, al-Maqdisī is the only one to give a "systematic" account:

There are four types of counter-objection of which three are valid:

1. Question to question: e.g., If Q asks, "What do you say about x?" R says "What do you say about y?"
2. Thesis (*daʿwā*) to thesis: e.g., If R says that the world is eternal *a parte ante*, then Q asks "What is the difference between (*mā al-farq*) you and someone who claims that the world is created in time (*muḥdath*)?"
3. Cause (*ʿilla*) to cause: e.g., A monotheist says to a "corporealist," "If you say the Creator is a body because it is impossible to think of any non-corporeal actor, then why do you not say He is complex and composite, since all bodies are such?"
4. Proof (*dalīl*) to proof: e.g., Q says "If you prove that y is the case on account of x, what is the difference between you and someone who claims that y is the case on account of q?"[85]

These examples are interesting for they finally do present *muʿāraḍa* as a question. But the systematic garb is deceiving. al-Maqdisī outright rejects the first kind, while the second kind is controversial—al-Qirqisānī, al-Jubbā'ī, al-Kaʿbī and al-Maqdisī all accept it, while al-Ashʿarī and Abū Hāshim both reject it.[86]

In the course of presenting examples of *muʿāraḍa*, al-Qirqisānī also argues for its being a valid part of *jadal* from another perspective: "The one who uses counter-objection asks for a distinction between the two theses; however, this is nothing more than asking for a proof (*dalīl*) that confirms his thesis and refutes yours."[87] Even if we grant al-Qirqisānī's thesis, then we might still object that devoting a separate chapter to *muʿāraḍa* is superfluous since the topic is covered by the second and third of the "four questions." The question, however, is not superfluous if we assume that Q is not obliged to have an opinion of his own, which he is trying to defend—if he is only interested in silencing his opponent or proving that his "system" is inconsistent. Such an assumption points to *muʿāraḍa* as being part of the "native" pre-systematic techniques of disputation. When systematization finally came, this technique was too important to ignore. Everything possible was done to bring it into the new system, even though the arguments brought forth cloud the difference between it and distinction (*faṣl*, *farq*).

The stock of theological examples used to illustrate it also points to an earlier period when there were frequent debates between Muʿtazilites and various Islamic and non-Islamic opponents.

---

[85] Al-Maqdisī, *al-Bad'*, p. 33, line 3 ff.

[86] Ibid., p. 33, lines 2–5. Ibn Fūrak, "Mujarrad," fol.146b: 15. al-Qirqisānī, *al-Anwār*, p. 478, line 18 ff. al-Juwaynī, *al-Kāfiya*, p. 421, lines 1–3.

[87] Al-Qirqisānī, *al-Anwār*, p. 479, line 6 ff.

A later author, Abū Hilāl al-ʿAskarī (d. after 1010) contrasts *muʿāraḍa* with the fourth question (applying the cause to its effects). In the latter, he says, Q admits R's reasoning from the cause (*iʿtilāl*); this is not true of *muʿāraḍa*.[88] If we take al-Maqdisī's third example (cause against cause), we see that if the "corporealist" were willing to grant that God is complex and composite, then the counter-objection would fail. Counter-objection tests P's willingness to apply his reasoning systematically, while the fourth question tests the cause's commensurability to all instances of the given category. But this in turn leads to another problem.

In viewing the consistency of a given position within R's entire system of beliefs, Q might be charged with changing themes in the middle of a dispute. Changing themes (*intiqāl*), however, is one of the traditional indications of defeat. Thus, the technique of counter-objection is vulnerable on at least two fronts.

The Signs of Defeat

All our sources discuss the signs of defeat (*dalāʾil al-inqiṭāʿ*). Table 2.2 gives an overview of the signs of defeat according to our authors. A close study of Table 2.2 reveals that there is hardly any connection between the signs of defeat and the four questions.[89] The diversity of the signs points to their being taken from the practice of debate. This does not mean that they are not or cannot be given in a specific order.

If we consider al-Qirqisānī's list, we detect a principle that gives order to the signs of defeat, viz., the possible answers to any question. One must think along the lines of alternative propositions. Either R answers or he is silent. If he is silent, then this is due to his incapacity or to some other reason. If the former, then he has lost. If he does answer, then he either answers properly or not. If he does not answer properly, then he has either given an inadequate or unjustifiable answer (as in denying necessary evidence). An inadequate answer would be one in which he contradicts his original thesis, or does not answer the question at all, and, instead, moves on to some unrelated topic. al-Qirqisānī, however, explicitly applies these signs to both R and Q; presumably, because every question has a corresponding answer, so

---

[88] Al-ʿAskarī, *al-Furūq*, p. 55, line 20 ff. MS.804 (Lugha), Dār al-Kutub al-Miṣrīya [=MS.1279(Lugha), Alexandria and MS.258 Taimūr, Dār al-Kutub al-Miṣrīya all read *iʿtilāl*. At the bottom of the page one should add: "*fa-qul innahā muḥdatha li-anna ḥadathahā mutaṣauwar fī al-ʿaql fa-lā yutaṣauwar fī al-ʿaql mā lā ḥaqīqa lahū*." For al-ʿAskarī, see Sezgin, *GAS* 8, pp. 183–5. The method of *muʿāraḍa* is similar to that of the *methodos kata sugkrousin* of classical rhetoric, which consisted in placing the various charges of the plaintiff alongside one another and showing their inconsistency. R. Volkmann, *Die Rhetorik der Griechen und Römer* 2nd ed. (Leipzig: B. Teubner, 1885), p. 244, line 6 ff. Van Ess compares it with the *methodos kata peritropēn* in his "Disputationspraxis," pp. 53–54. See also van Ess, "Logical Structure," p. 41.

[89] On these questions cf. above.

Table 2.2 The signs of defeat

Signs	*al-Qirqisani*	al-Maqdisi	al-Ash'ari	al-Kātib
1. Silence	1	6	4	1
2. Peevishness	2	4	–	3
3. Contradiction	3	1	2	–
4. Digression	4	2	5	4
5. Appeal to crowd	–	5	–	–
6. Commensurability	–	(8)	1	–
7. Reductio ad absurdum	–	(7)	3	–
8. Distinction	–	–	6	
9. Answer other question	–	–	7	–
10. Incapacity	(4)	3	8	2
11. Mental confusion (khabaṭ, takhlīṭ)	5	–	–	–

Numbers indicate order in which they appear in each source (Al-Qirqisānī, *al-Anwār*, p484, line 20ff. Vajda, "Études," p. 34 ff., gathers together the signs from al-Maqdisī and al-Kātib but fails to note that al-Maqdisī's discussion goes on; cf. *al-Bad'*, p. 51, line 11ff. At the end of his study, Vajda offers an anonymous Hebrew Karaite fragment of the six signs of defeat wherein the title *re'iyyah* is made equivalent to *ḥaqīrāh* and *derīshah.* He suggests that the first term must render Arabic *kalām*, while the others might be terms of Jewish jurisprudence [(it is an expression normally used to signify painstaking (legal) examination (of evidence)]. In our view, however, *re'iyyah* is a literal translation of *naẓar* while the other terms are equivalent to either baḥth or faḥṣ or *taftīsh*

too must every sign of R's defeat have a corresponding one of Q.[90] Let us now turn to some of the individual signs of defeat.

Silence would seem to be an appropriate sign of defeat but one might ask why it is qualified with the phrase "on account of incapacity (*al-sukūt lil-ʿajz*)."[91] This is illustrated by a *ḥadīth* that al-Ashʿarī relates, in one of his other writings, about an encounter between ʿAbdallah b. al-Zibaʿrā and the Prophet. The former poses a question and the Prophet is silent, "…not in the manner of someone who is unable to reply (ʿajz), nor of someone who has been defeated in debate (*munqatiʿ*) but because he was astounded at the man's ignorance."[92]

al-Qirqisānī's second sign of defeat is "denial of necessary knowledge, rejection of evidence from the senses, and peevishness in debate."[93] This is apparently an old

[90] On this type of reasoning, see van Ess, "Logical Structure," pp. 40–1. al-Qirqisānī, *al-Anwār*, p. 485, lines 18–19; al-Maqdisī, *al-Bad'*, p. 51, line 3.

[91] Al-Qirqisānī, *al-Anwār*, p. 484, line 20; al-Maqdisī, *al-Bad'*, p. 51, line 5. Ibn Fūrak, "Mujarrad," fol.154a: 11.

[92] Al-Ashʿarī, *R. fī istiḥsān al-khauḍ fī ʿilm al-kalām*, ed. R. McCarthy, *The Theology of al-Ashʿarī* (Beirut: Imprimerie Catholique, 1953), p. 94, line 2 ff. For other versions of this story see the Qur'ān commentary of al-Ṭabarī to 21/101.

[93] Al-Qirqisānī, *al-Anwār*, p. 484, line 20 ff.: "*jaḥd al-ḍarūrāt wa-daf al-mushāhadāt wal-mukābara wal-buht.*" al-Maqdisī, *al-Bad'*, p. 51, lines 12–3: "*jaḥd al-ḍarūra wa-daf al-mushāhada.*" al-Kātib, *al-Burhān*, p. 242, line 1: "*al-mukābara wa-jaḥd al-ḍarūra* (correction in Vajda, "Études," p. 35)." Al-Bāqillānī refers to certain opponents who don't employ peevishness in disputation [*mimman la yaʿtamid al-buht fi al-munāẓara wal-mudāfaʿa*].

technique. Thus, we read in a protocol of a debate between Theodore Abū Qurra and a "Saracen," Theodore has the Saracen say, "Persuade me that you are right not by evidence from them (Isaiah and Matthew) but from necessary and agreed upon principles (*anagkastikōn kai homologoumenōn koinōn ennoiōn*)."[94] This "sign" also has a parallel in Aristotle. In the *Topics* he speaks about people who question contentiously and who, when responding, fail to grant what appears to be true (*mē dous ta phainomena*).[95] He also talks about people who behave peevishly (*duskolainontes*) in not granting the premises that Q seeks and about others who "refuse to grant an argument although unable to provide a counter instance nor an argument to the contrary.[96] Alexander of Aphrodisias calls this sort of behavior peevishness (*duskolia*).[97] It is conceptually the same as *mukābara*.

Examples of this sign of defeat are very common in theological literature. Al-Bāqillānī provides an example of this in his *Tamhīd*. The Barahima and the Muʿtazilites claim that speculation (*naẓar*) is something requisite upon all human beings, for through it one learns that one should thank ones benefactor and abstain from ingratitude [i.e. towards God]. In short, it is the mind, *ʿaql*, that uses speculation in establishing one's duties to man and God. Against this position, al-Baqillānā objects that "if this were so, then all people with sound minds would have to share in it, and be unable to deny [*jaḥd*] it since they would necessarily affirm statements based upon direct evidence of the senses [*mushāhada*] and incorrigibility [*iḍṭirār*]. But that various peoples deny their claims shows that their knowledge is not a priori.[98]

Of course appeals to the phenomena are not always accepted as self-evident. Al-Bāqillānī argues elsewhere against the partisans of "the nature of things"— people, who like the Greek natural philosophers, the *physikoi*, maintained that there is no God other than nature, and that they know this a priori. Thus they know through their senses and a priori [*ḥissan wa-iḍṭirāran*] that burning and drunkenness are the results of the heat of fire and the potency of alcohol. Their claim is misplaced since there are various opinions about what *causes* the burning and drunkenness. Some for instance claim that they are initiated by God. Others, that it is an act of the man who brings the fire to bear or drinks the alcohol. "But if there is a difference of opinion, how can they claim that they grasp its nature [*ḥaqīqa*] by means of the

[94] In J. P. Migne, *Patrologia Graeco-Latina* (Paris: Garnier, 1857–66), vol. 97, p. 1556b5-7 cf. 1553a2-3. Cf. Philoponus, *In APr.*, p. 2, line 27: "hai koinai ennoiai ex hōn ho sullogismos aei alētheis kai autopistoi." The concept of *koinai ennoiai* is Stoic. Cf. M. Pohlenz, *Die Stoa* 2 vols. (G öttingen: Vandenhoeck & Ruprecht, 1948–9) vol. 1, pp. 56, 427. On these as criteria of truth, cf. M. Schofield, "Preconception, Argument, and God," *Doubt and Dogmatism*, pp. 294–5. On Theodore, see J. Wansbrough, *The Sectarian Milieu* (Oxford, Oxford University Press, 1978), pp. 106–8. C. Becker, *Islamstudien*, 2 vols. (Leipzig: Quelle & Meyer, 1924–32), vol. 1, p. 445.

[95] Aristotle *Top.* 161b3-4.

[96] Ibid., 161b9; 160b2 ff. The term *mukābara* is used in the old translation of Aristotle *SE* 174a22 to translate *to parapan anaiskhuntein* Badawi, *Arisṭū*, vol. 3, p. 921, line -3.

[97] Alexander of Aphrodisias, *Topicorum commentaria*, pp. 559, line 5; 557, line 31 ff.

[98] *Tamhīd*, p. 122 lines 1–14; *iḍṭirār*, literally, "necessary", that which cannot be otherwise, *anangkē (Arist. Metaph. 1015b6)*.

testimony of the senses?... For clearly what is established by the senses is known incorrigibly. It is not possible that a group of people could conspire to deny it or doubt it ... just as we cannot doubt our own existence or that of the sky above us and the earth below...."[99]

Self-contradiction (*naqḍ* or *munāqaḍa*) was one of the traditional signs of defeat.[100] In it R denies something he said earlier, either due to weakness (*ʿajz*) or to his acceptance of Q's point. Our authors commend this since it is better to yield to the truth than to contend peevishly.[101]

Digression or randomness in debate is a concept that in all probability derives from Aristotle. He twice refers to a sophistic method of argumentation in which the opponent directs the conversation to an unrelated theme where he has more arguments.[102] Alexander of Aphrodisias calls this practice *metalēpsis* and *metabasis*,[103] where the latter term is literally equivalent to the Arabic term, *intiqāl*. An indication that this association is no chance one is provided in a debate of the seventh century. There, one of the opponents says: "But I implore you, let us stick to the same subject and not go from inquiry to inquiry (*stathōmen kai mē apo zētēmatos eis zētēmata metabainontes*) so that we do not wind up merely prattling."[104]

al-Ashʿarī mentions four signs that are ignored by al-Qirqisānī, although two of them are known to al-Maqdisī. The first is R's inability to answer the fourth question: he does not show that his cause is commensurate.[105] The second is where Q forces R to admit something absurd such as "fire is at one and the same moment (*ḥāl*) hot and cold."[106] al-Maqdisī, also, mentions that Q has two intentions "whether he be seeking the truth (*mutafaqqihan*) or merely quibbling: to make R tell the truth or to force him to say something absurd (*aḥāla*)."[107] The third sign is unique: "R holds an opinion such that he should hold another similar opinion, but he does not

---

[99] *Tamhīd*, p. 43.

[100] ʿAbd al-Jabbār attributes this technique to one of the early Islamic theologians, Abū l-Hudhayl. ʿAbd al-Jabbār, *Faḍl al-iʿtizāl*, ed. F. Saiyid (Tunis: al-Dār al-Tūnisīya lil-Nashr, 1974), pp. 259, line 8 ff.; 254, line 4, 258, line 5 ff.

[101] Al-Maqdisī, *al-Bad'*, p. 53, line -3 ff. al-Kātib, *al-Burhān*, p. 241, lines 3–6. Ibn Fūrak, "Mujarrad," 155a: 11–3.

[102] Aristotle, *SE* 172b19, 25–8; *Top*. 111b32 ff.

[103] Alexander of Aphrodisias, *Topicorum commentaria*, p. 168, lines 3–5.

[104] G. Bardy, "Les trophées de Damas," p. 243, lines 12–5. In Syriac law, one cannot start a new trial before the old dispute has been settled. E. Sachau, *Syrische Rechtsbücher.* 3 vols. (Berlin: G. Reimer, 1907–14), vol. 3, p. 185.

[105] Ibn Fūrak, "Mujarrad," fol.154a: 3–7; al-Maqdisī, *al-Bad'*, p. 52, line 11 ff. Both authors use the example of a good horse.

[106] Ibn Fūrak, "Mujarrad," fol.154a: 9–11. There is partial parallel in Aristotle *Top*. 159a19-22. Aristotle says, "The business of the questioner is so to develop the argument as to make the answerer utter the most extravagant paradoxes that necessarily follow because of his position." *Topica*, trans. W. Pickard-Cambridge, *The Works of Aristotle*, ed. W. Ross, vol. 1 (Oxford: Clarendon Press, 1928).

[107] Al-Maqdisī, *al-Bad'*, p. 51, lines 14–17.

and is unable to distinguish between the first and second case."[108] In this case R has fallen victim to counter-objection (*muʿāraḍa*) and has been unable to grant the counter-example nor show why it should not hold. Finally he mentions the case of R who answers a question other than the one posed by Q.[109]

Our authors all mention one sign of defeat that is seen as a sort of general rubric for the other: that R or Q fail to defend what they originally began with, or that they fail to meet (their) original goal.[110] Wherever this failure occurs the opponent wins.

I wish to turn briefly to the "practice" of disputation in order to illustrate how the signs of defeat and techniques of debate actually worked. The example comes from al-Bāqillānī and his dispute with the dualists.

One of the dualists' arguments is that they perceive two corporeal forms [*shakhṣ*] inseparable from the world—the heavy and the light; the former they associate with Darkness, the latter with Light. Al-Bāqillānī objects to this argument by pointing out that it is compatible with the argument of the "naturalists" that there are four natures— heat, cold, wetness, and dryness. "If they grant this, they abandon their religion; if they seek a distinction [*faṣl*] they find none". Similarly, one can counter [*yuʿāriḍ*] the claim of the "naturalists" that if they argue for their position on the grounds of what they see and perceive [*bil-shāhid wal-wujūd*], then they are forced to concede [*yulzamuna*] the arguments of the dualists. Finally, both the dualists and "naturalists" are criticized for being inconsistent. We perceive endless genera of body: motion, rest, smell, taste, color etc., that are "inseparable" from body. If they were to include them, they would abandon their opinion [that there are only two or four principles]; but if they denied it, they would contradict their own method of argumentation [r. *naqaḍu istidlālahum*] and would be unable to find a distinction [*faṣl*] [to save them] from this counter-objection [*muʿāraḍa*].[111]

The Rules of Jadal (*Adab al-Jadal*)

The final part of the early systematic *jadal* books was devoted to the rules of politeness in dialectic, the *adab al-jadal*. Of the works of our period, al-Maqdisī's stands out as the only one that neglects to mention these rules.[112]

---

[108] Ibn Fūrak, "Mujarrad," fol.154a: 13–15.

[109] Ibid., fol.154a: 15. Cf. al-Baghdādī, *al-Faqīh*, vol. 2, p. 57, lines 1–6 where he mentions all of al-Ashʿarī's signs in a slightly different order. At line 3, read *an yuʿallila wa-lā yujrī* (i.e., *al-ʿilla fī maʿlūlātihā*).

[110] Ibn Fūrak, "Mujarrad," fol.154a: 15–17. al-Qirqisānī, *al-Anwār*, p. 485, lines 14–18. al-Kātib, *al-Burhān*, p. 241, line -1. al-Maqdisī, *al-Bad'*, p. 51, line 12.

[111] *Tamhīd*, pp. 62–4.

[112] Ibn Fūrak, "Mujarrad," fol.154a: 18 entitles his chapter *fī ādāb al-jadal*. al-Qirqisānī treats these rules in two separate chapters, one on the *adab al-jadal*, and the other on duties that the disputant (*mujādil*) must obey.

The chapters on the *adab al-jadal* offer a rather mixed assortment of rules of debate, conduct and advice to the participants. al-Qirqisānī's treatment, which may well be the earliest, does not appear to have any specific order or ordering principle. al-Ashʿarī's long chapter, although extremely influential with respect to al-Juwaynī's account of the subject, is Ibn Fūrak's compilation of what al-Ashʿarī said in various writings.[113] This compilation too seems to lack a guiding principle. The greater part of these treatments concerns advice to opponents and rules of politeness, where it is often difficult to distinguish the one from the other. But what is most striking is that there are very few correspondences among the various reports so that we would be hard pressed to say that one author got this idea from the other. Rather, the hodge-podge manner of composition and the range of advice offered all point to the practice of dialectical disputation as the chief source of our author's inspiration. The literary tradition that describes such debates in terms more reminiscent of street-brawls than learned amicable disputation finds its confirmation in these rules.[114] The solemn prohibitions put forward point to the free-for-all practice.

al-Kātib begins his discussion by warning the opponents that they should seek the truth.[115] al-Ashʿarī recommends a prayer at the beginning of the disputation.[116] One should not shout or wildly gesticulate.[117] The ideal disputant preserves his *waqār*, his *gravitas*. You should face your opponent when debating; if he does not do so, you should abstain from disputing with him.[118] One should be nice to one's opponent.[119] These are just a few of the rules of politeness that our authors bring.

At the end of his account al-Qirqisānī contrasts the disputant and the person who knows (*al-ʿālim*). The former has need of the latter but not vice versa. These thoughts lead him to a second observation. Since no human being can always hope to be victorious, "It is the mark of the skilled disputant (*al-ḥādhiq al-mujādil*) that his method (i.e., his comportment) be praiseworthy (*maḥmūd*)."[120] Both these remarks seem to be loosely based upon Aristotle's *Topics*. At the beginning of his account of dialectic, Aristotle contrasts the dialectician with the *philosopher*, a comparison that may lay at the bottom of al-Qirqisānī's first statement.[121] Later Aristotle asserts that the good respondent is one who grants nothing that is "not wholly praiseworthy (*maḥmūd*)" and should he be defeated, makes it appear that defeat stems from the

---

[113] Ibid., fol.154a: 19–20.

[114] For a description of the practice see van Ess, "Disputationspraxis," pp. 23 ff.

[115] Al-Kātib, *al-Burhān*, p. 232, lines 2–3.

[116] Ibn Fūrak, "Mujarrad," fol. 154b: 5–7. al-Juwaynī's account in the *Kāfiya* shows many similarities in structure and language and is probably dependent upon it. Cf. al-Juwaynī, *al-Kāfiya*, pp. 529 ff.

[117] Ibn Fūrak, "Mujarrad," fol.154b: 9. Cf. al-Jāḥiz, *Kitāb al-Bayān wal-Tabyīn*, ed. ʿA. Hārūn, 4 vols. (Cairo: Maṭbaʿat al-Khānjī, 1960–1), vol. 1, p.91, line 10 ff.

[118] Al-Kātib, *al-Burhān*, p. 240, line 7. Ibn Fūrak, "Mujarrad," fol.155a: 8–10. al-Qirqisānī, *al-Anwar*, p. 491, lines 2–8.

[119] Ibn Fūrak, "Mujarrad," fol.154b: 10–1. al-Qirqisānī, *al-Anwār*, p. 489, line 9.

[120] Al-Qirqisānī, *al-Anwār*, p. 493, lines 9–15.

[121] Aristotle *Topics*, 155b7 ff.

thesis and not him.[122] In the second case, Aristotle refers to the praiseworthy or plausible propositions, while al-Qirqisānī refers to the praiseworthy comportment of both disputants.

Other rules concern strategy. al-Qirqisānī warns not to answer a question hastily since this can lead to defeat.[123] The opponents should let the truth be their guide and not be swayed by the audience.[124] So too they should avoid arguing with contentious opponents and beware those who dissemble in debate.[125]

The advice that we find in these treatments may in part derive from the advice that Aristotle gives in the *Topics* and *Sophistical Refutations*.[126] However, the rules of conduct seem to belong to another tradition—that of classical rhetoric and the law courts of classical antiquity. We must bear in mind that in the early ninth century, *jadal* or *jidāl* was also associated with the arguments of the law courts. Thus, the theologically minded traditionalist al-Muḥāsibī argues in favor of the "good sort of *jidāl*" where one argues, in court, in favor of someone whom one knows to be in the right.[127] In this meaning, *jadal* approaches the meaning of the *altercatio* of antiquity. Quintilian devotes part of his work on rhetoric to a discussion of the rules of forensic debate (*altercationis praecepta*) and the parallels are striking.

Quintilian warns his man to know his subject thoroughly for otherwise he may be "reduced to silence" or forced to grant something which he should not grant. The skilled debater must avoid anger, and bear with fortitude his opponent's impudence, even should he interrupt him in the middle of a sentence. If one sees that defeat is inevitable, one should yield gracefully. On the other hand, if you have trouble making your point, try to divert the judge's attention by raising another point where you have better arguments.[128]

Conclusion

In the above, we have attempted to give a systematic account of theological *jadal* as it was understood in the tenth century. We have suggested that the structural similarities of the works at our disposal indicate that they derive from a common tradition and that this tradition was initiated by Ibn al-Rīwandī. But in the absence of

---

122 I.e. *endoxa*. Ibid., 159a20-24; cf. 101b5-10. Badawi, *Arisṭū*, vol. 3, p. 743, line 8 ff.; cf. vol. 2, p. 493, line 3 ff.

123 Al-Qirqisānī, *al-Anwār*, p. 490, lines 7–10. Cf. al-Kātib, *al-Burhān*, 240, line 11.

124 Al-Qirqisānī, *al-Anwār*, p. 492, line 15 ff. Ibn Fūrak, "Mujarrad," fol.154b: 12–14.

125 Al-Kātib, *al-Burhān*, p. 236, line 15 ff.

126 Summarized by van Ess, "Disputationspraxis," pp. 52–3.

127 Cf. J. van Ess, *Die Gedankenwelt des Ḥārith al-Muḥāsibī* (Bonn: Selbstverlag des Orientalischen Seminars der Universität Bonn, 1961), index s.v. *jadal, jidāl*. al-Ḥārith al-Muḥāsibī, *al-Masā'il fī a'māl al-qulūb wal-jawāriḥ wal-makāsib*, ed. A. 'Atā (Cairo: 'Ālam al-Kutub, 1969), pp. 140 ff.

128 Quintilian, *Inst. Or.*, VI.iv.1 ff.

texts, we must abstain from saying that our account is the same as the one given by him.

Leaving aside then the question of these texts' relation to Ibn al-Rīwandī's book, we still possess a fairly reliable idea of what the theologians thought about theoretical *jadal* in the early tenth century. We see a virtually complete system of the rules of disputation; we have rules about how a debate gets started; what sort of questions are allowed; what sort of objections are allowed; how to determine who has lost the debate; and even rules of general conduct. While all the various parts are not systematically thought out, the theory still is basically sound.

In the next chapter we shall explore what the philosophers thought about *jadal* and then return to the tradition of Islamic dialectics as it was carried on by the jurists.

Chapter 3
Dialectic and Arabic Philosophy

The Arabic Aristotelian philosophers' views on *jadal* are available in their commentaries and paraphrases on Aristotle's *Topics*. This book was known under three titles; *Ṭūbīqā*, *Kitāb al-Mawāḍiʿ* (literally a translation of Greek *topika*, places) and *Kitāb al-Jadal*.[1] In the longer works on this subject represented by those of al-Fārābī, Avicenna, and Averroes, the book is most often referred to as *K. al-Jadal*.

In what follows I do not wish to summarize the contents of the *Topics* but I do wish to pick out a few themes which are relevant to the topic of *jadal* as dialectics.[2] Thus, I will present its purpose, its benefits, how a debate works, who are the participants and what rules if any regulate it.

What Is Dialectic?

At the beginning of the *Topics* Aristotle defines dialectic as a *method* (*methodos*) whereby we shall be able to reason from opinions that are generally accepted (*endoxa*) about every problem propounded to us and also shall ourselves, when supporting an argument avoid saying anything contrary (*hypenantion*).[3] The Arab

[1]Yaʿqūb b. Isḥāq al-Kindī, *Rasā'il*, ed. M. Abū Rīda, 2 vols. (Cairo: Dār al-Fikr al-ʿArabī, 1950–1953), pp. 367, lines 5–6; 382, line 1 ff. Ibn al-Nadīm, *Fihrist*, ed. R. Tajaddud (Tehran: Maktabat al-Asadī, 1971), p. 309, line -3. al-Khwārizmī, *Mafātīḥ al-ʿulūm* (Cairo: Maṭbaʿat al-Sharq, 1342), p. 91. Abū Ḥaiyān al-Tauḥīdī, *al-Muqābasāt*, ed. T. M. Ḥusain (Baghdad: Maṭbaʿat al-Irshād, 1970), p. 206, line 2.

[2]On the importance of dialectics for scholasticism, cf. M. Grabmann, *Geschichte der scholastischen Methode*, 2 vols. (Freiburg: Herder Verlag, 1909–11), vol. 2, pp. 18ff. U. Gerber, *Disputatio als Sprache des Glaubens* (Zürich, EVZ Verlag, 1970) p. 109.

[3]Aristotle *Topics* 100a18-21.

L. B. Miller, *Islamic Disputation Theory*, Logic, Argumentation & Reasoning 21,
https://doi.org/10.1007/978-3-030-45012-0_3

philosophers, however, consider dialectic an *art* (*ṣināʿa*).[4] This is not surprising since it is called in the Arabic translation of the *Topics*, a *ṣināʿa*, art (=*technē*), and *ṭarīq*, method,[5] Aristotle contributes to the translators' confusions by often comparing the method of dialectic with the *faculties* (*dunameis*) of medicine and rhetoric[6] and this probably led to the association of dialectic with the *stochastic* arts.[7] At one point, Aristotle himself virtually refers to the art of dialectic.[8] In the Arabic translations of Aristotle, reference is often made to the "art of dialectic (*ṣināʿat al-jadal*)."[9] al-Fārābī defines the *art* of dialectic as follows:

> The art (*ṣināʿa*) of dialectic is the art through which a man acquires the capacity to (1) fashion from commonly accepted premises a syllogism that destroys a thesis whose subject is universal, and that he obtains through questioning a respondent who was entrusted with defending either part of a contradictory alternation, whatever that happens to be; and (2) to defend any proposition with a universal premise by opposing himself to a questioner entrusted with destroying either part of a contradictory alternation, whatever that happens to be.[10]

al-Fārābī's definition expands upon Aristotle's. It makes clear that this art involves universal propositions, a question, a respondent and their roles. Avicenna's definition of dialectic is practically the same as that of Aristotle:

[4] This opinion is of Stoic origins. Cf. G. Ryun, "*Ratio et Oratio*: Cicero, Rhetoric and the Sceptical Academy" (Princeton University Ph.D. thesis, 1983), pp. 216 ff, 280 ff. In scholastic philosophy, *disputatio* is conceived of as a *technē*.

[5] cf. A. Badawi, *Manṭiq Arisṭū*, 3 vols. (Beirut: Dār al-Qalam, 1980); for *sināʿa*, see *Sophistic Elenchi* 169b30 (Y;b. Z.; Ov); 171b11 (Y); 172b8 (Y,b.Z.); 183b13 (Y, b. Z.); 184 b4, (Y,b. Z., Ov); for *ṭarīq* 100a18, 102b36. The confusion cannot originate in Syriac which has calques for both words. Cf. T. Noeldeke, *Kurzgefasste syrische Grammatik*, (Leipzig: T. Weigel, 1898), p.59.

[6] Aristotle *Topics* 101b5-6. Aristotle also calls sophistic a *dunamis* and not a *technē* or *epistemē* since the last two terms reveal the truth. Cf. S. Ebbeson, *Commentators and Commentaries on Aristotle's Sophistic Elenchi*, 3 vols. (Leiden: E.J. Brill, 1981), vol. 2, pp. 203; 153–4; 160–2. Aristotle *SE* 165a27 ff. Alexander of Aphrodisias, *In Topicorum libros octo commentaria*, ed. M. Wallies, vol. 2, pt. 2 (Berlin: G. Reimer, 1891), *Commentaria in Aristotelem Graeca* (CAG), edita consilio et auctoritate Academiae Litterarum Regiae Borrusicae (Berlin: G. Reimer, 1883–1909), pp. 4, line 29 through 5, line 2. H. Throm, *Die Thesis*, *Rhetorische Studien* 17 (Paderborn: F. Schöningh, 1932): 26. Throm quotes Aristotle *Rh.* 1356b28 ff where Aristotle denies that rhetoric or dialectic can be sciences. Heidegger observes that rhetoric is *technikon*, not a *technē because it has no specific subject matter (referring to Arist. Rh. A2 1355 b 33 sq.: διό καί φαμεν* αὐτὴν οὐ περί τι γένος ἴδιον ἀφωρισμένον ἔχειν *τὸ τεχνικόν*. Heidegger, *Grundbegriffe der aristotelischen Philosophie*, 116.

[7] Alexander of Aphrodisias, *Topicorum commentaria*, p. 32, line 11 ff.

[8] Aristotle *Rh.* 1355a34; cf. 1354a1.

[9] Badawi, *Arisṭū*, 169b25; 170a35; 172a2 (Y, b. Z.); 172a18 (b.Z.); 172a35 (Y; cf Ov). Cf. *APo.* 77a31.

[10] al-Fārābī, *Kitāb al-Jadal*, fol.187b, MS.231 TE41, Bratislava, ed. typescript of Miriam Galston.

> Dialectic is an art which enables us to (1) bring an argument (*ḥujja*) about any thesis (whose proof is) sought by means of generally accepted propositions[11] and such that (2) if we respond, we not grant anything contradictory to our thesis.[12]

Averroes' version is modeled upon al-Fārābī's. Considering all three definitions and their relation to one another and to Aristotle, we note that all three consider dialectic an *art* involving question and answer.[13] This duality of purpose is already transparent in Aristotle's definition. Aristotle calls the dialectical thesis a problem (*problēma/ mas'ala*), while the Arab philosophers refer to a thesis, *waḍ'*.[14] All three agree that dialectic uses *endoxa*, generally accepted opinions, as premises; however, al-Fārābī and Averroes refer to "fashioning syllogisms," while Avicenna refers to "bringing an argument (*ḥujja*)." This is a more serious objection or change of Aristotle's definition. Avicenna considers the term *ḥujja* as more encompassing than *qiyās*, the term used by Aristotle, al-Fārābī, and Averroes, for the former includes both *qiyās*, syllogism and induction, *istiqrā'*, another means of dialectic to achieve its goal.[15] al-Fārābī is the only one to mention that dialectical questions involve contradictory alternatives, although the commentators have occasion to mention this fact in other places in their commentaries. To sum up, the Arab Aristotelians are agreed that dialectic is a syllogistic *art* which uses *endoxa* in order to defend or destroy any thesis.

In the *Topics*, Aristotle discusses dialectical syllogism in relation to their kinds of syllogism: demonstrative (*burhān*), eristic (*mumārī*) and fallacious (*mughālaṭāt*).[16] Reasoning is demonstrative if it uses valid syllogisms based upon true and primary premises; eristic, if it uses syllogism based upon pseudo-*endoxa*, or non-valid syllogisms based upon true *endoxa*; and fallacious, if it argues syllogistically from premises foreign to the science that it deals with. In the beginning of the *Sophistical Refutations*, which is actually the ninth book of the *Topics*, Aristotle refers again to four types of syllogistic conversation: didactic (*didaskalia*) dialectical, peirastic, and eristic. Didactic arguments turn out to be the demonstrative arguments discussed

[11] *Mashhūra*. On this and other terms used to translate *endoxa* see R. Walzer, *Greek into Arabic* (Oxford: B. Cassirer, 1962), pp. 94 ff.

[12] Avicenna, *Kitāb al-Jadal*, ed. F. al-Ahwānī, *al-Shifā': al-Manṭiq*, gen. ed. I. Madkour, vol. 6 (Cairo: General Egyptian Book Organization, 1965), p. 21 lines 4–5. Avicenna goes on to call it a "psychological *habitus* (*malaka nafsānīya*) used volitionally…" but notes that it is an art since all the sciences (*'ulūm*) are arts (p. 21, lines 6–10).

[13] Only al-Fārābī notes that "Aristotle in defining this *art* calls it a method." "al-Jadal," fol.187b.

[14] al-Fārābī explains: dialectical *quaesita* are called theses (*auḍā'*) for *waḍ'* is the name of the genus that contains some species, which are named after it (Ibid., fol.227a). Earlier, he defines dialectical *quaesitum* as a "proposition (*qaḍīya*) whose nature it is to be obtained by questioning. It is posited so that the questioner destroy it, or the respondent preserve it dialectically." On other terms for thesis cf. Avicenna, *K. al-Jadal*, Arabic introduction of al-Ahwānī. pp. 28–9.

[15] Ibid., *al-Jadal*, text, p. 25, lines 3–4.

[16] Aristotle *Topics* 100a25 ff. Badawi, *Arisṭū*, p. 489, line -5 ff. On this division in later Arabic logic, see Sirāj al-Dīn al-Urmawī, *Maṭāli' al-anwār*, p. 349 margin where the pseudo-dialectician is called *mushāghibī* and the pseudo-philosopher *sufisṭā'ī*. For the division in Latin logic, of. L.M. de Rijk, *Logica Modernorum*, 3 vols. (Assen: Van Gorcum, 1962–7), vol. 1, pp. 91–2 and index s.v. *disputatio*. For Thomas of Aquinas's teaching, cf. Gerber, *Disputatio*, pp. 126–7.

in the *Analytica*, while dialectical and peirastic arguments have been discussed in the *Topics*. In the *Sophistical Refutations*, Aristotle wishes to treat "eristic and contentious arguments."[17]

Aristotle's discussion of the types of syllogistic discussion had its echo in the writings of the Arab Aristotelians. al-Fārābī and Avicenna devote much thought to the difference between dialectic and the other sorts of syllogistic discussions. al-Fārābī notes that dialectic differs from an epistemic (*'ilmī*) discussion since there, one seeks the truth. A typical discussion of this sort takes place between a student and teacher or between a person who knows and one who is ignorant. But such a discussion could also take place when a man takes counsel with himself.[18] Avicenna avails himself of another terminology. The discussion between a student and teacher he calls *mujārāt*.[19] The person who teaches himself engages in *ta'līm*, instruction.[20] The syllogism used in this sort of discussion, says Avicenna, is certain (*yaqīn*), that is, it is a proof.[21]

al-Fārābī treats eristic discussions as a sub-group of sophistical ones. The non-syllogistic type of arguments he calls *qaul mirā'ī* or *mirā'* contentiousness or eristic reasoning.[22] Avicenna, however, calls such a conversation *mu'ānada*, pure contentiousness.[23] "The practitioners of these syllogisms are called sophists, if they pretend to seek the truth, like the philosophers, and eristic (*mushāghib*) if they allege like the dialecticians that they wish to persuade fairly."[24]

al-Fārābī calls a discussion with someone who argues fallaciously (*mughāliṭ*) peirastic, *imitiḥān*, in the sense of probative.[25] He thus identifies the peirastic discussion of the *Sophistical Refutations* with the fallacious type of the *Topics*. Avicenna too refers in the same breath to the peirastic (*mumtaḥin*) and fallacious type of syllogism.[26] Elsewhere, he explains that to a certain extent, peirastic questions are epistemic "since their principles are related; in another way they are not the same since they do not both intend to establish knowledge."[27]

---

[17] Aristotle *SE* 165a38 ff.

[18] al-Fārābī, "K. al-Jadal," fol.210a-b. Aristotle *Topics* 155b16 and Badawi, *Arisṭū*, vol. 3, p. 727, line 2 [*hoi epistēmonikoi sullogismoi* = *al-qiyāsāt al-'ilmīya*]. Cf. Aristotle *SE* 165b1-3. al-Fārābī, *Kitāb al-Ḥurūf*, ed. M. Mahdi (Beirut: Dar el-Machreq, 1970), p. 173, line 22 ff.

[19] Avicenna, *K. al-Jadal*, p. 18, line 9. Avicenna, *Kitāb al-Burhān*, ed. A. 'Afīfī, *al-Shifā': al-Manṭiq*, gen. ed. I. Madkour, vol. 5 (Cairo: General Egyptian Book Organization, 1956), p. 194, line 15. Cf. Aristotle *APo.* 77b10 with Badawi, *Arisṭū*, vol. 1, p. 365, line 11. *Yujārī qaulan* is used to translate Greek *dialego*.

[20] Aristotle *APo.* 71a1. Ibid., *SE* 164a39, b1. Avicenna, *al-Burhān*, p. 57, line 12 ff.

[21] Avicenna, *K. al-Jadal*, p. 7, lines 10–12.

[22] al-Fārābī, "K. al-Jadal," fol.196b ff.

[23] *Mu'ānada* is often used to translate Greek *enstasis*, objection: e.g., Aristotle *APo.* 73a33; 77b34, 38; *Topics* 156b1-3; 157b21; 160b39.

[24] Avicenna, *K. al-Jadal*, p. 16, line 3 ff.

[25] al-Fārābī, "K. al-Jadal," fol.211a ff.

[26] Avicenna, *K. al-Jadal*, p. 16, line 6 ff.

[27] Avicenna, *al-Burhān*, p. 193, lines 3–4. Cf. Aristotle *APo.* 77a35 ff.

Dialectic differs from these as said before in that it is based upon generally accepted opinions. But it also differs in respect to its intentions and the benefits that it provides. Aristotle mentions three benefits for practice (*gumnasia/riyāḍa*), encounters (*enteuxeis/munāẓara*), and for the philosophical sciences.[28] al-Fārābī considers the last two purposes or benefits as one unit. When dialectic is philosophical, it follows philosophy in five benefits:

1. preparing the student for exact sciences by (a) giving him practice in research.[29]
2. by (b) giving the student an acquaintance with the *endoxa* which are the subjects of the exact sciences.[30]
3. in subjects where it is difficult to think abstractly dialectic plays a role, since demonstration (*burhān*) can cause doubt to cease but cannot deal with opposing syllogisms.[31]
4. in arriving at the universals through induction, a practice "extremely useful in correcting the opinions and customs (*sunan*!) of people that don't hit the mark."[32]
5. it protects the philosopher from sophistical arguments.[33]

As can be seen, al-Fārābī takes Aristotle's reference to the role of dialectic in philosophy extremely seriously. al-Fārābī understands the philosophical side of dialectic as *faḥṣ*, investigation. For him, a dialectical discussion can take place between two people where both are ignorant about the status of something, but where they undertake in common to search for it (*mushārik fī al-faḥṣ*); one of them takes the role of questioner, the other that of respondent. They investigate helping each other out (*muta'āwinūn*) to find the syllogism since it is easier for a number of people to find something than it is for the individual.[34] In the *K. al-Ḥurūf*, al-Fārābī relates the important role played by dialectic in the discovery of the true methods of

[28] Aristotle *Topics* 101a25 ff. Badawi, *Arisṭū*, vol. 2, p. 492, line 3 ff. Cf. Throm, *Die Thesis*. According to Gerber, *Disputatio* p. 67, dialectic, in early scholastic philosophy, was either totally rejected (Petrus Damiani) or used to find the truth in specific questions (Anselm of Canterbury) as in the *disputationes quodlibetales*.

[29] al-Fārābī, "K. al-Jadal," fol.197a. Cf. Aristotle *Topics* 101b2.

[30] al-Fārābī, "K. al-Jadal," fol.199b.

[31] Ibid, fol.201a. Cf. Avicenna, *K. al-Jadal*, p. 11, line 16 ff. Averroes, *Talkhīṣ kitāb al-Jadal*, ed. C. Butterworth and A. Harīdī (Cairo: General Egyptian Book Organization, 1979) p. 32, line 1 ff, for this and the following two notes.

[32] al-Fārābī, "K. al-Jadal," fol.202a, 218 ff. Cf. Plato *Republic* 519a. Avicenna, *K. al-Jadal*, p.14, line 31.

[33] al-Fārābī, "K. al-Jadal," fol.203b.

[34] Ibid., fol.214b-215a; cf. fol.195a where one should perhaps read *al-munāzirāni* in accord with Aristotle *Topics* 101a27. al-Fārābī later takes back part of what he says. When the two disputants do not have syllogisms to support their positions, then their opinions belong to the category of things that are investigated and not such that are made into dialectical theses (fol.225a ff.). Cf. Aristotle *Topics* 104b12-17. G. Vajda, "Autour de la Théorie de Conaissance chez Saadia," *Revue des Études Juives* 126 (1967): 387.

proof.[35] This use of dialectic is also mentioned by Averroes.[36] Avicenna, however, separates the inquisitive part of dialectic that is useful in philosophy from *jadal*. Indeed, he mentions a discussion called *munāẓara* but this sort of discussion is far removed from *jadal*:

> It is derived from speculation (*naẓar*) and reflection (*iʿtibār*). Its purpose is to investigate (*mubāḥatha*) the two opposing opinions which have been entrusted— I mean that each one of the interlocuters is entrusted with each one of them (the opposing opinions) in order that it may become clear to them which one of them is holding the true opinion (*al-muḥiqq*) and that the second may help him (*fa-yusāʿiduhū*) to this end. These two have no other purpose than to attain knowledge, and they are essentially only benefited by what attains knowledge and transmits it.

> The word *munāẓara* is derived from *naẓar* and *naẓar* signifies neither victory (*ghalaba*) nor contention (*muʿānada*). But *jadal* signifies prevailing through speech in forcing one's opponent to accept one's position (*ilzām*) as well as an abundance of power and craft (*ḥīla*) slightly removed from what is thoroughly moral and fair (*al-ṭabīʿi…al-ʿadl al-ṣirf*)[37]

Avicenna then thinks that dialectic primarily refers to an altercation between questioner and respondent. The primary benefit of a dialectical syllogism does not accrue to a man when he uses it by himself except accidentally, for the benefit of dialectic occurs through a "common pursuit" (*amr mushtarak*).[38]

The different interpretations of al-Fārābī and Avicenna originate in partly contradictory statements that Aristotle makes. At the beginning of the eighth book of the *Topics*, Aristotle compares the inquiries (*skepsis, faḥṣ*) of the philosopher and the dialectician.[39] They both are on the same level with respect to deriving the topos (*mauḍiʿ*); but the knowledge of how to arrange questions is peculiar to the dialectician, "… for the philosopher and the person inquiring by himself (*man yatafarrad bil-faḥṣ, tōi zētounti kath' heauton*) doesn't care a whit if the respondent doesn't accept his premises because he sees that defeat will result. In contrast to the dialectician perhaps all his effort is devoted to making the premises of his syllogism as familiar and close to the matter at hand as possible."[40] Here the investigator in the Arabic text is identified with the philosopher. But later Aristotle refers to dialectical discussions (*dialektikoi sunodoi/al-mufāwaḍāt al-jadalīya*) which are "not pursued

---

[35] al-Fārābī, *al-Ḥurūf*, p. 209. Cf. Aristotle *Topics* 104b1-2. al-Fārābī, "K. al-Jadal," fol.224a. Avicenna, Ibid., pp. 82–3.

[36] Averroes, *K. al-Jadal*, p.32, line l ff.

[37] Avicenna, *K. al-Jadal*, p. 15, line 14 through p.16, line 2; p. 20, lines 6–10. Cf. Abū Ḥaiyān al-Tauḥīdī, *al-Muqābasāt*, Number 91, p. 360. He quotes al-ʿĀmirī who defended *jadal* as an investigation whose purpose is to force (*ījāb*) an argument upon the opponent such that he has to accept it and cannot repel it.

[38] Avicenna, *K. al-Jadal*, p.11, line 9. Cf. Aristotle *Topics* 161a37: *to koinon ergon*. Badawi, *Arisṭū*, vol. 3, p. 754, line -5 has *al-ʿamal al-mushtarak*.

[39] Aristotle *Topics* 155b8. Badawi, *Arisṭū*, vol. 3, p. 726, line 12.

[40] Aristotle *Topics* 155b10 ff. Badawi, *Aristū*, vol. 3, p. 726, line -3 ff. The translation is adapted from that of W. Pickard-Cambridge, *Topica, The Works of Aristotle*, ed. W.D. Ross, vol. 1 (Oxford: Clarendon Press, 1928).

for the sake of experience (*peira*/*ikhtibār al-ma'ānī*) and inquiry (skepsis/*faḥṣ*)."[41] Here Aristotle places inquiry, *faḥṣ*, in the realm of dialectic.[42] In his commentary to the above passage, Avicenna refers to practice dialogues (*muḥāwarāt irtiyāḍīya*) where one seeks to uncover the things (*istikshāf al-ma'ānī*) and to make clear what is preferable (*istīḍāḥ al-rujḥān*) He makes no mention of inquiry (*faḥṣ*).[43] So too in commenting on the first passage above,[44] he does not mention "the inquirer" nor "inquiry" when referring to the dialectician and philosophers. In his commentary upon this passage, Averroes does mention the dialectician as researcher. There he quotes the translation to *Topics*. However he understands this practice as *training* the mind for scientific knowledge, and not as a separate intention of dialectic.[45]

Avicenna emphasized the contentious and doxological aspects of dialectic. Both he and Averroes understand the second benefit that Aristotle mentions, its use in encounters (*enteuxeis*), as referring to political philosophy—debating with the masses (*munāẓarat al-jumhūr*).[46]

But what of Aristotle's "first benefit" of dialectic training? al-Fārābī understands it as a preparatory art for practice. "It is like wrestling, racing, sword-play and the other practical arts where victory is sought. A man learns all the things through which victory comes about and uses them well against any opponent whether in the role of questioner or respondent."[47] Avicenna too sees victory (*ghalaba*) as playing a major role in dialectic. The person by himself should avoid using dialectical syllogisms—the conclusions which they yield are never free from doubt, as in scientific proof (*burhān*). The syllogisms of dialectic are quā syllogism inferior to those of science, since the premises of the former are *endoxa* or granted by the opponent while those of the latter are true and prior.[48] Here Averroes follows a different path. He understands "practice" as related to the "third benefit," use in the philosophical

---

[41] Aristotle *Topics* 159a33 ff. Badawi, *Arisṭū*, vol. 3, p. 744, line -7 ff. In the translation of the *Topics* the following terms are used for dialectic discussion: *jadal* (108a34, 36 [= Badawi, *Arisṭu*, vol. 3, p. 520, lines 3, 5]; *muḥāwara* (158b [= Badawi, vol. 3., p. 741, line 10); *munāẓara* 101a27 [= Badawi, vol. 2, p.492, line 8]; *mufāwaḍa* 161a12 [= Badawi, vol. 3, p. 753, line 3]. Cf. SE 169a39 and Badawi, vol. 3, p. 847, lines 5–6.

[42] J. Le Blond, *Logique et Méthode chez Aristotle*, (Paris: J. Vrin, 1938), pp. 24–5. Cf. Abū l-Ḥusain al-Kātib, *Kitāb al-Burhān fī wujūh al-bayān*, ed. A. Maṭlūb and Kh. al-Ḥadīthī (Bagdhad:Jāmi'at Baghdād, 1967), p. 224, line 16 ff. J. van Ess, "The Logical Structure of Islamic Theology," *Logic and Classical Islamic Culture*, ed. G.E. von Grunebaum (Wiesbaden: Harrasowitz, 1970), p. 25.

[43] Avicenna, *K. al-Jadal*, p. 321, lines 10–13.

[44] Cf. above note 40 and 41.

[45] Averroes, *Kitāb al-Jadal*, ed. G. Jehamy, *Averroes Paraphrase de la Logique d'Aristote*, 3 vols. (Beirut: Imprimerie Catholique, 1982), p. 641, line 13. This is the same as in Averroes, *Talkhīṣ kitāb al-Jadal*, ed. Butterworth and Ḥarīdī, p. 221, lines 16–17. cf. Alexander of Aphrodisias, *Topicorum commentaria*, p. 83, line 32 for dialectics as preparation for philosophy.

[46] Averroes, *Talkhīṣ kitāb al-Jadal*, ed. Butterworth, p. 31, lines 1, 10ff. Avicenna, *K. al-Jadal*, p. 14, line 3 ff. Cf. Alexander of Aphrodisias, *Topicorum commentaria*, p. 28, lines 1–2: "*enteuxeis legōn tas pros tous pollous*. Throm, *Die Thesis*, p. 21 and note 2 quotes Aristotle *Rhetoric* 1355a29.

[47] al-Fārābī, "K. al-Jadal," fol.203b-204a.

[48] Avicenna, *K. al-Jadal*, p. 11, line 5; p. 9, line 12 through p. 12, line 8.

sciences. "It is preparatory to philosophy as horse-back riding games prepare for war. This practice consists in applying oneself to and learning the principles whereby a thing is affirmed or denied."[49] His account of dialectic omits the subject of victory.

There are grounds for this omission. He identifies the search for victory at all costs as the "opinion which the masses hold as to the nature of *jadal*."

> Since the word *jadal* in the opinion of the masses only signifies a discussion between two people, where each one aims at defeating (*ghalaba*) his opponent by any sort of speech at hand, Aristotle used this name *tropically* to refer to that meaning (*maʿnā*) which the masses intend and this is the very thing (*maʿnā*) which we just defined (in giving our definition of *jadal*).[50]

The "masses" to which Averroes refers are most probably the masses who practice *jadal* in the theological or juristic style whose origins we investigated in the previous chapter. In order to understand the turnabout which has taken place in the ancient tradition from the Greek commentators until Averroes, it is useful to cite the opinion of Ammonius on this topic:

> Aristotle aims at only defeating his opponent and to make him say something contradictory, while Socrates' goal is not victory but rather the grasping of the truth.[51]

Averroes does not claim that *jadal* leads to the truth. His claim is only that its aim is not victory at all costs, but preparation for advanced study.[52]

To sum up, we have seen that Averroes relates all the benefits of dialectic to philosophy, while al-Fārābī and Avicenna distinguish between philosophical and non-philosophical benefits of dialectic. al-Fārābī recognizes the role of dialectic in helping to discover the truth in subjects which have not been sufficiently investigated, while Avicenna lays more weight upon the opinionative aspects of dialectic. But all three philosophers are agreed that the proper method for revealing or presenting the truth, that is certain knowledge, is the method of proof described by Aristotle in the *Analytica*. Only this method yields certain results.

Dialectical Questions — Form and Content

In the preceding chapter we had occasion to discuss the difference between dialectical and epistemic questions. I would like to expand on those remarks here.[53]

---

[49] Averroes, *K. al-Jadal*, p. 31, lines 7–9. Cf. Alexander of Aphrodisias, *Topicorum commentaria*, on *Topics* 161a23-4 where Aristotle discusses peevish argumentation. "To dispute agonistically and to use anything at hand is to argue against the opponent and not the thesis."

[50] Averroes, *K. al-Jadal*, p. 130, line 5 ff.

[51] Ammonius, *In Aristotelis De Interpretatione commentarius*, ed. A. Busse, "CAG" vol. 4, pt. 5 (Berlin: G. Reimer, 1897), p. 202, line 18 ff.

[52] Cf. Aristotle *Topics* 104b1 ff.: "*pros alētheian kai gnōsin*."

[53] For the following see Throm, *Die Thesis*, pp. 30 ff. and pp. 74 ff.

al-Fārābī knows two sorts of dialectical questions: choice questions (*mas'alat takhyīr*) and confirmation questions (*mas'alat taqrīr*). The former question is put in the form "hal…am..?", or "Is it the case that x or not x?". The latter sort of question has the form "*a-laisa*?" or "Is it not the case that…?" This distinction derives from the *Topics* and following where Aristotle distinguishes between a dialectical problem (*problēma*) and a dialectical proposition (*protasis*).[54] They differ only in the way (*tropos*) that they are formulated. A dialectical proposition would be "Isn't (*ara ge*) two-footed animal the definition of man?" or "Isn't (*ara ge*) animal the genus of man?" A problem would be "Is (*poteron*) two-footed land-animal a definition of man or (*ē*) not?" Alexander comments on this passage by noting that the distinction which Aristotle draws is between "*poteron*" and "*ara ge*" questions. The difference, he says, between a problem and proposition is perhaps that in the former the respondent may choose (*helesthai*)[55] whichever alternative he desires. "Or perhaps in a proposition you ask for the answer of one of the contradictory alternatives while in a problem you ask for the demonstration (*deixis*) of one of the alternatives. This is why 'problem' seems to resemble *pusmatic* questions and propositions dialectical questions…."[56] The distinction of the early "translation" of Aristotle's *Peri Hermeneias* is mentioned by Avicenna in connection with Aristotle's discussion of dialectical propositions in the *Topics*.[57] There he identifies the "*hal*" question with the *su'āl tafwīḍ*, the "choice question" and the "*a-laisa*" question with the *su'āl al-ḥajr*, the restrictive question.[58] Hints of this older terminology are to be found in al-Fārābī and Averroes. al-Fārābī notes for example that in "choice" questions "the respondent is allowed the choice between granting either of the contradictory alternatives, which he desires; the matter is his to choose whichever one he likes or thinks is better for him to grant."[59] Averroes, too, remarks upon questions where the respondent is granted a choice (*fawwaḍa*) in replying.[60] In the second type of questions where the respondent is asked to grant one *specific* alternative, to the exclusion of its opposite, acting on the principle that this alternative alone is the proper one to be granted."[61]

---

[54] al-Fārābī, "K. al-Jadal," fol.219b ff. He identifies *muqaddima/protasis [πρότασις]* with *taqrīr* questions and *mas'ala/problēma* [πρόβλημα] with *takhyīr* questions "even though the proposition (*qaḍīya*) be part of a syllogism, preparatory to it or even a *queaesitum*."

[55] Cf. Aristotle *De Interpretatione* 20b28.

[56] Alexander of Aphrodisias, *Topicorum commentaria*, p. 40, line 12 ff; cf. p. 37, line 15 ff; 69, line 1ff.; 94, lines 17–24. Boethius, *Anicii Manlii Severini Boetii commentarii in librum Aristotelis peri hermeneias*, ed. C. Meiser, 2 vols., *secunda editio* (Leipzig: Teubner, 1880) pp. 357 ff.; 359, line 10 ff.

[57] Aristotle *Topics* 158a14 ff.

[58] Avicenna, *K. al-Jadal*, p. 308, line 3ff. Cf. van Ess, "Disputationspraxis in der islamischen Theologie. Eine vorläufige Skizze," *Revue des Études Islamiques* 44 (1976): 41.

[59] al-Fārābī, "K. al-Jadal," fol. 205a-206b.: "*huwa alladhī yufawwaḍ bihī ilā al-mujīb an yusallim aiya al-naqīḍaini.*" Cf. Idem, *K. al-Ḥurūf*, p. 201, lines 18–19; p. 222, line 4 ff.

[60] Averroes, ed. Jehamy, p. 138, lines 15–19; cf. p. 112, lines 1–2. Aristotle *APr*. 24a22 ff. Averroes, *Talkhīṣ K. al-Qiyās*, ed. C. Butterworth and A. Harīdī (Cairo: General Egyptian Book Organization, 1983), p. 63, lines 5–11.

[61] al-Fārābī, "K. al-Jadal," fol.206a-b; Idem, *K. al-Ḥurūf*, p. 202, line 2; p. 222, line 14.

The above two question types are strictly dialectical. The three great commentators never confuse them with the questions of science and, indeed do their best to keep them apart. The "what is" question which Aristotle reserved for epistemic questions is clearly excluded from dialectic. Questions like "What is man? or "How many ways is the good said?" are not dialectical.[62] Of all the discussions of dialectical questions, al-Fārābī's is the most systematic. He devotes himself in more than one treatise to explaining the significance of the Arabic interrogative particles. In his commentary to Book I, Chapter Nine of the *Topics* where Aristotle relates the ten categories to the "four things mentioned earlier" (definition, property, genus and accident),[63] al-Fārābī notes that the interrogative particles refer primarily to the categories and are as such epistemic.[64] The particle "*hal*" for example is exceptional in that it can be either epistemic or dialectical. "It is epistemic when it asks for information about the *true* alternative for which there is a *proof* of one of the *contrary* propositions or when it seeks the proof of some questions. In truth, it was necessary that a special expression had existed to signify each type of question."[65] In epistemic questions the choice is between *contrary* alternatives, in dialectic the choice is between *contradictory* alternatives.[66] Epistemic questions may occur in the course of a dialectical discussion when one seeks to understand (*tafhīm*) or conceptualize (*taṣwīr*) a word's meaning. But epistemic questions, *per se*, are out of place in dialectic. This especially is the case with the particle "mā" which asks about a thing's essence (*jauhar*). "It may be used in an extended, metaphorical, and loose sense…as in the question 'What is your opinion about such and such?' where it becomes a question asking for information or instruction about such and such."

The question "what is your opinion about x?" which sounds so natural to our ears is not proper to dialectic says al-Fārābī.[67] This is a rather thinly veiled attack upon the theologians *jadal*. For other than this remark, al-Fārābī's account of epistemic questions follows the argument given by Aristotle in the second book of the *Posterior Analytics*. The reference to "extended, metaphorical, and loose usage" is a codeword that al-Fārābī uses when he wishes to criticize the Islamic theologians. A passage in the *Ḥurūf* brings this out rather nicely:

> If we consider what common expressions signify (*al-alfāẓ al-mashhūra*), we only take into consideration those situations (*al-amkina*) in which we use them in our conversations with one another to signify the generally accepted meanings (*al-ma'ānī al-mashhūra*) for whose sake these expressions were originally posited. Now if we take from these expressions, those words which have been referred (*manqūla*) to philosophical concepts (*al-ma'ānī al-falsafīya*), then we are only considering (*na'khudhu*) those concepts (*al-ma'ānī*) on whose account these (words) were originally referred (*auwalan nuqilat*). We do not con-

[62] Aristotle *De Int* 20b22; cf., *Topics* 158a14 ff.

[63] Aristotle *Topics* 102a37.

[64] Ibid., 103b20 ff. al-Fārābī, "K. al-Jadal," fol.206a-207a; fol.208b-209b.

[65] Ibid., fol.208b. Cf. Aristotle *APo.* 87b38 ff: "Scientific knowledge is knowledge of the universal" and therefore the scientific question must involve contraries. Le Blond, *Logique et Methode*, p. 18.

[66] al-Fārābī, "K. al-Jadal," fol.207a; Idem, *al-Ḥurūf* p. 206, line 16 ff.

[67] al-Fārābī, "K. al-Jadal," fol.208a, 209b.

sider those metaphorical, tropical, and extended concepts extended meanings which are used *after* the original transfer (*ba'da naqlihim*), by the philosophers; although many of these concepts are connected with or similar to the philosophical ones, to which these (words) had been originally transferred.

This, indeed, occurs in many commonly accepted expressions which originally (*auwalan*) signify everyday things; their meanings are later transferred to, (*nuqilat*) and used for philosophical ones. (This is fine.)

Then, the orators, poets, and the rest of the people appropriated them and used them in other meanings that resembled the philosophical ones, or that were connected with them in some way—i.e., metaphorically, tropically, or in an extended manner (*musāmaḥa*).[68]

For al-Fārābī, questioning is intimately bound to metaphysic and science. The questions expressed by the Arabic particles (*ḥurūf*) play an important role and should therefore, be used in their veritative sense, in philosophy, dialectic and sophistic.[69] In poetry and rhetoric, on the other hand, these particles may be used in a wider sense, or metaphorically, or tropically. Tropical usage occurs in sophistic, when the opponent pretends that he is using a word in its veritative sense, but is not. In dialectic, it may occasionally crop up in order to "establish the language of question and response." It has, however, no place in philosophy proper.[70]

al-Fārābī is compelled as a loyal Aristotelian to take issue with the method of the theologians. Of paramount importance is the distinction between dialectical and epistemic discussions.[71] In epistemic discussions, says al-Fārābī, the questioner, if he is a student, asks the respondent for a proof of "x" so that he may also come to know it. In dialectic, however, the questioner asks questions in order to refute the respondent's thesis.[72] Epistemic discussion is concerned with proof; dialectic is concerned with defending or attacking any thesis. The questioner does not seek to know what establishes the respondent's thesis, but rather what refutes it. He can refute the thesis without bothering to refute his opponent's proof.[73] For al-Fārābī, there is thus a radical difference between the method and aims of epistemic and dialectical discussions and the "ancient" opinion that may be the same opinion held by the modern Islamic theologians of his time:

Some of (our) predecessors used to think that it was incumbent upon the person who questions in accord with the arts of dialectic to ask the respondent for a proof of his thesis after having first obtained it (by questioning). After having obtained this proof, the questioner should forget about the thesis and attack the proof, doing his utmost to refute it. This is because they did not know the difference between the methods of *rhetoric* and those of *dialectic*. Furthermore, they were content to believe that when the proof of the thesis was destroyed the thesis itself is destroyed....They also used this method when they were hard-

[68] al-Fārābī, *al-Ḥurūf*, p. 165, lines 6–15; cf. Arist. Metaph. 1021b15ff.

[69] On this tripartition, cf. Walzer, *Greek into Arabic*, pp. 133–4.

[70] al-Fārābī, *al-Ḥurūf*, p. 165, lines 6–15.

[71] Cf. Throm, *Die Thesis*, pp. 65 ff.

[72] al-Fārābī, "K. al-Jadal," fol.206a.

[73] Ibid., fol.213a-b.

> pressed for arguments to destroy the thesis, and it was otherwise impossible for them to continue the argument because they were too stupid to find a syllogism and so destitute that they could not find anything to destroy the thesis….They therefore demanded that the respondent provide them with a proof for his thesis. In that way they could change the subject (of the discussion) and substitute the proof for the thesis. Thus, they found an easier way to refute him…since proof can be attacked in three ways: either in respect to the major or minor premise, or in respect to the form of the syllogism. But the thesis can only be destroyed or defended in one way….When they had trouble destroying the syllogism…they demanded that the respondent prove the syllogism's premises …and so on in the hope of stumbling upon something that might allow them to refute the original thesis, or anything else that the respondent said in the course of the debate. This is clearly a sophistic-method of argumentation. It is used in rhetoric but is clearly different from the (proper) method of dialectic.[74]

This paragraph could be taken as an attack on the method which we mentioned in the previous chapter. In the *jadal* of the philosophers it is the questioner who carries the weight of the argument, and who must disprove the respondent's thesis, while the respondent does not have to do anything positive. In the theological *jadal* of our last chapter, it was the respondent who was required to give proof. After this, he was required to show that his reasoning was valid for other similar situations. There, too, the questioner is out to destroy the respondent's proof, and thereby his thesis.

If I am right in supposing that al-Fārābī's exposition is an attack upon theological *jadal*, one might well ask, "Why does al-Fārābī refer to 'some of his predecessors' (*qaum min man taqaddama*) instead of saying 'the theologians'…?" Here, I think there are a number of factors at play. First, it seems to be al-Fārābī's intention to distinguish the dialectic that is a part of logic from that of the *jadal* of the theologians. Second, he does not feel that the theological type of *jadal* is on a par with that of Aristotle. Finally, he may have thought that such ideas did not deserve to be expressly mentioned by name in a philosophical commentary on a work of logic, just as citations from the Qur'ān and from the prophetic traditions would be out of place. Every genre has its proper subject-matter. But in as much as the theological type of *jadal* was wide-spread, it was necessary to show that it has little in common with the *jadal* of the philosophers. That al-Fārābī calls this method rhetorical and sophistic corresponds very well with al-Fārābī's known opinions about the nature of *kalām*. The above citation indirectly confirms that the method which described in our chapter on theological *jadal* was the method known to and criticized by al-Fārābī.

Avicenna too emphasized this distinction between epistemic and dialectical questions. The dialectician is not permitted to ask outright about the whatness (*mā'īya*) of a given thing or its wherefore (*limmīya*) since these are learning questions (*su'āl taʿallum*).[75] He may however reformulate them as "*hal*" questions—e.g., "Do you say that the essence (*mā'īya*) of x is y?" or he can ask for the whatness of an expression used by the respondent. He can also reformulate "why?" questions and say, "Why did you say what you said?" as long as he is not asking for the

---

[74] Ibid., fol.213b ff.

[75] Avicenna, *Kitāb al-ʿIbāra*, ed. M. Khudairī, *al-Shifā': al-Manṭiq*, gen. ed. I. Madkour, vol. 3 (Cairo: Dār al-Kitāb al-ʿArabī,1970) p. 97, line -1 ff.

"wherefore." He could also ask "Is the reason for x's being y or not?" Avicenna notes by way of concluding the discussion, that dialectic shares many themes with the sciences, that is, such *quaesita* as are true and at the same time *endoxa*, "for the way to these *quaesita* by means of what is prior and true is blocked.[76]

The Rules of Debate

While the functions and duties of the questioner and respondent become apparent through the positive advice which Aristotle provides, in the *Topics* the rule of conduct governing the debate become apparent only through considering his admonitions. Aristotle does not tell us explicitly how a debate ends, nor does he discuss in detail his understanding as to how the discussion begins. The ambiguity of Aristotle's account fathered various interpretations of dialectic, speculation which has continued down to the present.[77]

In as much as Aristotle treats this subject indirectly, it is not surprising that the Arab commentators act accordingly. In what follows I will show how this material was interpreted.

al-Fārābī's discussion had two forms:

Type I

1. The questioner obtains the thesis from the respondent through asking a question.
2. Once this has been posited, the questioner should obtain premises which will be useful in refuting the respondent in questioning him.
3. The questioner asks each premise separately.
4. When he has obtained sufficient premises, he announces to the respondent that he has refuted him and presents his syllogism.
5. If the questioner is successful, then an *elenchus* has occurred.
6. The respondent is allowed to question the form of the syllogism, but since he has granted each premise, he is not allowed to renege on his previous answers, unless the questioner has distorted one of his previous answers, and used this distortion as the basis of his conclusion. In this case, the respondent must inform the questioner that he has falsified his response and that his *elenchus* is therefore not valid.[78]

6a. In bringing an objection to the form of the questioner's syllogism, the respondent brings a syllogism which is called *ʿinād*. *ʿinād* is the preserve of the respondent, just as *tabkīt* (*elenchus*) is that of the questioner. In the first part of the debate, the respondent preserves (*ḥifẓ*) the thesis. Only after the questioner has brought his proof is he allowed to defend it.[79]

---

[76] Avicenna, *K. al-Jadal*, p. 79, line 15 through p. 80, line 5.

[77] P. Moraux, "La Joute dialectique d'apre's le huitie'me livre des *Topiques*," *Aristotle on Dialectic*, ed. G.E.L. Owen (Oxford: Clarendon Press, 1968): 277.

[78] al-Fārābī, "K. al-Jadal," fol.188b ff.

[79] Ibid., fol.213b; cf. fol.247b. Idem, *al-Ḥurūf*, p. 207, lines 18–22; p. 208, lines 5–7.

Type II

1. The questioner obtains the thesis from the respondent through asking a question.
2. The questioner may obtain premises contrary to the thesis by asking questions.
3. The questioner presents a syllogism refuting the thesis in which premises not consented to by R are used. He does so when he supposes that the respondent would grant them.
4. In this case, the respondent must consider both the content and form of the *elenchus*.
5. If he disagrees with any of the premises, he informs the questioner by making a statement, not by posing a question.
6. If the respondent objects to the form of the syllogism, he proceeds as in Type I.6.
7. If the respondent successfully refutes the *elenchus*, he has accomplished opposition (*ʿinād*).[80]

Of the two types, al-Fārābī espouses the first type as the more useful in dialectic.

al-Fārābī's account of dialectic would make the discussion fairly similar to a Socratic dialogue. Unlike a Socratic dialogue, there seem to be only two participants in this discussion, no more, no less. Again, the discussion starts from a question of contraries and not a simple question. While Socrates would ask "Is virtue teachable?" al-Fārābī dialectician would ask "Is virtue teachable or not?"

Avicenna gives a somewhat different account of dialectical discussion. The discussion does not begin with the questioner asking the respondent his opinion about something (*su'āl al-madhhab*) for, "this question is superfluous, even if it is indispensable. It is preparatory to what is needed as the object of a disputation, in the same way that setting up a target is not part of the act of throwing something, but rather a necessary preliminary (step) to something's being thrown in its direction."[81] Otherwise, Avicenna's dialectical discussion follows the course described by al-Fārābī. The initiative is ever on the side of the questioner. Should the respondent produce any evidence in favor of this thesis, the questioner is not bound to consider it at all.

Averroes' account is also similar to that of al-Fārābī. In as much as his commentary follows Aristotle's *Topics* more closely than those of al-Fārābī and Avicenna, we can guess what passage inspired al-Fārābī original interpretation. The passage occurs in the *Topics*. Here Aristotle advises the respondent how to reply to various types of questions: "for thus the respondent does not seem to suffer anything through any fault of his own if he grants each (premise) with his eyes open."[82] From al-Fārābī onwards, it appears that the above passage was taken to mean that each premise is granted separately, one after the other.

---

[80] al-Fārābī, "K. al-Jadal," fol.188b ff.

[81] Avicenna, *K. al-Jadal*, p. 30, lines 5–7.

[82] Aristotle *Topics* 160a11–12, trans W. Pickard-Cambridge, *Topica.* Aristotle *Topics* 160a11–12: "houtō gar ho apokrinomenos ouden doxei di' hauton paskhein, *ean proorōn hekasta tithēi.*" Badawi, *Arisṭū*, vol. 3, p. 748, lines 2–3: "*matā kāna waḍʿuhū li-wāḥid wāḥid min al-ashyā' allatī yadaʿuhā baʿda taqdīmihī al-naẓar fīhī wal-ta'ammul lahū.*"

Naṣīr al-Dīn al-Ṭūsī also knows about two methods of dialectical discussion, that of the Ancients and that of the Moderns.[83] The ancient method corresponds to Type I of al-Fārābī. The modern method is one in which the questioner asks no other question than what the respondent's opinion is (*madhhab/ra'y*). He then proceeds to bring a proof of the contrary. The respondent listens in silence, only speaking when the questioner mentions a premise which he doesn't accept. After the questioner brings his conclusion, the respondent may attempt to dispute it.

Avicenna prefers the first type of discussion. He refers to the second type of discussion in his commentary to the *Sophistic Elenchi* as follows:

> Sometimes they depart from the (correct) method of questioning; nay, they bring a syllogistic argument with the conclusion, as if it were self-evident and as if there were no consent needed (from the respondent). And this is the very custom, in our own times, of contentious argumentation of those who are called dialectical theologians (*mutakallimūn*).[84]

Averroes makes a similar statement in his commentary to the *Sophistic Elenchi.* The context of both statements reveals that the origin of this second form of dialectical discussion derives from a remark by Aristotle in the *Sophistical Refutations.* "One should not ask the conclusion in the form of a proposition, and some propositions should not be asked at all but treated as admitted."[85]

The problem of this method, according to Averroes, is that "in this case the respondent is forced to consider not only the form of the syllogism but all of the premises as well."[86] Averroes' comment is a virtual repetition of al-Fārābī's second type of dialectical discussion; thus, the latter is probably based on an interpretation of the above passage from the *Sophistic Elenchi.*

The Participants in the Debate

The standard term for dialectician is *jadal.* The questioner is called the *sā'il* and the respondent the *mujīb*. These terms are taken from the translations of Aristotle. The Arab philosophers recognize the various intentions of the participants in a dialectical discussion as well as their shared purpose. Here again their views are based upon Aristotle's writings. The greater part of Aristotle's teaching is contained in the eighth book of the *Topics*, where he gives advice to questioner and respondent. In Aristotle's dialectical discussions, the burden of proof rests upon the questioner.

---

[83] Naṣīr al-Dīn al-Ṭūsī, *Āsās al-iqtibās*, ed. M. Riẓavi_ (Tehran: Intishārāt-i Dānishgāh-i Tihrān, 1947), p. 449, line 9 ff.

[84] Avicenna, *al-Safsaṭa*, ed. F. al-Ahwānī, *al-Shifā': al-Manṭiq*, gen. ed. I. Madkour, vol. 7 (Cairo:General Egyptian Book Organization, 1958) p.75, lines 8–10.

[85] Aristotle *SE* 174b38-40.

[86] Averroes, *Talkhīṣ kitāb al-Safsaṭa*, ed. S. Sālim (Cairo: Dār al-Kutub wal-Wathā'iq al-Qaumīya, 1972), p. 110, lines 5–9.

This is also the case with respect to the Arab Aristotelians. al-Fārābī gives as is his custom a precise overview of the goals of both parties:

> The aim of the questioner is to destroy (*ibṭāl*) that which the respondent was entrusted to defend (*ḥifẓuhū*) and this is his victory (*ghalaba*) over the respondent; while the defense of that which the questioner was entrusted to destroy is the aim of the respondent and this is his victory over the questioner. Aristotle thinks that it is the primary concern of the dialectician to destroy opinions, although this only comes about through producing something opposed to that which he seeks to destroy.[87] Nevertheless, his concern in accord with his primary intention is to destroy; affirmation (*ithbāt*) is his concern only secondarily.[88]

Avicenna also holds the same opinion. The questioner must *per se* raise questions from which he can fashion premises to support a thesis opposed to the original one.[89] The respondent is not required to raise any questions at all. He need only put forward the grounds for his beliefs since he is only defending his thesis.

He does not however have to bring forward a proof since quā respondent his role is defense (*dhabb*):

> Defense means that he not grant anything from which something opposed to a premise could be constructed or a contradictory premise or something which results in the contradictory of his thesis. In general, he should not grant anything which results in the destruction *(naqḍ)* of that through which his activity reaches its perfection.[90]

Jadal in Theology and Philosophy: An Overview

In the previous two chapters, we have discussed the various interpretations placed by theologians and philosophers on *jadal.* We have seen that the philosophers objected to the epistemic oriented *jadal* of the theologians since for them *jadal* is opinion oriented. One could see in this a rekindling of the clash between Aristotelians and Stoics or Platonists. For the Stoa, philosophy had three parts: physics, ethics, and logic.[91] The division is perhaps of Aristotelian origin.[92] Of interest is the division of the logical part into *dialectic* and rhetoric. Dialectic in this division deals with the "canons or criteria they admit as a means for discovery of truth."[93] Aristotle too knows dialectic as *a* means for discovering the truth, but hardly as a canon or criterion of truth. The latter understanding of dialectic goes back to suggestions made in

---

[87] Cf. Aristotle *Topics* 164b2-4.

[88] al-Fārābī, "K. al-Jadal," fol.188a.

[89] Avicenna, *K. al-Jadal*, p. 30, lines 1–4. Avicenna sometimes uses the term *da'wā* (On this see the Arabic introduction p. 29).

[90] Avicenna, *K. al-Jadal*, p. 32, lines 10–13.

[91] Diogenes Laertius, *Lives of Eminent Philosphers*, ed. and trans, R. Hicks, VII.39 (translation by Hicks). Cf. P. Moraux, *Le Commentaire d'Alexandre d'Aphrodise aux "Secondes Analytiques" d'Aristote* (Berlin: de Gruyter, 1979), p. 9, fragment 1.

[92] Aristotle *Topics* 105b19 ff.

[93] Diogenes Laertius *Lives* VII.42 (translation by Hicks). Cf. above, note 92.

various Platonic dialogues.[94] Platonic dialectic was a sort of sifting through the various beliefs (*doxa*) held by the participants in the dialogues in order to arrive at an opinion which is consistent and irrefutable. Aristotle, while recognizing the role of belief (*doxa*) in helping to arrive at the truth, gives belief an inferior place, in his philosophy, to that of knowledge. For him, demonstration is an art and science, dialectic merely a method or faculty.[95] While the Arab philosophers know dialectic as an "art", perhaps following some late Byzantine tradition, they still rank it below the art of demonstration. Thus, their disagreement with the theologians as to the nature of *jadal* has its roots in antiquity.

[94] e.g. Plato's *Gorgias* and *Republic*.

[95] Alexander of Aphrodisias, *Topicorum commentaria*, p. 19, lines 15–16. Following Aristotle, he remarks that the questions between the various philosophical schools are *endoxa*; for example, "Is the soul immortal as Plato holds or a fifth substance as Aristotle holds?" For Aristotle dialectic is not suited to discussing scientific questions since, among other things, it allows the use of false premises. E.g. Aristotle *Topics* 161a27 ff. Cf. *The Works of Aristotle*, vol. 1, s.v. premises.

Chapter 4
Dialectic (Jadal) in Jurisprudence

The method of *jadal* that was originally applied to exclusively theological subjects later became used in jurisprudence. This is not surprising in itself, given the long and close association between theology and jurisprudence from the very beginning of Islamic thought. What is surprising is the way in which *jadal* took hold of jurisprudence and became an integral part of it. During the tenth century, there arose two genres of juristic literature, both of which were the products of the incursion of *jadal* in jurisprudence: works with the *jadal* method devoted to the *uṣūl al-fiqh* (Islamic legal philosophy or principles of law) and works devoted to the *furū'* (or case law). The former usually had the word *jadal* somewhere in their title while the latter were generally called *ṭarīqa* "method." In what follows, we shall discuss works written on juristic *jadal*. The study is divided into three periods. The earliest preserved books on juristic *jadal* comprise the first group; the second group is represented by assorted texts from approximately a century or so later when logic first became mated to jurisprudence; the third group is basically the group that shows the transition from strictly legal debate to the universal theory of debate represented by the *R. al-Samarqandīya*.

The Early Period

Our first direct sources for *jadal* in the *uṣūl al-fiqh* are from the eleventh century. The earliest one is an introductory work of Abū Isḥāq al-Shīrāzī, *Ma'ūnat al-mubtadi'īn wa-tadhkīra lil-muntahīn fī al-jadal.*[1] Other works on this subject

[1] [Fīrūzabādī] al-Shīrāzī, Abū Isḥāq Ibrāhīm ibn 'Alī ibn Yūsuf. "Ma'ūnat al-mubtadi'īn wa-tadhkirat al-muntahīn fī al-jadal." MS.867 Garrett Collection, Princeton University Library, Princeton. On al-Shīrāzī, see *Encyclopedia Iranica*, s.v. "'Abū Esḥāq," by W. Madelung.Cf. Abū Isḥāq al-Shīrāzī,*K. Tabaqat al-fuqahā'*, ed. I. 'Abbās, 2nd ed. (Beirut: Dār al-Rā'id, 1981), introduction pp. 5 ff.

L. B. Miller, *Islamic Disputation Theory*, Logic, Argumentation & Reasoning 21,
https://doi.org/10.1007/978-3-030-45012-0_4

were composed by his students Ibn ʿAqīl and al-Bājī. The latter composed a *jadal* work entitled *al-Minḥāj fī tartīb al ḥijāj*, while the former composed a work whose title has come down to us as *K. al-Jadal ʿalā ṭarīqat al-fuqahā'*.[2] The final work which we have from this period is that of Imām al-Ḥaramayn al-Juwaynī, *al-Kāfiya fī al-jadal*.[3] The works of al-Bājī and al-Juwaynī are by far the most detailed. al-Shīrāzī's long treatise on dialectic, *al-Mulakhkhaṣ fī al-jadal* that was among the manuscripts microfilmed by the Arab League in 1976 is still unavailable.[4]

Of these four works, Ibn ʿAqīl is very much dependent on al-Shīrāzī; al-Bājī is also somewhat dependent on him but will occasionally profess a different opinion or explicitly criticize al-Shīrāzī. al-Juwaynī on the other hand comes from the Islamic east, and from an apparently different tradition. He often refers in his work to al-Ustādh Abū Isḥāq, referring most probably to the Ashʿarite theologian al-Isfarāʿinī (d. 1027). At other times, al-Juwaynī refers to Ibn al-Suraij, Ibn Fūrak, b. al-Qāṣṣ, al-Kaʿbī and even Abū Hāshim and al-Jubbā'i; that is to say, he refers to both theological and juristic personages who wrote on *jadal* or expressed opinions about it.[5] al-Bājī and Ibn ʿAqīl, too, cite other authors,[6] other opinions. This is, indeed, not very surprising. Our authors were writing a good century after b. al-Rīwandī's opus on *jadal* and about a half century after the first attempts at making *jadal* part of jurisprudence were carried out, if we can believe our sources, by the likes of Ibn al-Suraij, A. ʿAli al-Ṭabarī, and others.

---

[2] Abū l-Walīd al-Bājī, *Kitāb al-Jadal ʿalā ṭarīqat al-fuqahā'*, ed. G. Makdisi with an introduction "Le livre de la dialectique d'ibn ʿAqīl," *Bulletin d'Études Orientales* 20 (1967): 119 ff. On b. ʿAqīl, see *EI*[2], s.v."Ibn ʿAḳīl," by G. Makdisi, and G. Makdisi, *Ibn ʿAqīl et la resurgence de l'Islam traditionalist au XI*[e] *siecle*. (Damascus:Institut Francais de Damas, 1963). On al-Bājī, see *EI*[2], s.v. "al-Bādjī," by D. Dunlop. C. Brockelmann, *Geschichte der arabischen Litteratur* (GAL), 5 vols (Leiden: E.J. Brill, 1949) I,p. 534. SI, pp. 743–4. A. M. Turki, *Polémiques entre Ibn Ḥazm et al-Bājī sur les principes de la loi musulmane, essai sur le littéralisme zahirite et la finalité malikite* (Algiers: Societe Nationale d'Édition et de Diffusion, 1976).

[3] Imām al-Haramayn Abu al-Maʿāli ʿAbd al-Malik al-Juwaynī, *al-Kāfiya fī al-jadal* ed. F. Ḥusain Maḥmūd (Cairo: Maṭbaʿat ʿĪsā Ḥalabī, 1978). On al-Juwaynī, see EI[2] s.v. "al-Djuwaynī," by C. Brockelmann [and L. Gardet]. Brockelmann, *GAL* I, pp. 486 ff., SI, pp. 667–8.

[4] Abū Isḥāq al-Shīrāzī, "al-Mulakhkhaṣ fī al-jadal," MS.39 (uṣūl al-fiqh), Maktabat al-Jāmiʿ al-Kabīr bi-Ṣanʿāʾ, Sana (Yemen),76 fols. Cf. "al-Makhṭūṭāt allatī ṣauwarahā baʿathat al-Maʿhad ilā al-Jumhūrīya al-Yamanīya," *RIMA*, 22, fasc. 1 (May 1976): 47, number 295. A. ʿĪsawī and M. al-Māliḥ, eds., *Fihris al-Makhṭūṭāt al-Maktaba al-Gharbīya bil-Jāmiʿ al-Kabīr bi-Sanʿāʾ* (Cairo: Maṭbaʿat Aṭlas, 1978?), p.345. The *incipit* shows that the work began with definitions of the *termini technii*; while the *explicit* shows that it included a chapter on the *adab al-jadal* and most probably contained another chapter on the signs of defeat.

[5] al-Juwaynī, *al-Kāfiya*, pp. 144, 248, 307–8, 362, 409, 609 note 56.

[6] al-Bājī, *Minhāj* cites b. al-Qaṣṣār, al-Karkhī, Abū ʿAlī al-Ṭabarī and many others Cf. 255 ff. (index). Ibn ʿAqīl *al-Jadal*, cites Abū Yaʿlā b. al-Farrā, Abū ʿAlī al-Ṭabarī, al-Karkhī, and others pp. 126–7 (index).

Question and Answer (The Four Questions)

For our authors, *jadal* means question and answer. Their debt to theological *jadal* is, thus, most evident in their discussions of "question and answer." al-Bājī, b. ʿAqīl, and al-Juwaynī all discuss the "types" of questions used in *jadal*. The discussions show that the "four questions" of the theologians were subject to scrutiny and disagreement. Let us start out by considering al-Juwaynī's account:

There are four types (*aqsām*) of dialectical questions.

Someone said there are five; for, he said "The first question is about the existence (*hāliya*) of the opinion; that is, 'Do you have an opinion or not?' (2) Then (you ask) about the opinion itself. (3) Then you ask about the proof (*burhān*). (4) Then you ask about the verification of the proof (*taṣḥīḥ al-burhān*). (5) Then you ask about the way he escapes from being refuted (*ilzām*)."

Now someone else said, "If he asks about the opinion (i.e. question 2) then he (also) asks about the existence of the opinion [that is, question 1]."

Other people added another question:(6) "the whatness of the opinion [read *wa-su'āl ʿan mā'īyat al-madhhab*]"; but [in al-Juwaynī's opinion] this is the same as the question about the opinion, since one says, "What do you say?" or "What is your opinion?"

Some said that there are two types of questions: one about the opinion and the other about its verification (*tasḥīḥ*). But refuting the opponent by opposition (*al-ilzām bil-muqābala*) and the like are not questions about anything at all. Rather, like the question[7] about the proof of the opinion and its mode, it falls under the second type of question (i.e. the verification of the opinion)". But this opinion is not correct. For refutation by opposition and its like, as well as the question about the proof and its mode, are not the same (sort of question) as the question about the verification of the opinion.

The commonly accepted view is that there are four types of question and that each one corresponds to a type of response, whether it be valid or invalid; the number of questions must correspond, whether they be more or less than four in number.

When Q asks for the mode of proof, he asks R to show "on account of what" is the proof consistently true. For no proof is sound if it is known that the juristic qualification (*ḥukm*) of the principal case is either disallowed or contradicted, or that it can be stood on its head. Since this question seeks to find out what reveals the (true) juristic qualification (of R's proof), the answer will not be of the desired type unless it be free from the sort of objections which we just mentioned.

However, if Q brings his question in the manner of contradiction, reversal, or objection, then he is actually asking for the "mode of signification," so that some people remarked "The fourth question, that is opposition (*muqābala*), is really a sub-division of the question about the "mode of signification," because his oppo-

[7] al-Juwaynī, *al-Kāfiya*, read *kal-su'āl*, p. 77, line −1.

sition by means of contradiction (*munāqaḍa*), counter-objection (*muʿāraḍa*), reversal (*qalb*), and distinction (*farq*) is (really) asking for the mode of signification."

Thus, some people say: "There are two sorts of question" although the common view is the one we just mentioned.[8]

al-Juwaynī's discussion presents a summary of the state of *jadal* in eleventh century Islamic jurisprudence. In Ibn ʿAqīl, for example we have the bi-partite division of questions, while al-Bājī allows that there are five types of questions.[9] If we now turn to al-Bājī's detailed account of the questions, we will get an accurate understanding of how *jadal* became juristic.

Questions One and Two

al-Bājī devotes his first chapter on "questions" to the question about the existence of R's opinion:

The question "Does R have an opinion about this point of law (*ḥāditha*) or not?" is of two sorts. One is to ask, "Does he have an opinion on this question?" as if you asked him "Do you have an opinion about whether it is permitted to sell fruit and vegetables for its like at a profit or not?"[10]

The second sort is to give two statements stemming from the person whose opinion (*madhhab*) R follows and to ask him if he chooses one of them (instead of the other): for example, Q says, "There are two opinions reported on Malik's authority about wiping the soles of the sandals in the case of people who are in residence.[11] Do you choose one of them or are they both equal in your eyes so you do not prefer one at the other's expense?" All these questions are proper in disputation (*naẓar*)....[12]

al-Bājī's first question is the restrictive question of the theologians, but it is here firmly in the fold of jurisprudence. al-Juwaynī is the only author who knows the distinction between restrictive and non-restrictive questions:

Next Q's questions are divided up into various types (*wujūh*): one which specifies the juristic qualification through questioning; for Q says, "Is date-brandy forbidden or allowed?" For (in this sort of question) it is necessary that the response be

[8] Ibid., p. 77, line 8 ff.

[9] Ibn ʿAqīl, *al-Jadal*, p. 42, par. 219–20. al-Bājī, *Minhāj*, p. 34, par.= 64.

[10] Cf. Schacht, *An Introduction to Islamic Law* (Oxford: Clarendon Press, 1964), p. 146.

[11] Cf. Schacht, *The Origins of Muhammadan Jurisprudence* (Oxford: Clarendon Press, 1959) p. 263. Van Ess, *Das Kitāb an-Nakth des Naẓẓām* (Gottingen: Vandenhoeck & Ruprecht, 1972).

[12] al-Bājī, *Minhāj*, p. 34, par. 65.

from a part of the question, so that you reply "Forbidden" or "Allowed." This type of question is called restrictive (*su'āl ḥajr wa-man'*).

Another type is when you ask the question in a general manner (*mujmalan*) where you intend to give R the choice in the matter, for you say, "What do you think about date-brandy?" and this is called a non-restrictive question (*su'āl tafwīḍ*).[13]

al-Khaṭib al-Baghdādī also knows about the non-restrictive type of question.[14] But as in al-Juwaynī's account, he makes no reference to the "logicians." His source for this question is the Qur'ān—Abraham's "dispute" with the idolaters.[15] By the time of al-Juwaynī and al-Baghdādī it would seem that these technical questions have lost their previous association with logic.

al-Bājī's second question concerns "what the opinion is." His discussion is as follows:

> Sometimes (this) question concerns the juristic status (*ḥukm*) and sometimes "the manner in which the status is applied (*ṭarīq al-ḥukm*)." An example of the first sort would be to ask "Is date wine permitted or forbidden?", or to ask "Does the law against usury (*ribā*) apply to the sale of fruits or not?" or other such questions about whose juristic status the jurists disagree. As for the question about the way in which the status is applied, it could be through (1) its appellation (*ism*), as when you ask about *nabīdh* (date brandy) "Is it called wine (*khamr*)?" ... Or it could be about (2) an attribute (*ṣifa*) connected with the juristic status, as when you ask (about the hair of an unclean animal), "Does the animal's being alive render it permissible (that is non-polluting)?"....Or it could be about (3) the *ratio legis* (*'illa*) for the prohibition against selling corn for corn at a profit? or "What is the reason for prohibiting wine?" (Finally), it can (stem) from a (4) report (*khabar*), as when you ask, "Was the conquest of Mecca by force or by treaty?" All these questions are valid since their establishment leads to the establishment of the juristic status (of the case at hand).[16]

al-Bājī's examples are again almost always restrictive questions and are all concerned with legal matters. In the second sort of question, which is the question about the manner in which the juristic status is applied, we find terms commonly associated with juristic analogy: *ṣifa*, *'illa*, *ḥukm*. We shall have occasion to discuss these terms in our treatment of the third question. Now although al-Bājī does not use the technical term for nonrestrictive questions, he is certainly aware of them, and, indeed, specifically rejects their use in disputation. Non-specific questions (*mujmal*) such as "What do you say about usury?" or "Is it necessary to do things in a certain order in matters of ritual cleanliness?" should be avoided since R is at a loss as to which thing he is being asked about. Q should always make plain his question.[17] In his short epistle on juristic principles, the Ḥanafite jurist al-Karkhī (d. 952) notes the following principle:

---

[13] al-Juwaynī, *al-Kāfiya*, p. 80, line 3 ff.

[14] al-Khaṭīb al-Baghdādī, *Kitāb al-faqīh wal-mutafaqqih*, ed. I. al-Anṣārī, 2nd ed., 2 vols. (Beirut: Dār al-Kutub al-'Ilmīya, 1981), vol. 2, p. 51, line 13 ff.

[15] Qur'ān, 26/71. Cf. Isḥāq b. Ibrāhīm al-Kātib, *Kitāb al-burhān fī wujūh al-bayān*, ed. A. Maṭlūb and Kh. Ḥadīthī (Baghdad: Jāmi'at Baghdād, 1967), p. 222, line 12 ff.

[16] al-Bājī, *Minhāj*, p. 35, par. 67.

[17] Ibid., 36, line 4 ff.

> Should a questioner ask a question, the respondent should not give an unqualified answer in response. Instead, he should first consider whether the question has one, two, or more parts, and then he should answer each part accordingly since often, an unqualified response will lead him to contradict himself.[18]

Aristotle, too, has a chapter on the use of ambiguous questions in debate.[19] There, he brings out the situation rather clearly—R should not be afraid to say "I do not understand what you are talking about" and he should be careful that the question does not have more parts than he thought at first sight. More likely than not, we have here a coincidence of themes rather than a case of Aristotle's influence.

There are other pitfalls in this question. al-Bājī, al-Baghdādī, and al-Juwaynī all mention that care must be taken in formulating the question so as not to cede the respondent's position before he has given his evidence:

> If Q asks: "Is it the case that the fast of a person who fasts during Ramaḍān is valid when this person has first expressed his intention to do so in the morning [that is, after the fast had already begun]?", he has in effect conceded the point which he wished to dispute; for his statement "the person who fasts" is a report that he concedes that what this person did was to fast.[20]

Among our jurists, however, there was not universal agreement. al-Baghdādī for example did not believe that such "carelessly" formulated questions amounted to conceding the opponent's point. When the question is restored to its basic form (*taqdīr*), it would run something like, "That person *whom you say* fasts during Ramaḍān, why do you say that if he expresses his intention in the morning, his fast is valid?"[21] The problem which our authors are talking about is one which we already encountered in al-Qirqisānī's explanation of the specific order of the questions: one must avoid conceding something and then going back and denying it.[22] This consideration played a role not only in the order in which the four questions were asked, but also, as we shall shortly see, in the sub-divisions of these questions.

Question Three: What Is Your Evidence?

It is in the formulation of this question that the *jadal* of the jurists most sharply differs from that of the theologians. For the standards and definitions of "what is evidence (*dalīl*)" differ. al-Shīrāzī understands *dalīl* (lit. sign) as "that which leads to the *quaesitum*;" al-Bājī understands it as "what *can* lead to the *quaesitum*;"

---

[18] al-Karkhī, *al-Uṣūl allatī 'alaihā madār kutub asḥābinā* (Cairo: al-Maṭba'a al-Adabīya, 1320), p. 86, line 3 ff. On al-Karkhī, see F. Sezgin, *Geschichte des Arabischen Schrifttums* (GAS), (Leiden: E. J. Brill, 1967) 1: 444.

[19] Aristotle *Topics* 160a17 ff.

[20] al-Juwaynī, *al-Kāfiya*, p. 99,line 8 ff. Cf. Qur'ān, 2/185.

[21] al-Khaṭīb al-Baghdādī, *al-Faqīh*, vol. 2, p. 52, line 9 ff.

[22] Cf. Our treatment of the four questions of theological *jadal*.

al-Juwaynī understands it (*dalāla*) as "that which through sound reasoning (*bi-saḥīḥ al-naẓar*) leads to the cognizance of something not previously known." (He notes that *dalāla* and *dalīl* are at times used synonymously.)[23] The definitions which we just mentioned are broad enough to include syllogistic reasoning; however, syllogism is not at home in jurisprudence, or for that matter in juristic *jadal*.

The rules of evidence here are those of the *uṣūl al-fiqh*. al-Shīrāzī and al-Bājī, for example, understand three categories of evidence in the *uṣūl al-fiqh*: *aṣl* (source), *aṣl maʿqūl* (reasoned source), and *istiṣḥāb al-ḥāl* (*praesumptio*). Under the first category, they understand in order of priority the evidence of scripture, tradition, and consensus. Under the second category, they understand such hermeneutic devices as liberal interpretation (*fakhwā al-khiṭāb*), and the reasoned interpretation (*maʿnā al-khiṭāb*), of one of the sources (*aṣl*). The final type of evidence *praesumptio*, is the principle that the status of a given thing remains as it was in the past—if we see someone who was married yesterday, we assume that, if we see him today, he is still married.[24]

For our purposes, the most important "source" is the second type, and of that category, the one known as (*maʿnā al-khiṭāb*). Of it, al-Shīrāzī says: "It is analogical reasoning (*qiyās*) and consists in (1) the understanding of the "test case" (*farʿ*) on the basis of the principal case (*aṣl*) by means of some *ratio legis* which connects them both; (2) and the application of the juristic qualification of the principal case to the test case."[25]

	It is intoxicating (*jāmiʿ* = *ʿilla*)	
Wine (*aṣl*)		Date-brandy (*farʿ*)
is		is
forbidden (*ḥukm*)		(?) (Point of dispute).

In the analogy which we have described graphically above, the proponent argues on the basis of the *ratio legis* (*ʿilla*) that wine is intoxicating; and, therefore, its juristic status (*ḥukm*) is "that it is forbidden;" so, too, date-brandy should be forbidden since it is also intoxicating. The above example is called by al-Shīrāzī an "analogy from the *ratio legis* (*qiyās al-ʿilla*)," since it is "...the understanding of the test case (*farʿ*) on the basis of the principal case on account of some *causative entity* (*maʿnā*) with which the juristic status is connected in the Law. This is like comparing date-brandy to wine because the former is (also) strongly intoxicating."

[23] Abū Isḥāq al-Shīrāzī, *al-Lumaʿ fi uṣūl al-fiqh* (Cairo: M. B. Ḥalabī, 1957), p. 3, line 20. al-Bājī, *Minhāj*, p. 11, lines 11–2. al-Juwaynī, *al-Kāfiya*, pp. 46 ff., 48, line 10 ff. On the concepts of sound reasoning and *dalīl*, see J. van Ess, *Die Erkenntnislehre des ʿAḍudadīn al-Īcī* (Wiesbaden: Steiner, 1966) pp. 364 ff. Van Ess shows that al-Shīrāzī's definition is probably of muʿtazilite origins.

[24] al-Bājī, *Minhāj*, par. 19. Abū Isḥāq al-Shīrāzī, "Maʿūnat," fol.1b: 8 ff.

[25] Ibid., fol.3a: 11. The word maʿnā occurs in the writings of al-Shafiʿi in the meaning of common characteristic accoring to R. Brunschvig, *Études d'Islamologie*, ed. A. Turki, 2 vols. (Paris: G. P. Maisonneuve et Larose, 1976) 2:357.

The jurists were well aware that such reasoning was not stringent. al-Juwaynī puts it most succinctly when he remarks that "the causes in law (*'ilal shar'iya*) are different from the causes in intellectual matters. The latter are coextensive with their causata (that is, A <=> B), while the former owe their existence to the imposition of the lawgiver. *Qiyās*, juristic analogy, only exists because "the Lawgiver made it signify and hint at the juristic status."[26] Similar remarks are made by al-Bājī, al-Shīrāzī and Ibn 'Aqīl.[27]

The conventional character of analogical reasoning made it the chief object of juristic controversy. As early as the ninth century, the theologian al-Naẓẓām and various Islamic sects (for example, Khārijites) rejected analogical reasoning.[28] By the eleventh century, however, the objections to analogical reasoning *per se* were dying out. Authors of books on the *uṣūl al-fiqh* from the four major law schools availed themselves of this method. But the objections to particular analogical arguments, especially those used by members of opposing law schools, became the rule of the day.

The jurist's lenient attitude towards stringency met opposition from the theologians. al-Khaṭīb al-Baghdādī gives an overview of this situation:

> The jurists call *ḥadīth* with one line of transmission "*dalīl*". They also called analogical reasoning (*qiyās*) and anything which to a preponderant opinion (that "x" is the case) demonstration (*ḥujja*) and proof (*dalīl*).
>
> Now the great experts among the theologians and theoreticians (*ahl al-naẓar*) criticized them for doing this. They said "*Ḥujja* and *dalīl* are what cause the person using them to obtain *knowledge* of the thing signified and lead to certain knowledge (*yaqīn*). But properly speaking, *dalīl* does not lead to preponderant opinion; for, what does this is called *amāra* (hint)."
>
> al-Khaṭīb al-Baghdādī says: Neither the jurists nor the theologians have erred! The theologians reported the truth about "*dalīl*," and "*ḥujja*." But the jurists called what they were religiously obligated (*kullifa*) to have recourse to (such as *ḥadīth* with one line of transmission, analogy, and other such things which don't afford knowledge but preponderant opinion instead) "*dalīl*" since God obligated them to pass judgment by using probable evidence obtained by speculation...."[29]

The jurists had an even better reason for arguing that their evidence was not stringent. A Mu'tazilite jurist argued against theologians, that if the statutes deriving from the *uṣūl* by analogical reasoning and *khabar wāḥid* (*ḥadīth* with a single line of transmission) were valid apodictically, then whoever did not obey these laws must necessarily be branded as heretics.[30] The catholic nature of the Islamic system

---

[26] al-Juwaynī, *al-Kāfiya*, pp. 9, line 7 ff.; 148, line -5, *et alia*.

[27] Ibn 'Aqīl, *al-Jadal*, p. 159, par.236. al-Bājī, *Minhāj*, p. 177, par. 389. Abū Isḥāq al-Shīrāzī, "Ma'ūnat," fol. 17b: 10ff.

[28] On al-Naẓẓām, see van Ess, *Kitāb al-Nakth*. al-Juwaynī, *al-Burhān fī uṣūl al-fiqh*, ed. 'A. al-Dīb, 2 vols. (Cairo: Dār al-Anṣār, 1980), vol. 2, p. 750. Ibn 'Aqīl, *al-Jadal*, p. 191, par. 68.

[29] al-Khaṭīb al-Baghdādī, *al-Faqīh*, vol. 2, p. 23, line -2 ff.

[30] Abū l-Ḥusain Muḥammad al-Baṣrī, *Kitāb al-mu'tamad fī uṣūl al-fiqh*, ed. M. Hamīdullāh, 2 vols. (Damascus: Imprimerie Catholique, 1963), vol. 2, pp. 987–8 ff. On the relation of this work to 'Abd al-Jabbār's *al-'Umad*, see Sezgin, *GAS* I: 625 ff.

of jurisprudence, its acceptance of diverse rules of law as being equally "orthodox," made the non-stringency of laws derived from the *uṣūl* a prerequisite if not a *desideratum.*

There were, of course, as early as al-Shāfiʿī, books composed about the *quaestiones disputatae* among the leading jurists. Writings on the subject by al-Shāfiʿī, al-Qāḍī, al-Nuʿmān, al-Ṭabarī, and al-Dabūsī have survived.[31] If we take al-Ṭabarī's *K. Ikhtilāf al-fuqahā'*, as our model of early juristic "disputation" literature, we find that is totally free of the *jadal* technique. His custom is to report the opinion and reasoning of some leading jurist on a given controversial issue; sometimes he gives the reason (*ʿilla*) for the jurist's choosing that opinion; and sometimes he goes on to give his own opinion about which statement, if any, solves the problem. The detailed study of these works as a whole would most probably reveal that they were intended to acquaint the reader with the points of dispute and the various solutions that were current. The reader could then choose that opinion which he most readily assented to; for, in these texts there is no argumentation as to what is faulty in the other school's reasoning. The techniques of argumentation are ignored.[32]

This is also true of the books on *uṣūl al-fiqh*. They are not polemical in intention. Rather, they aim at explaining how the various statutes derive from the principles of the law. Indeed, it was probably the widespread acceptance of the science of *uṣūl al-fiqh* which was responsible for the penetration of the *jadal* method into jurisprudence. Once the points of dispute had been identified, it was but a short step to consider whether the opposing school's opinion had missed the point of dispute or had argued improperly. Or, when a new case arose, and different opinions prevailed concerning its juristic status, the method of reasoning again became the focus of attention. al-Shīrāzī tells us, for instance, that he wrote his short introduction to dialectical jurisprudence because he noticed the people's pressing need for such works.[33] al-Bājī makes similar remarks,[34] and granted, the complexity of the *uṣūl al-fiqh*, it is not unexpected that "the people" were at a loss when it came to juristic disputation.

The audience to which our authors were addressing their books were jurists who had already studied the *uṣūl al-fiqh*. al-Juwaynī tells us that his book is written for those who already have a good knowledge of "law and the principles of jurisprudence." He later notes that the "discussion of how to derive the *rationes legis* (*ʿilal*)...

---

[31] Some of al-Shāfiʿī's *ikhtilāf* works are printed in his *Kitāb al-Umm*, 7 vols. (Cairo: Bulaᵃq, 1321–26), vol. 7. On that see Sezgin, *GAS*, 1: 487. For al-Ṭabarī's work, see, Sezgin *GAS*, 1: 328. al-Qāḍī al-Nuʿmān, *Kitāb ikhtilāf uṣūl al-madhāhib*, ed. S.T. Lokhandwalla (Simla: Indian Institute of Advanced Study, 1974). Cf. The review of the latter by J. van Ess, *Der Islam* 51 (1974): 300–1. Sezgin, *GAS*, 1: 456. R. Brunschvig, "La Theorie du *qiyās* juridique chez le Hanafite al-Dabūsī," *Orientalia Hispanica sive studia* F. M. Pareja *octogenaria dicata*. Ed. J. M. Barral (Lugduni Batavorum: E. J. Brill, 1974), pp. 150–4.

[32] Abū Jaʿfar Muḥammad b. Jarīr al-Ṭabarī, *Kitāb Ikhtilāf al-fuqahā'*, ed. F. Kern, 2 vols. (Beirut: n.p., n.d.), vol. 2, pp. 25ff.; p. 46, line -8 ff.

[33] Abū Isḥāq, al-Shīrāzī, "Maʿūnat," fol.1b: 2 ff.

[34] al-Bājī, *Minhāj*, p. 7, par. 2.

is peculiar to the *uṣūl al-fiqh*. This art should be known before one takes up the study of the rules of *jadal*."[35] We have just mentioned al-Bājī's and al-Shīrāzī's treatment of the various principles (*uṣūl*) of jurisprudence. But the treatment is brief because their main concern is how to argue for or against any given juristic opinion.

Let us now return to the third question: What is your evidence?

According to al-Bājī,[36] R has three possible methods of demonstration (*dalāla*): (1) he may bring evidence concerning the problem or (2) evidence that the juristic qualification (*ḥukm*) applies to a part of the whole and then extrapolate to the whole or (3) he may base one question upon another. The first method is exemplified by the analogical reasoning discussed above. The second case is a restricted instance of the first. It is more dangerous than the first type of demonstration since R may have initially stated his thesis unrestrictedly, and then proceeded to prove it restrictedly. In such a case R loses because he fails to accomplish his original goal.[37]

The third method of proof is more controversial than the others. It is a remnant from that period of *jadal* where the experts were undecided as to whether Q was obliged to follow R's method (*madhhab*). This becomes clear when we examine al-Bājī's example:

> If a Ẓāhirite asks a Mālikite about interest on honey, the Mālikite says, "We prove this question on the basis of analogical reasoning (*qiyās*). If you allow me to use analogy, then I will use it to solve this question; if not, then I will prove that analogy is a sound basis for argumentation.[38]

If Q rejects both options, he is behaving eristically and loses. Now the situation can get complicated. If R should announce his intention of using this "controversial" method at the beginning of the dispute, then this is permissible. However, should he use this method after having started out on the basis of some other piece of evidence, there is disagreement as to whether he is allowed to do this or not. Abu ʿAli al-Ṭabarī, one of the founding fathers of *jadal* in jurisprudence, declared that this is not allowed since it is a digression (*intiqāl*).[39] But al-Bājī and al-Shīrāzī and Ibn ʿAqīl all permit it.[40] In order to avoid such problems, our authors stipulate that in cases of doubt, Q is obliged to follow R's method (*madhhab*) even if it be a paltry one.

---

[35] al-Juwaynī, *Kāfiya*, p. 89, line -3 ff.; p. 130,line -1 ff.

[36] al-Bājī, *Minhāj*, p. 37, par. 71.

[37] Ibid., p. 38, lines 5–6: "*wa-ʿajaza ʿan bulūgh mā qaṣadahū, fa-ḥukima ʿalayhī bil-inqitāʿ*." On the signs of defeat, see below.

[38] al-Bājī, *Minhāj*, p. 38, line 10 ff. Cf. al-Khaṭīb al-Baghdādī, *al-Faqīh*,vol. 2, p. 41, line -5 ff. Abū Isḥāq al-Shīrāzī, "Maʿūnat," fol.11b: 1.

[39] al-Bājī, *Minhāj*, p. 39, line 7.

[40] Ibid., 39, lines 8–9.

Question Four: The Mode of Signification

al-Bājī tells us that this question is exclusively used against arguments based upon Qur'ānic verse and prophetic tradition, and then only when the proof verse or tradition is obscure in meaning or application.[41] In the *jadal* of the theologians, the question about the mode of signification was used against "rational evidence." It operated under the old Mu'tazilite scheme of argumentation from the signifier (*dalīl*) to the signified (*madlūl*), where often the *way* in which the sign signifies this significate or its connection with it is not clear. But in juristic analogy, the mode of signification or the *ratio legis* was evident. In regard to it, the question about the mode of proof had become superfluous. But come what may, the old system had to be preserved, so the third question (of theological *jadal*) was kept but significantly reinterpreted to include only argument from the Qur'ān and *sunna*.[42]

Question Five: Objection

In following al-Bājī's scheme, we have picked up an extra question. This happened at the very beginning where the first question of theological *jadal* became two questions. In any event, the fifth question is the one in which Q was able to use the arsenal of weapons at his disposal. In the other questions, the questioner is seeking information and so has no call to object. al-Juwaynī notes, in apparent reminiscence of theological *jadal*:

> Most of the theoreticians (*ahl al-naẓar*) say: If Q knows R's thesis, and it is so well known to him that he cannot doubt, he may begin by asking for its demonstration. If he knows P's evidence (*dalīl*) and that P has no other evidence to offer, Q may begin objecting to his evidence![43]

This question is of course the same as the old "fourth question" of theological *jadal*. But now, the question has been greatly enlarged. We noted earlier how certain ancient debating techniques such as counter-objection (*mu'āraḍa*) and distinction (*farq*) were haphazardly sheltered in the "new systematic" theological *jadal*.[44] In juristic *jadal*, this fault has been repaired. The new fourth question is called "question in the manner of rejection of evidence (*dalīl*)."[45] This new appellation succeeded in encompassing all the techniques of debate at Q's disposal under the rubric of one question. al-Juwaynī, as we stated earlier, had another name for this question:

---

[41] Ibid., p. 39, par. 76; cf. Ibn 'Aqīl, *al-Jadal*, p. 163, par. 219.

[42] Cf. van Ess, *Īcī*, pp. 358 ff. al-Khaṭīb al-Baghdādī, *al-Faqīh*, vol. 2, p. 43, line 1 ff.; Ibn 'Aqīl, p. 42, par. 220; Shīrāzī, Mulakhkhaṣ 123b3ff.

[43] al-Juwaynī, *al-Kāfiya*, p. 79, line -3 ff.

[44] Cf. above our chapter on theological *jadal*.

[45] al-Bājī, *Minhāj*, p. 40, line -3 ff.: "*al-su'āl 'alā wajh al-qadḥ fī al-dalīl.*" Cf. al-Khaṭīb al-Baghdādī, *al-Faqīh*, vol. 2, p. 40, line 8.

opposition (*muqābala*). He gave three types of opposition: contradiction, reversal, and counter-objection. He later identifies this question as *ilzām bil-muqābala* or *ilzām 'alā al-dalāla* which he defines as "making the person demonstrating [that is, R] show the proof's commensurability."[46] The demand to show the proof's commensurability was the fourth question of theological *jadal*. al-Juwaynī explicitly associates the new juristic question with the old theological one.[47]

Turning to the objections used, we find that al-Shīrāzī, al-Khaṭīb al-Baghdādī, and al-Bājī all discuss objections against opponents who use Qur'ān, *ḥadīth*, *ijmā'* and *qiyās*; that is to say, in descending order with respect to their probative value. But al-Bājī and al-Juwaynī also give us a catalogue of the objections used, so before turning to the detailed study of the specific objections, let us turn to al-Bājī's analysis. We will be confining our remarks to objections against analogical reasoning since the argumentation there was at its most technical level and because it reveals the strongest bond with the old theological system of *jadal*.

According to al-Bājī, all objections against any type of argument are of three types: *muṭālaba*, *i'tirāḍ*, and *mu'āraḍa*.[48]

Muṭālaba *(Request)*

Muṭālaba is al-Bājī's name for the objection that takes the form of asking for verification that such and such is the case (*muṭālaba bi-taṣḥīḥ*). Thus, when R uses a *ḥadīth* as the basis of his argument, Q may *request* that R verify the wording of the *ḥadīth* or its chain of transmission (*isnād*); or if R uses analogical reasoning, Q might ask him to verify that the *ratio legis* (*'illa*) applies to both cases or whether it applies at all.[49] Here al-Juwaynī disagrees. al-Juwaynī understands *muṭālaba* as a sub-division of *i'tirāḍ* ("objection").[50] It is sometimes used synonymously with *man'* and *mumāna'a* (lit. obviation, disallowance) which al-Juwaynī defines as "the making known of a claim that disagrees with R's."[51] He defines *muṭālaba* as "making the opponent explain his proof (*ḥujja*). It is of two sorts: (1) asking him to explain the basis (*aṣl*) of his proof (dalāla), and its establishment; and, (2) asking for an explanation of the 'mode of proof'."[52] Thus, in al-Juwaynī's system, *muṭālaba* is a subdivision of the third question about the verification of the proof (*burhān*), although it could be used in the fourth question where objections are brought for-

[46] al-Juwaynī, *al-Kāfiya*, p10.. 79, line 10.

[47] Ibid., p. 79, line 10: al-Juwaynī uses the term *ṭard* which is a later equivalent of the old *jarayān al-'illa fī ma'lūlātihā*. Cf. our chapter on theological *jadal*.

[48] al-Bājī, *Minhāj*, p.40, line -2.

[49] Ibid., p.40, line -1 ff.

[50] al-Juwaynī, *al-Kāfiya*, p. 67, line 15.

[51] Ibid., p. 68, line -9.

[52] Ibid., p. 68, line 4 ff.

ward.[53] al-Juwaynī allows that Q may object to what R says only in the third and fourth questions (al-Juwaynī is operating in the old theological four question scheme) since "in them he seeks to make objections (*ṭaʿn*) and to destroy (*ifsād*) R's thesis; this can only take place after R has mentioned his thesis and its proof." Thus, to object before the last two questions would be out of place.[54]

Iʿtirāḍ *(Objection)*

al-Bājī says that *iʿtirāḍ* is an objection that goes to the heart of the evidence (*dalīl*), rendering it void.[55] Against analogical reasoning (*qiyās*) al-Bājī knows fifteen different sorts of objection (*iʿtirāḍ*) while al-Juwaynī knows, or rather lists nine types.[56] al-Juwaynī defines *iʿtirāḍ* in the following manner:

> It is opposing (*muqābala*) the opponent's argument by means of something which prevents him from attaining his goal.... Others say, "it is preventing (*mumānaʿa*) the opponent (from proving his point) by taking a stand of equal probative force (*bi-musāwatihī*) against the argument that he brings."[57]

Iʿtirāḍ in its non-technical meaning has the sense of interposing something between a person and his goal, so that tropically, the one who makes an *iʿtirāḍ* prevents R from proving his point.[58]

Muʿāraḍa *(Counter-Objection)*

This is al-Bājī's final category, but it is no stranger to us. We met it before in theological garb and it has not changed its aspect here. al-Bājī defines it as "Q's opposing the demonstrator (R) with a piece of evidence of similar or greater probative force."[59] In that case R must respond by using all the weapons that Q would normally use against R, such as the request to verify information (*muṭālaba)* and objection (*iʿtirāḍ*); that failing, R must show why his evidence is to be preferred to that of Q.[60] al-Bājī's *muʿāraḍa*, thus, includes a reversal of the roles of R and Q. R must change his tactics if he is to escape from the claws of this deadly technique. But *muʿāraḍa* was still controversial, as al-Juwaynī notes:

---

[53] Ibid., p. 77, line 13.

[54] Ibid., p. 79, lines 15–17.

[55] al-Bājī, *Minhāj*, p. 41, line 3.

[56] Ibid., pp. 148–9. al-Juwaynī, *al-Kāfiya*, p. 67 line 13 ff.

[57] Ibid., p. 67, lines 3–6.

[58] Ibid., p. 67, line 8.

[59] al-Bājī, *Minhāj*, p. 41, line 6, p. 14, lines 7–8.

[60] Ibid., p. 41, line 6 ff.

Table 4.1 The order of the objections

Al-Juwaynī	Al-Shirāzī	Al-Bājī	Ibn ʿAqīl
1. Mumānaʿa, Manʿ Muṭālaba	4. Manʿ al-ḥukm fī al-aṣl wal-farʿ; 5. Muṭālaba bi-taṣḥīḥ al-ʿilla	5. Mumānaʿa al-aṣl, al-farʿ, al-waṣf; Muṭālaba bi-taṣḥīḥ al-ʿilla	1. Mumānaʿa 2. taṣḥīḥ al-ʿilla
2. Fasād al-waḍʿ	11. Fasād al-waḍʿ	10. Fasād al-waḍʿ	9. Fasād al-waḍʿ
3. ʿAdam al-taʾthīr	6. ʿAdam al-taʾthīr	14. ʿAdam al-taʾthīr	3. ʿAdam al-taʾthīr
4. Ishtirāk fī al-dalāla, qalb	14. Qalb	9. Qalb	7. Qalb
5. Munāqaḍa, Naqḍ	7. Naqḍ	11. Naqḍ	5. Naqḍ
6. al-Qaul bi-mūjib al-ʿilla	9. al-Qaul bi-mūjib al-ʿilla	8. al-Qaul bi-mūjib al-ʿilla	6. al-Qaul bi-mūjib al-ʿilla
7. Farq	15. [Muʿāraḍa]	15. [Muʿāraḍa]	–
8. Muʿāraḍa	–	15. Muʿāraḍa	–
9 [Ilzām]	–	–	–

> Some of the dialecticians (*jadalīyūn*) argued that muʿāraḍa is not to be accepted from Q, since in it, Q sets himself up as a demonstrator (*mustadill*), but the rules of dialectic (marāsim al-jadal) stipulate that Q restrict his discourse to objections (al-iʿtirāḍāt al-maḥḍa); however, the "reason" (*ʿilla*) which Q brought as counterevidence is done so in the form of bringing evidence, for, in order to establish this "reason" he is forced to bring forth all the evidence....[61]

al-Juwaynī does not agree with this opinion. He argues that *muʿāraḍa* is of objection *iʿtirāḍ* and as long as R's proof is not free of objections, his thesis has not been firmly established. It is Q's job, he says, to bring objections while it is R's duty, according to the rules of dialectic, to ward off any objections. Therefore, if Q brings a *muʿāraḍa*, R is obliged to reply to it:

> Thus, they both will be aiding the progress of the investigation (mutaʿāwinūn ʿalā al-baḥth) Q by objecting and R by responding...for after all the purpose of dialectic is that each party help the other to investigate the matter thoroughly (*wal-gharḍ min al-munāẓara al-taʿāwun ʿalā al-baḥth wal-faḥṣ*).[62]

al-Juwaynī and his fellow *uṣūlī*s did not distinguish between disputation (*munāẓara*) and dialectic (*jadal, jidāl*, and *mujādala*). They are all equivalent in the technical language of the experts in *fiqh* and *uṣūl al-fiqh*, although they derive from different roots.[63]

We shall now turn to the objections used against analogical reasoning. It is here that the terminology is at is most difficult level, and it is here that the tradition of *jadal* has been expanded upon. According to al-Juwaynī these objections follow a specific order one necessarily following the other, there being no way to journey back after a later objection has been put forth (See Table 4.1). We will now look at

[61] al-Juwaynī, *al-Burhān*, p. 1050, par. 1053 ff.

[62] Ibid., p. 1053, line 2 ff.

[63] al-Juwaynī, *al-Burhān*, p. 1050, par. 1053 ff.

al-Juwaynī's catalogue following the order in which he gave them and then discuss his remarks as to why these objections must come in a specific order.

Mumāna'a, Man'

As we noted above, al-Juwaynī makes these terms at times synonymous with *muṭālaba*. The word *man'* or *mumāna'a* is used synonymously with objection (*i'tirāḍ*) and disagreement (*nizā'*).[64] "However, the word *mumāna'a* has become a *terminus technicus* among the jurists denoting the disallowance of the characteristic (*waṣf*) peculiar to the principal case (*aṣl*), or to the test case (*far'*), or to both together, or to the juristic qualification (*ḥukm*) of the principal case (*aṣl*).[65] Here is an example that al-Juwaynī uses in order to make this technique more apparent:

> An example of this against the principal case (*aṣl*): Q objects when R argues that a "hire contract" (*ijāra*) is rendered void by the death of one of the contracting parties because it is a contract for mutual benefit, and, therefore, is to be treated similarly to the case of marriage (*nikāḥ*). Q disallows this: "Death does not render the marriage void; rather marriage reaches its *conclusion* just as the 'hire contract' reaches its conclusion upon the completion of the [stipulated] time period."[66]

In the above example,[67] Q has disallowed R's allegation about the juristic quality (*ḥukm*) of the principal case, and has, thus, performed the objection known as *mumāna'a*.

al-Juwaynī's example is also used by al-Shīrāzī, al-Bājī, and Ibn 'Aqīl. The role of R is filled in by a Ḥanbalite, while the role of Q is filled by a Shāfi'ite in al-Shīrāzī, a Mālikite in al-Bājī, and a Ḥanbalite in Ibn 'Aqīl.[68] There are other instances where common examples are used. This coincidence reveals the "*topos*" character of the examples. They are without a doubt gleaned from the earlier literature on the divergence of the jurists (*ikhtilāf al-fuqahā'*).

al-Juwaynī and all the other jurists of our period also give detailed advice as to how to answer this objection. While the answers to this and the other objections are not without interest, most of them are of an obvious nature and their detailed explanation would take us very far afield. Nevertheless, I wish to mention al-Shīrāzī's solution to this example in order to show to what extent Ibn 'Aqīl relied on his short

---

[64] Ibid., p. 67, par. 159.

[65] Ibid,. p.131, lines 10–12. Ibn 'Aqīl, *al-Jadal*, p. 158, par. 240.

[66] al-Juwaynī, *al-Kāfiya*, p. 140, lines 1–5. *EI*² s.v. *"Idjāra"*.

[67] The example is based upon van Ess, *Ici*, p. 321.

[68] al-Bājī, *Minhāj*, p. 163, par 349. Ibn 'Aqīl, *al-Jadal*, p. 158/par. 245. Abū Isḥāq al-Shīrāzī, "Ma'ūnat," fol. 12a: 8–12.

treatise (or on some treatise on which al-Shīrāzī relied?). al-Shīrāzī says there are three solutions[69]:

(1) to explain that the principal case is (commonly) accepted (*mauḍi'uhā musallam*); (2) to explain away (*tafsīr*) the dissallowed part of his argument; (3) to demonstrate it (*an yadulla 'alaihī*). In al-Shīrāzī's examples of these solutions we learn that "demonstrating it" (3) amounts to referring it back to some *ḥadīth* or to the Qur'ān. In Ibn 'Aqīl, we learn that there are "three solutions."[70] He then lists al-Shīrāzī's solution in the order (1),(3),(2), where this account is preceded by a confusing paragraph about (4) defending the principal case by establishing that the line of transmission, on which it is based, is valid. The real confusion in Ibn 'Aqīl's account is that while he lists four solutions, he promises to give only three! The explanation for this and other places where Ibn 'Aqīl has the same material and presentation as al-Shīrāzī is that Ibn 'Aqīl's treatise is based on his study of al-Shīrāzī's "Ma'ūnat," or more likely on his own personal study under the tutelage of al-Shīrāzī. In this sense we could be dealing with Ibn 'Aqīl's reworking of his "school-notebooks."

Fasād al-waḍ' *(False Construction)*

al-Juwaynī defines this as "turning back the construction by means of that which necessitates the falsification of the constructed."[71] Now what all this jargon means becomes clear from his example: R tries to base a juristic qualification that is *permissible* upon a principal case (*aṣl*) whose juristic qualification is *obligatory*, "for obligation and permissibility are opposed to one another; thus, the founding (*binā'*) of one upon the other, and that is the construction of one upon the other, is a false construction."[72]

al-Shīrāzī and al-Bājī define this objection in other terms: it is the attaching to the *ratio legis* (*'illa*) the contrary of what it requires.[73] al-Shīrāzī gives the example of the Ḥanafite who argues that the saliva (*su'r*) of a predatory animal brings about ritual impurity since a predatory animal has fangs, so that its saliva causes ritual impurity as in the case of dogs. A Shāfi'ite objects using a *ḥadīth* to show that being a predator with fangs is a cause (*'illa*) of ritual purity and not ritual impurity. His objection amounts to saying: "You should have made being predatory with fangs a cause for not bringing about ritual impurity." But by stating what the real juristic

---

[69] Ibid., fol.12a: 4 ff.

[70] Ibn 'Aqīl, *al-Jadal*, p. 47, par. 240 ff.

[71] al-Juwaynī, *al-Kāfiya*, p. 68, lines 10–12.

[72] Ibid., p. 155.

[73] Abū Isḥaq al-Shīrazī, "Ma'ūnat," fol.15b: 16–17. al-Bājī, *Minhāj*, p. 178, line 10.

quality should be, Q has turned the argument around, using R's principal case to bring about the contrary of his thesis.[74]

This is what the Greek rhetoricians knew as the *methodos kata peritropēn*.[75]

As we shall later see, the usual technical term for this ancient method was *qalb*, reversal. It would appear that at this stage, some of the technical terms of juristic dialectics had not yet been given their permanent technical meeting.

al-Bājī, for instance, treats as a sub-group to false construction, the category of false perspective (*fasād al-iʿtibār*). This he defines as considering a thing in the light of something which should not be considered. He explains later that "false perspective may occur in considering a juristic qualification with another one that is incompatible with it, or in considering the test case with the (wrong) *ratio legis*."[76]

al-Shīrāzī considers the "false perspective" as a separate type of objection. But he gives a good example of what al-Bājī has in mind:

> It consists in considering the test case (*farʿ*) on the basis of a principal case (*aṣl*) although both have conflicting juristic qualifications in similar cases. For instance, considering the minor and person of age as equals with respect to paying the alms tax (*zakāt*) although the law treats them differently with respect to the obligations of prayer and fasting.[77]

R has chosen a false perspective.

ʿAdam al-taʾthīr (Ineffective *Ratio Legis*)

We again possess conflicting accounts about the meaning of this "question." al-Juwaynī knows it as "...when R claims a connection between a juristic qualification (*ḥukm*) and a certain thing (*maʿnā*) and this claim is not apparent.[78] al-Shīrāzī defines it as "the existence of a juristic quality (*ḥukm*) together with the absence of the (alleged) *ratio legis* (*ʿilla*)."[79] This question is a form of the old fourth theological question, then called *jarayān al-ʿilla fī maʿlūlātihā*, applying the cause to its causata.[80] Here I think al-Juwaynī is being rather cautious in his definition.

---

[74] Abū Isḥāq al-Shīrāzī, "Maʿūnat," fol.15b: 16 ff. Cf. E. Gräf, *Jagdbeute und Schlachttier im islamischen Recht* (Bonn: Selbstverlag des Orientalischen Seminars der Universität Bonn, 1959), pp. 132–137.

[75] R. Volkmann, *Die Rhetorik der Griechen und Römer* (Leipzig: Teubner, 1874), p. 243. Cf. Our remarks on *muʿāraḍa* in our chapter on theological *jadal*.

[76] al-Bājī, *Minhāj*, p. 178, par. 392.

[77] Abū Isḥāq al-Shīrāzī, "Maʿūnat," fol.16b: 3–4.

[78] al-Juwaynī, *al-Kāfiya*, p. 68, line 13 ff.

[79] Abū Isḥāq al-Shīrāzī, "Maʿūnat," fol.13a: 11.

[80] See note 46, *supra*, and text thereto.

He avoids calling it the absence of the relation between the juristic quality and the *ratio legis*. As he tells us more than once, the *ʿillal* of the law are unlike the *ʿilla* of the intellect for the latter are correlative while the former are not.[81] al-Bājī is also very wary about the value of this objection:

> It is the "non-absence" of the juristic quality on account of the absence (*ʿadam*) of the ratio legis in some case (*mauḍiʿ*). But in our view, being effective (*ta'thīr*) is evidence that the *ratio legis* is sound, but its being ineffective does not (necessarily) mean that it is unsound, for it could be shown to be sound by another piece of evidence. Indeed, in our view it would have been more appropriate to include this objection in the category of "requesting the verification of the *ratio legis* (*al-muṭālaba bi-taṣḥīḥ al-ʿilla*)" but since the majority of our teachers (*shuyūkhunā*) say "being ineffective renders the *ratio legis* void" ...we have devoted a chapter to it in the category of objections against the *ratio legis*.[82]

al-Bājī's protest that this objection should be put in another category appears to be valid. In al-Shīrāzī's account, the "request to verify the *ratio legis*" comes directly before this one, and this would suggest that he saw a very close association between the two. al-Shīrāzī had the habit of breaking up the objections into many separate ones. So, for instance, he has separate adjoining chapters on false construction and false perspective (numbers 10 and 11 in his list). An example from al-Shīrāzī's chapter on the verification of the cause will help illustrate this connection:

> (A Shāfiʿite) says: Date-brandy is forbidden because it is an intoxicating drink, so it is forbidden as in the case of grape-wine. A Ḥanafite objects: How do you know that this *ratio legis* is the proper one? He replies: The proof that this is the proper one is the existence of the juristic quality (*ḥukm*) on account of the *ratio legis*, and its absence when it is absent. Don't you see that it is the consensus that when it has been pressed, it is permissible before the appearance of the intoxicating factor? But when the latter does not appear, and nothing else in addition, it is the consensus that it is forbidden. But, should the intoxicating factor cease to exist, it is the consensus that it is permitted....[83]

Here R conclusively shows the effectiveness of the *ratio legis* in bringing about the juristic quality. If Q had objected: "But pressed grapes before they become intoxicating are forbidden," then he would have been making the claim that the *ratio legis* was ineffective.

---

[81] al-Juwaynī, *al-Kāfiya*, p. 9, line 5 ff.

[82] al-Bājī, *Minhāj*, p. 195, par. 443.

[83] Abū Isḥāq al-Shīrāzī, "Maʿūnat," fol.13a: 1 ff.

Qalb or *Ishtirāk fī al-dalāla (methodos kata peritropēn)*[84]

al-Juwaynī defines it as "Q's agreeing with R's evidence in order to derive an incompatible conclusion."[85] He later tells us it is a type of opposition (*muqābala*).[86] al-Bājī defines it as Q's sharing R's evidence.[87] He also gives us insight into the history of this technique:

> It is a sound question. Abū 'Alī al-Ṭabarī mentioned that it is the subtlest thing that occurs between two disputants. Certain Shāfi'ites, however, claimed that "*qalb* is not a sound question since it amounts to imposing a (new) question upon R and Q is not allowed to demand a proof (*dalāla*) of anything other than the point of dispute."
>
> But this (view) is incorrect, for Q only intends to render R's *ratio legis* null and void, and to show R that the juristic qualification (*ḥukm*) which he has attached it to has no connection with it; rather, that its contrary or something else incompatible is connected to it. This is what excludes it from being a *ratio legis* for this particular juristic qualification.

Abū Isḥāq al-Shīrāzī was of the opinion that *qalb* is a type of counter-objection (*mu'āraḍa*), and that it does *not* render the *ratio legis* void.[88] But this is not entirely correct, for I think we must make a distinction (*taqsīm*) since there are really two sorts of *qalb*: (1) One with respect to all the qualities of the *ratio legis*, and (2) another which attaches to only some of them.[89]

In type one, Q's objection destroys R's *ratio legis*; for, Q's argument for connecting it with a contrary or incompatible juristic qualification necessarily renders it void. al-Juwaynī offers an example of *qalb* which we earlier used to demonstrate al-Shīrāzī's and al-Bājī's conceptions of false construction. But as we remarked earlier, it is a perfect illustration of how the same *ratio legis* can be used to arrive at a contrary juristic qualification. Now although the technique was widely used, there was apparently a certain amount of disagreement as to what it was properly called. al-Juwaynī tells us that certain people referred to the example of the predatory animal as an instance of counter-objection (*mu'āraḍa*):

> This, however, is a great mistake. Since the 'proof' (*ḥujja*) (which stems) from the two principal cases is one thing, and one *ratio legis* (*'illa*): since, the proof is none other than the *ratio legis* of the two principal cases, and the proof is one, (there can be no counter-objec-

---

[84] al-Bāqillānī provides a nice example of *qalb* at *Tamhīd*. p. 156, lines 6–10. He notes that the Jews, Christians, and Magians object to the Muslim claim that Muhammad challenged the Arabs to bring forth verses on the same level of the Qur'an, saying "How do you know that he actually challenged them?" The Muslim reply is to turn [*qalb*] the question against them by saying "How do you know that Jesus and Moses and Zarathustra challenged their people to emulate their deeds?"

[85] al-Juwaynī, *al-Kāfiya*, p. 68, line -1: "*Musāwāt al-khaṣm khaṣmahū fī mā yūriduhū 'alā al-tanāfī.*"

[86] Ibid., p. 217, line 3.

[87] al-Bājī, *Minhāj*, p. 14, line 7.

[88] Cf. Abū Isḥāq al-Shīrāzī, "Ma'ūnat," fol.17a: 15–6. Ibn 'Aqīl, *al-Jadal*, p. 143, par. 295. al-Juwaynī, *al-Kāfiya*, p. 225, line 14. al-Juwaynī attributes this view to Shāfi'ites.

[89] al-Bājī, *Minhāj*, p. 174, par. 385.

tion here) because a thing cannot be opposed to itself (*lā yuʿāriḍ nafsahū*) nor can it be preferred to itself.[90]

al-Juwaynī gives a very clear example of this difference:

R claims to know that "x is the case" *a priori*.
Q objects: Why do you deny that your opponent knows that "x" is *not* the case *a priori*?[91]

As we saw in our chapter on *muʿāraḍa* earlier, and as al-Juwaynī clearly states, this must be an example of *qalb*, because the evidence is one thing. In order for this example to be one of *muʿāraḍa*, one must imagine Q objecting; "Why do you deny that your opponent knows that ʽx is not the caseʽ by means of necromancy?" In the device known as *qalb*, Q shares R's evidence in order to slyly draw a contrary conclusion.

Although al-Shīrāzī, as we noted above, identifies certain species of *qalb* as "false construction," he is still aware of this technical word, and identifies several types. One he calls *qalb al-taswīya*, "turning around the juristic qualification where one accepts R's proof in its entirety, with a small addition."[92]

An example:

R, a Ḥanafite, argues: The minor ritual ablution (*wuḍūʾ*) is an act of ritual purification by means of a liquid so it requires no profession of intention as in the case of removing ritual impurity.
Q, a Shāfiʿite says: I reverse (your argument) I say that liquids and *solids*[93] are on the same level with respect to expressing intention, as in the case of removing ritual impurity, (so that a profession of intention is necessary).[94]

Q here adds something to R's argument in order to draw his contrary conclusion. The "equalization" is at one and the same time the "addition:" making the status of liquids and *solids* equal in the principal case. This leads to the contrary conclusion. al-Juwaynī knows this type of reversal under several appellations: *qalb al-taswīya*, *qalb al-tafriqa*, and *qalb al-iʿtibār*.[95] The method itself was subject to controversy—some people argued that it should be disallowed because it is too general (*mujmal*) and, thus, does not lead to any practical rules.[96] al-Juwaynī refutes this and other objections.[97]

---

[90] al-Juwaynī, *al-Kāfiya*, p. 233, line -2 ff; cf. p. 253, par. 396. J. van Ess, "The Logical structure of Islamic theology," *Logic in Classical Islamic Culture*, ed. G.E. von Grunebaum (Wiesbaden: Harrasowitz, 1970): 41.

[91] al-Juwaynī, *al-Kāfiya*, p. 217.

[92] Abū Isḥāq al-Shīrāzī, "Maʿunat," fol.17a: 17 ff. Cf. Ibn ʿAqīl, *al-Jadal*, p. 143, par .297. al-Bājī, *Minhāj*, p. 176, par 388. There, at p.176, line 19, read *al-taswīya* for *al-sawīya*.

[93] The reference is to the practice of *tayammum*, using a substitute for water to perform the ritual ablution.

[94] Abū Isḥāq al-Shīrāzī, "Maʿūnat," 17a: 17 ff. Cf. al-Juwaynī, *al-Kāfiya*, p. 238.

[95] Ibid., p. 238, lines 16–8.

[96] Ibid., p. 240, line 10 ff.

[97] Ibid., p. 241, par. 379.

There were other types of *qalb*. One is called by al-Shīrāzī *qalb li-ḥukm maqṣūḍ*, the reversal of the intended juristic qualification.[98] al-Juwaynī calls this same technique explicit reversal (*al-qalb al-ṣarīḥ*):

> It is called explicit reversal since Q can explicitly state what he finds incompatible in the intended juristic qualification that R derives from his *ratio legis*. An example: R says: Prayer in seclusion (*i'tikāf*) is not allowed unless the person fasts, since (*i'tikāf*) is tarrying in a specific place, so it does not become an act of piety except by some (external) nexus (*qarīna*) (to piety), as in the case of standing at Arafat (during the pilgrimage).
>
> Q says: This *ratio legis* requires that no fasting be stipulated (in it), as in the case of standing at Arafat.
>
> (al-Juwaynī says:) It is called explicit since the disagreement about fasting was explicitly mentioned by Q in his denial that amounted to the contradiction of R's opinion; this (objection) turns R's argument on its head.[99]

al-Juwaynī's account is a graphic description of how Q reverses R's argument.

Now there were some people who objected to *qalb per se* and they brought the same arguments that we previously encountered in discussing juristic "counter-objection," namely, that this technique amounted to reversing the roles of R and Q, since R seems to be bringing forward an argument. al-Juwaynī rules that this is not the case, since Q brings it in the form of an objection.[100]

Naqḍ *or* munāqaḍa *(Inconsistency)*

al-Juwaynī offers two definitions of *naqḍ*:

(1) It is the denial that the juristic qualification
has the alleged *ratio legis*...
(2) Thie existence of the *ratio legis* with the absence
of its alleged juristic qualification.[101]

This type of objection is reminiscent of the "ineffective cause", but here it is allowed that the cause (*'illa*) *is* effective but not in all cases (*ṣuwar mawāḍi'*) and is, therefore, invalid. There was disagreement about this type of objection just as there was in the case of the "ineffective cause." Most of the writers on *uṣūl al-fiqh* and juristic dialectics accepted it, but certain Ḥanafites did not.[102] Together with the ineffective cause, it comprises the old category of applying the cause to its causata.[103]

---

[98] Abū Isḥāq al-Shīrāzī, "Ma'ūnat," fol.17a: 9 ff.

[99] al-Juwaynī, *al-Kāfiya*, p. 236, line 14 ff. Cf. EI² s. v. "*Ḥādjdj*.

[100] al-Juwaynī, *al-Burhān*, vol. 2, par. 1041.

[101] al-Juwaynī, *al-Kāfiya*, p. 69, line 1 ff. Cf. al-Juwaynī, *al-Burhān*, vol. 2, p. 977, lines 11–12. He defends it there as "the absence (*takhāluf*) of the *ḥukm* with the presence of P's alleged *'illa*. Cf. Abū Ish·āq al-Shīrāzī, "Ma'ūnat," fol.14a: 1 ff. al-Bājī, *Minhāj*, p. 185, par. 412; p. 14, line 6.

[102] al-Juwaynī, *al-Burhān*, vol. 2, p. 977, line -2 ff.

[103] Cf. note 46, *supra*, and text thereto. Van Ess, *Īcī*, pp. 384 ff.

In his treatment of "inconsistency," al-Juwaynī mentions another category of objection, *munāqaḍa*, contradiction or self-contradiction.[104] al-Juwaynī is somewhat careless in his use of these terms, sometimes using *naqḍ* and at other times using *munāqaḍa* to describe this phenomenon.[105] It seems, however, that he understands *munāqaḍa* as a general category of which *naqḍ* is a species, where the name of the genus is at times used in place of the name of the species.

A special case of *naqḍ* is treated as a separate objection by al-Bājī, al-Shīrāzī, and Ibn ʿAqīl.[106] They call it *kasr* (literally, breaking up). They describe it as the existence of the meaning (*maʿnā*) of the *ratio legis* without the existence of the corresponding juristic qualification. In it Q attacks one of the "characteristics" (*auṣāf*) of the *ratio legis* or substitutes its meaning for it. al-Juwaynī mentions it in his chapter on "inconsistency" as a controversial objection, and gives much space to the arguments of those who deny it.[107] Sometimes its supporters called it refuting R by referring to the "spirit of law" (*ilzām ʿalā al-maʿnā*).[108] al-Juwaynī sees this method as the very last resort of a questioner who has first unsuccessfully used the objection of "inconsistency" against an expression in R's proof, and now decides to show that its "intention" is inconsistent.[109]

al-Qaul bi-mūjib al-ʿilla *(Limited Acceptance)*

al-Bājī says that this technique involves "Q's accepting the *ratio legis* while excluding its application to the disputed point."[110] al-Juwaynī calls it, "Q's agreeing with R's argument as to the juristic quality of the *ratio legis*, while excluding its application to the point of dispute".[111] An example:

R: A Kufī argues that fasting is necessary in the case of prayer in seclusion (*iʿtikāf*) because: Prayer in seclusion is characterized by tarrying in a special place, and this act does not become *per se* an act of worship as in the case of standing at Arafat.

Q: In my view no act of worship becomes such without a profession of intention, and this is the very act of *iʿtikāf*, just as being in a state of ritual consecration (*iḥrām*) is added to standing at (Arafat) so that it becomes an act of worship.[112]

---

[104] al-Juwaynī, *al-Kāfiya*, p. 67, line -2.

[105] Ibid., pp. 67, line -2; 69, line 1; 132, line -2; 172 ff.; 133, line 3 ff.

[106] Abū Isḥāq al-Shīrāzī, "Maʿūnat," fol.14b: 18 ff. al-Bājī, *Minhāj*, p. 191, line 3 ff. Ibn ʿAqīl, *al-Jadal*, p. 140, par. 305 ff.

[107] al-Juwaynī, *al-Kāfiya*, 212, line 5 ff.; cf. p. 264.

[108] Ibid. p. 213, line 11 ff.

[109] Ibid. p. 212, line 5 f.

[110] al-Bājī, *Minhāj*, p. 173, par. 381 ff. Cf. Abū Isḥāq al-Shīrāzī, "Maʿūnat," fol.15a: 4 ff.

[111] al-Juwaynī, *al-Kāfiya*, p. 69, line 5; cf. 161, line 4 ff.

[112] Ibid., p. 162, par. 258. Cf. *EI*² s.v. "Iʿtiḳāf."

al-Juwaynī notes that Q has literally stripped away R's evidence from the point of dispute.[113]

Farq *(Distinction)*

al-Juwaynī defines it as "a type of counter-objection (*muʿāraḍa*) which contains an objection that the case at hand (*farʿ*) and the principal case (*aṣl*) differ with respect to the *ratio legis* of the juristic qualification.[114] al-Shīrāzī and al-Bājī consider *farq* to be a special case of counter-objection, and, thus, they mention it in their chapters on counter-objection.[115] al-Bājī says:

> It is the most legal (*afqah*) objection that occurs in the debate, for through it the juristic status of the problem becomes known. It consists in mentioning something which necessitates a difference between the test case (*farʿ*) and the principal case. That is, to mention something (*maʿnā* [in the sense of the *ḥukm* of the *ʿilla*]) and its contrary (*ʿaks*) in the point of dispute. Some say there is no need for him to give its contrary in the case in dispute.
>
> But this is wrong, for, if it is not given, then no distinction has been made. For, if he confines his objection to the principal case and does not give its contrary in the case at hand, his argument does not harm R; for, in that case, R can either say: "My cause is convertible" as some theoreticians have suggested; or he can say, "Your *ratio legis* in the principal case is not incompatible with what I say. It only reinforces its juristic qualification." This in no way amounts to an objection (*yamnaʿu*) against the soundness of his explanation (*taʿlīl*).[116]

al-Bājī's discussion indicates that in using this method Q makes a distinction between R's test case and his principal case in order to render void the *ratio legis* which R alleged was common to both of them. In order to do this properly, Q is obliged to specify that his objection applies to both cases.

This "question" is not unfamiliar to us. We have already mentioned it in our chapter on the theologians. It also seems to have been used as early as the tenth century as a technical term in jurisprudence.[117] al-Bājī mentions the opinion of b. al-Qaṣṣār (d.940), a Mālikite jurist famous for writings on *khilāf* and *uṣūl al-fiqh*:

> Some said: Q must attribute R's principal case to (another) principal case, and the *ratio legis* of the test case to (another) principle. But Abu l-Ḥasan b. al-Qaṣṣār says: Q does not have to attribute either one of them to another principle.[118]

al-Bājī does not, unfortunately, tell us how b. al-Qaṣṣār understood *farq*, but he does cite an opinion of al-Shīrāzī which is not to be found in his *Maʿūnat*:

---

[113] al-Juwaynī, *al-Kāfiya*, p. 162, line 14.

[114] Ibid., p. 69, lines 7–8.

[115] Abū Isḥāq al-Shīrāzī, "Maʿūnat," fol.18a: 1 ff. al-Bājī, *Minhāj*, p. 201, par. 456 ff.

[116] Ibid., par. 456.

[117] On this term, cf. van Ess, *Īcī*, p. 322.

[118] al-Bājī, *Minhāj*, p. 202, par. 457.

> Abū Isḥāq al-Shīrāzī said: "The *ratio legis* of the *aṣl*, need not be attributed to another *aṣl*, but the *ratio legis* of the *far'* must be attributed to another *aṣl*."[119]

	(AṢL$_2$)		*(AṢL$_3$)*
		'ILLA$_a$ ('ILLA$_f$)	
	AṢL$_1$		*FAR'*
(ḤUKM$_2$)	*ḤUKM$_1$*		*ḤUKM$_1$(ḤUKM$_3$)*

In the first type of "distinction" that al-Bājī mentions, there is a clean break—Q associates R's *ratio legis* (*'illa$_a$*) to a new principal case and asserts a different *ratio legis* (*'illa$_f$*) for the test case. Q may assert that not only does the test case have another *ratio legis* and, thus, another juristic qualification (*ḥukm$_3$*), but he can also claim that R's *ratio legis* derives from another principle and yields a wholly different juristic qualification (*ḥukm$_2$*). In this first sort of *farq*, we see the mirroring effect which it brings about. Q is in effect bringing a counterclaim with respect to both the test case and the principal one. The association with counter-objection (*mu'āraḍa*) is transparent. In al-Shīrāzī's statement, the "counter-objection" only occurs in the test case, where Q differentiates between R's *ratio legis* and the "real" *ratio legis* which derives from another principal case (*aṣl$_3$*).

Mu'āraḍa *(Counter-Objection)*

al-Juwaynī says that according to the technical language of the jurists it is "preventing one's opponent's argument (from prevailing) by making an equal and opposing claim; or it is matching the opponent's claim to prove his thesis with another opposed to it."[120] al-Bājī defines it as "Q's opposing (*muqābala*) R with a proof of equal weight or weightier."[121]

al-Juwaynī's account of counter-objection is confusing. It seems at times that he understands it as a species of *munāqaḍa* (inconsistency or contradiction) and at other times as another entirely different species of objection.[122] al-Juwaynī lists some of the old theological types of counter-objection along with some new ones: for example, thesis (*da'wā*) versus thesis; proof versus proof (*ḥujja*); and expression (*lafẓ*) versus expression.[123]

[119] Ibid., p. 202, lines 3–4. Cf. al-Juwaynī, *al-Kāfiya*, p. 307, line 9 where the *Ustādh* Abū Isḥāq is probably al-Shīrāzī and not al-Isfarā'inī.

[120] Ibid., p. 69, lines 11–2. "Mumāna'at al-khaṣm bi-da'wā al-musāwā au musāwāt al-khaṣm fī da'wā al-dalāla."

[121] al-Bājī, *Minhāj*, p. 14, line 7.

[122] Ibid., p. 213, par 343; p. 418, par. 604. Cf. above in our chapter on theological *jadal*.

[123] al-Juwaynī, *al-Kāfiya*, pp. 412, line 9; 413, line 4; 413, line 6 ff.

What is new and important is that al-Juwaynī provides a formula for using counter-objection. In arguing that counter-objection is a "valid question," he presents the following argument:

> The proof that it is a question is that when you use counter-objection against R's thesis using a "similar thesis," then you express it by saying: "*If you say this, why don't you say it is also true of this similar case? Indeed, why do you distinguish between the two although they are alike* (*nazīrāni*)?"[124]

The old controversy about the status of *mu'āraḍa* as a question has here given birth to formalism in phrasing objections, a new addition to the usual method of bringing definitions of the technique and practical examples.

This brings to a close al-Juwaynī's list of objections. But before we close this discussion, we wish to mention one other "technique," *ilzām*. al-Juwaynī defines it in passing:

> It is rejecting (*daf'*) R's discussion by showing something which brings about a difference ([or "distinction"] *faṣl*) between what R says and what R was entrusted to defend.[125]

That is to say Q claims that R has proved something other than the thesis entrusted to him. We shall have cause to return to this technique later in our discussion of the *ādāb al-baḥth*.

The Order of the Objections

al-Juwaynī stipulates that there is an order in which these objections must be brought, "without bringing the anterior before the prior in any way."[126] We have given examples and definitions of the various "questions" that he mentions in the order in which he first presents them in his work.[127] This, however, is not the order in which he treats them in his work, for either he or the copyist has slipped up. He does give an explanation of the order used in bringing the questions and he does follow this order in the course of his book. I give here a sample of his argumentation:

> Some say: "Disallowing (*man'*) is the first objection (*da'wā*) and not false construction, because what is disallowed is similar to the non-existent. False construction (however) must come after it since it is based on the premise that (part) of what R claims is existent.
>
> Others claimed that false construction should be given precedence since what is disallowed is subject to becoming established be it by (R's) revealing (his) intention or by (R's bringing) evidence; for the person disallowing must needs admit that what he initially disallowed is correct should R be able to stop his objection by means of the two methods; this being so, it would be impossible for Q to return to the claim that R has made a "false construction" after this admission (that the claim cannot be disallowed)....

---

124 Ibid., 419, lines 2–5; of. p. 412, line 14.

125 Ibid., p. 70, lines 17–8.

126 Ibid., p. 131, line 6 ff.

127 Ibid., p. 66, par. 59.

> When Q claims that the juristic qualification is not connected to what he claimed it was (that is, the ineffective cause) he may not (afterwards) go back and use the objections of "disallowance" or "false construction"...
>
> (This is also true of the claim of inconsistency (*naqḍ*)...for it only takes effect after first granting that the *ratio legis* is valid with respect to the point in dispute although it does not cover all the cases which R claims it does (*ghair muṭṭarid*).
>
> After reversal (*qalb*) one cannot go back to the prior objections. They disagreed, however, about whether one could return to the objection of "inconsistency" after using reversal because (some claimed) it is a type of counter-objection (while others claimed) that it is a type of "refutation" (*munāqaḍa*).[128]

al-Juwaynī's long account emphasizes that Q may not grant the existence of something and then go on to challenge it. But even so, the explanation is rather wanting.

Fortunately, we have another account of the order of the questions from al-Ghazzālī's book on juristic dialectics, *al-Muntaḥal*.[129] al-Ghazzālī was al-Juwaynī's student and although his book is lost to us, Fakhr al-Dīn al-Rāzī cites it in his work on dialectics:

> The second part (*ṭaraf*) concerns objection (*i'tirāḍ*). We shall mention in it what al-Ghazzālī says in his *Muntaḥal*... al-Ghazzālī says in his *Muntaḥal*: "the first question is disallowing (*man'*) and the last one is counter-objection (*mu'āraḍa*): between them there are three types of objection—one type (1) connected with destroying the basis (*aṣl*) of the argument as in the case of false construction and false perspective, commensurability (*ṭard*) and ineffective cause: this type follows directly after disallowance. Then there is another type (2) that is connected with objecting to the "text" (*matn*) of the *ratio legis*, such as requesting (that the *ratio legis* be textually verified = *muṭālaba*) and denying that the *ratio legis* applies consistently (*naqḍ*), and this is the second type. Finally, the third type (3) is the question of 'limited acceptance' with a denial that the *ratio legis* applies to the disputed point."[130]

al-Ghazzālī is the first author who names his guiding principles that Q should first attack the principal case and afterwards the *ratio legis*. The guiding principle is again not to deny what one has previously conceded.

If we go back and compare the order of questions of al-Shīrāzī's "school" with that of al-Juwaynī's "school," we note that if we discount the first questions of al-Rāzī's school, which concern how to argue against people who reject the use of analogical reasoning, then the first and last questions of the school are disallowance and counter-objection respectively. The disagreement came about the order of the questions which came in between them.

If we look at some of the works on dialectics written about a century later, we find again a certain confusion about the order in which the questions should brought, or rather a number of opinions. al-Barawī (d.1172) names thirteen types of objects

---

[128] Ibid., p. 132, line 8 ff.

[129] Cf. A. Badawi, *Mu'allafāt al-Ghazzālī* (Cairo: Dār al-Qalam, 1961) p. 32.

[130] Fakhr al-Dīn al-Rāzī, "Kitāb al-Jadal," fol.139a: 14 ff. MS.519/3 Köprülü, [Arab Leaugue (Tauḥīd wal-milal wal-niḥal) MS.191 *Fihris al-Makhṭūṭāt al-Muṣauwara*, ed. F. Saiyid (Cairo: Dār al-Riyāḍ, 1954),p. 135.] In the latter the passage occurs at 17a: 14 ff.

starting with "false perspective" and including "inconsistency" (*naqḍ*), (12) counter-objection and (13) limited acceptance.[131]

Fakhr al-Dīn al-Rāzī follows the method of al-Ghazzālī and al-Juwaynī in providing explanations about the order of his questions. His first three questions are (1) asking for an explanation of R's terminology, (2) false perspective, and (3) false construction:

1. Asking for explanation (*istifsār*) is the first question...since how can you object to something as long as you do not understand it?
2. (The argument) for placing false perspective, false construction, and ineffective cause after disallowance is baseless: since disallowance is an admission that the *ratio legis* is sound, while the other questions contend against the *ratio legis* and are therefore prior to disallowance.[132]

Unlike al-Ghazzālī, al-Rāzī apparently thought that one should attack the *ratio legis* before going after the principal case (*aṣl*). The objection of consistency (*ṭard*) follows as the fifth question. His last questions are (11) reversal, (12) counter-objection, and (13) limited acceptance.[133]

If we turn to the objections briefly described in b. al-Ḥājib's famous *uṣūl al-fiqh* work, *Muntahā al-wuṣūl wal-amal fī 'ilmai al-uṣūl wal-jadal*, we find that he has the same first three objections as al-Rāzī, but that his fourth question is disallowance.[134] Counter-objection comes as his fifteenth objection but there are others that come after it. His last objection is "limited acceptance."[135]

From the evidence of these three sources, it would appear that the jurists had, as late as the thirteenth century, still disputed about the order of questions used against analogical reasoning. But they seemed to have agreed that the first question commits Q to asking R for an explanation of his thesis or proof. This, however, is not a new addition to dialectic. al-Juwaynī knows it and mentions that it is useful to ask about the meaning of terms before objecting. But this question, that is asking for an explanation, is not counted as one of "the" questions. Asking for explanations is assumed to be done when necessary.[136]

---

[131] Abū Manṣūr Muhammad b. Muḥammad al-Barawī al-Shāfi'ī, "al-Muqtaraḥ fī al-muṣṭalaḥ," fols. 30b: 1 ff; 46a: 2 ff; 51b: 6 ff.; 53b: 17 ff. MS.693 Escurial. His work is contained in a commentary on it by Taqī al-Dīn Muẓaffar b. A. al-'Izz al-Shāfi'ī, known under the nick-name of al-Muqṭaraḥ. For details, see van Ess, *Īcī*, p. 51–2.

[132] al-Rāzī, "al-Jadal," 18a: 10 ff. [=140a: 10 Arab League microfilm.]

[133] Ibid., fol.18a: 14 ff. [=140 a: 14 ff. Arab League microfilm.]

[134] Ibn al-Ḥājib, *Muntahā al-wuṣūl wal-amal fī 'ilmai al-uṣul wal-jadal* ed. M. Ḥalabī (Cairo: Maṭba'at al-Sa'āda, 1326), p. 141, line -3 ff. al-Rāzī's fourth question is the "ineffective cause." On b. al-Ḥājib, cf. Brockelmann, GAL I pp. 367 ff., SI pp. 531 ff.

[135] Ibid., p. 150, line 3 ff.

[136] al-Juwaynī, *al-Kāfiya*, p. 131, line 3 ff.

The Signs of Defeat

al-Khaṭīb al-Baghdādī, b. Ḥazm Ibn ʿAqīl, and al-Juwaynī all give accounts of the signs of defeat. The vocabulary of their accounts is fairly standard and their authors' debt to the dialectic of the theologians is obvious. They all count digression (*intiqāl*) a sign of defeat although some recognize a good kind of digression.[137] There are four signs that come in approximately the same order in the accounts of al-Juwaynī and al-Baghdādī:

1. Self-contradiction (*munāqaḍa*).[138]
2. R's rejection of *a priori* knowledge or his being forced to say something absurd.[139]
3. R answers a question other than the one asked.
4. R fails to bring a distinction between two positions or answers that he holds are opposed.

al-Baghdādī also considers R's silence in response to Q's question and his arguing to no point, as other signs of defeat. Ibn ʿAqīl brings in several signs connected with the failure of R or Q to fulfill their duties as required by the "four questions:"

1. R's inability (*ʿajz*) to state his opinion.
2. R's inability to give a proof (*dalīl*).
3. R's inability to counter Q's objection.
4. Q's inability to properly formulate his question.
5. Q's inability to ask for a proof.
6. Q's inability to bring an objection.[140]

The relation of these signs to the four questions is so obvious that it requires no comment other than to note how the jurists on the whole took over elements of the theologians teaching on disputation.

But as in the case of the questions of juristic dialectic, there were new developments. al-Juwaynī mentions the false order of placing questions, such as using disallowance (*man*ʿ) after having used inconsistency (*naqḍ*), as a sign of defeat. He also discusses the problem of whether R is defeated should he give a proof when he is only asked to state his opinion.[141]

al-Juwaynī's account is also influenced by Aristotle. Thus, he gives four of Aristotle's five criticisms of an argument: ignorance of dialectic or proof, sound

---

[137] Cf. above our chapter on the signs of defeat of the theologians. On good and bad digression cf. Ibn ʿAqīl, *K. al-Jadal*, p. 133, par. 332; al-Juwaynī, *al-Kāfiya*, p. 551, par. 820 ff.

[138] al-Khaṭīb al-Baghdādī, *al-Faqīh*, vol. 2, p. 57; al-Ju- wainī, *al-Kāfiya*, p. 553, lines 15 ff. Ibn Ḥaẓm, *al-Taqrīb li-ḥadd al-manṭiq wal-madkhal ilaihī*, ed. I. ʿAbbās (Beirut: Dār al-ʿIbād, 1959) p. 197, line 9.

[139] Ibn ʿAqīl, *K. al-Jadal*, par. 335; Ibn Ḥaẓm, *Taqrīb*, p. 188, line 1 for this and the following note.

[140] Ibn ʿAqīl, *K. al-Jadal*, par. 331, 336.

[141] al-Juwaynī, *al-Kāfiya*, p. 557, line 9 ff; p. 558, line 13 ff.

proof of a thesis other than the one at hand, and inadequate proof either because the disputant has left something out or said too much.[142]

The Adab al-Jadal

al-Bājī, Ibn ʿAqīl, al-Juwaynī, and al-Khaṭīb al-Baghdādī all discuss the *adab al-jadal.* These basic rules of conduct during debate were taken over by the jurists from theological *jadal.* Ibn Ḥazm also has elements of this chapter in his own account of disputation.[143] But as we said above, these chapters also contained advice to R and Q. al-Juwaynī used this chapter as an opportunity to spell out precisely how he understands the duties of Q and R:

> Among the things that redound to the benefit of the art of dialectic is that each of the two disputants preserve his position (*martaba*). (This means that) he knows that it is the position of R to found and construct arguments while it is the position of Q to reject (*dafʿ*) and destroy arguments. It is R's duty (*ḥaqq*) to found the opinion that he is asked about on a firm foundation and sound principles such as proofs, and so forth. It is Q's duty and his position in questioning, should he wish to correct R (*tasḥīḥahū*), to reveal R's inability to found his opinion upon a sound principle (*aṣl*).[144]

al-Juwaynī adds that should R bring a proof and answer all Q's objections, then it is clear that Q loses.[145] One might at first suppose that the passage that we just cited more properly belongs in the account of the signs of defeat. But its placement here in the rules of conduct is not that hard to explain; for in order to tell R and Q how they should behave, one must have a clear idea as to what their responsibilities are during the debate.

The "Middle" Period of Juristic Dialectics

When later bio-bibliographical authors such as Hājji Khalīfa and others examined the phenomenon of juristic dialectics they turned to a section of Ibn Khaldūn's *Muqaddima* where he mentions this subject.[146] There he tells us that in his time there were two important methods (*ṭarīqa*) one of Abū al-Yusr Muhammad al-Pazdawī[147]

---

142 Ibid., p. 556, linr -1 ff. Cf. Aristotle *SE* 161a26 ff.

143 Ibn Ḥazm, *Taqrīb*, p. 196, line 5 ff.

144 al-Juwaynī, *al-Kāfiya*, p. 558, line -3 ff.

145 Ibid., p. 539, line 8 ff.

146 Ibn Khaldūn, *al-Muqaddima*, ed. M. Quatremère, 3 vols. (Paris: Institut Imperial de France, 1858), vol. 3, p. 23, line -7 ff.; p. 24, line -6 ff. This has been translated by F. Rosenthal, *The Muqaddimah* (New York: Pantheon, 1958), pp. 30–34.

147 Cf. Saiyid, *Fihris*, p. 253, Number 109. G. Makdisi, "Le Livre de la dialectique d'Ibn ʿAqīl," *BEO* 20 (1967), pp. 119–20. al-Bājī, *Minhāj*, intro. by Turki, pp. 9 ff. Turki, *Polémiques*, pp. 32 ff.

and another of Rukn al-Dīn al-ʿAmīdī.[148] The "method" of al-Pazdawī has not been preserved; but that of al-ʿAmīdī has. But there exist other "methods" from an earlier period, one of al-Marwazī (d. 1069)[149] and another of Raḍī al-Dīn al-Sarakhsī (d. 1149).[150]

If we examine these three "methods" as members of a genre of juristic literature, we find several shared characteristics in form and style. The most important characteristic is that they are all detailed arguments *for* the position of their authors' law schools *and against* the position of an opposing law school. The arguments that are found in the juristic dialectics books are brought here into play; but their theoretical foundations are ignored. The aim of these works is placed more on the side of practice than theory. If we turn to their organization, we find that they are arranged according to the subject-matter used in traditional "case-law" (*furūʿ*) works. Thus, the first chapters in these three works are on ritual purity, *zakāt*, fasting, and so forth. If we now turn to the argumentation used by these authors on a given topic, we find a uniformity of method employed.

Let us give a brief example taken from their chapter on *zakāt*. al-Marwazī's "method" is the following:

1. He states the problem: "There is no *zakāt* on permitted jewelry according to us (Shāfiʿites)...but the Ḥanafites say that there is; we both agree that there is a tax on forbidden (*maḥẓūr*) jewelry."
2. He explains certain terms used in problem: for example, what is meant by "forbidden".
3. He states what the types of his proof will be: "Our proof (*dalīl*) is based upon *ḥadīth* (*khabar*) and analogical reasoning(*maʿnā*)."
4. He states the opponents' objections in a general manner.
5. He gives his proof.
6. He gives *all* the opponents' objections.
7. He gives their refutation.[151]

After he is finished, al-Marwazī often offers a second "method" for proving his point. al-Sarakhsī's method is somewhat different[152]:

1. He states the problem: "Our *'ulamā'* say, *zakāt* is obligatory on all jewelry but al-Shāfiʿī said that …it is not."
2. He proceeds to give a proof.

[148] Brockelmann, *GAL* I, p. 568, SI, p. 785–6. G. Makdisi, *The Rise of Colleges* (Edinburgh: Edinburgh University Press, 1981), p. 109.

[149] Brockelmann, *GAL* SI p. 669, identifies him as al-Ḥu. M. b. A. al-Marwarrūdhī, but on MS.1523 (Fiqh Shāfiʿī) Dār al-Kutub al-Miṣrīya, "Ṭarīqat al-khilāf baina al-Shāfiʿīya wal-Ḥanafīya maʿa dhikr al-adilla li-kull minhumā," he is identified as al-Ḥasan b. Shuʿaib al-Marwazī. Cf. Makdisi, *Colleges*, p. 120 and note 199.

[150] M. b. M. Raḍī al-Dīn al-Sarakhsī, "al-Ṭarīqa al-Raḍawīya," MS.239 (Fiqh Ḥanafī), Dār al-Kutub al-Miṣrīya. Cf. Brockelmann, GAL I, p. 463, SI, p. 641. Makdisi, *Colleges*, pp. 108 ff., 118 ff.

[151] al-Marwazī, "Ṭarīqat," fol.43b: 13, 46b: 16.

[152] al-Sarakhsī, "al-Ṭarīqa," fol.4b: -3 ff.

3. He lists the opponent's objections in *kalām*-style: for example, "As for his statement...we say: we do not grant that" or "Even if we were to grant that..., why do you say that..."[153]
4. He then responds to the objections in *kalām*-style: "*Although the proof that you mentioned indicates* the preponderance of jewelry to all the other forms of material possessions used as currency, *however, we have another piece of evidence which shows that* they are all on the same level...."[154]

al-Sarakhsī will also often give a second "method" for solving the problem. al-ʿAmīdī's method is similar to al-Sarakhsī's in *form* and *style*.[155] Indeed, if we consider all three texts in a general manner, we see that even in al-Marwazī, the basic method is to state the problem, the evidence, the objections and their solutions.

This is the method that Makdisi discovered in the *Wāḍiḥ* of Ibn ʿAqīl and that he claimed derived from (juristic) sources prior to al-Qirqisānī.[156] This was a method which he said Ibn ʿAqīl applied "to any field" of investigation. His argument is implausible on several counts. First and foremost, there is a problem of chronology. While it is evident that these juristic *jadal* works are indebted to the earlier *khilāf* literature, we have shown that this earlier literature was not dialectical in character. Indeed, to judge from our bio-bibliographical sources, it would seem that the first books on juristic dialectics were written at the *end* of the tenth century—a good generation or two after al-Qirqisānī and long after b. al-Rīwandī's heyday.[157] The evolution of the concept of the "praiseworthy" and "blameworthy" types of dialectics is another sign of the transfer of dialectics from the controversy-steeped books of the theologians to the books of the jurists. In the preceding section, we have tried to show that the "quest" for ordering the objections is a continuation of the dialectical tradition first found in b. al-Rīwandī's book on the *Adab al-Jadal*. Another indication of the "theological" origins of juristic dialectic comes to the fore when we examine some of the terminology of the debate. In the first question of theology, you ask about R's opinion *(madhhab)*. This is the same question of juristic *jadal*. But in jurisprudence, the term *madhhab* usually has the meaning of "school of law."

Makdisi notes in his summary of Ibn ʿAqīl's method: "The objections to the arguments advanced for the thesis are called *al-as'ila*: a *su'āl* is not a question, it is an objection; the replies to objections are called *al-ajwiba* (sg., *jawāb*), which is

[153] Ibid., "*ammā qauluhū... qulnā lā nusallim*" (fol.5b: 9–11); "*la'in sallamnā... wa-lākin lima qultum....*" (fol. 6a: 1–5).

[154] Ibid., "*mā dhakartum min al-dalīl wa-in dalla ʿalā... wa-lākin hāhunā dalīl ākhar yadullu ʿalā l-musāwa bainahumā* ..." (fol.9b: 17 ff.).; cf. fol.13b: 10. This is an example of *muʿāraḍa* in its classic formulation.

[155] Cf. al-ʿAmīdī, "al-Ṭarīqa al-ʿAmīdīya fī al-khilāf wal-jadal," MS.236 (Fiqh Ḥanafī), Dār al-Kutub al-Miṣrīya.

[156] G. Makdisi, "The Scholastic Method in Medieval Education: An Inquiry into its Origins in Law and Theology," *Speculum* 49 (1974): 650. Makdisi, *Colleges*, pp. 117 ff.

[157] The first book on purely juristic *jadal* was written by al-Qaffāl al-Shāshī (d. 976), student of Abū l-ʿAbbās b. Suraij (d. 336/9). See, Abū Isḥāq al-Shīrāzī, *Ṭabaqāt al-fuqahā'*, p. 112. Makdisi, *Colleges*, pp. 108, 147. Sezgin, *GAS* I pp. 497–8.

also the term used for the refutation of the pseudo-arguments *[shubah]*."[158] Here again we must disagree with his account. Juristic *jadal* is part of that great tradition of *jadal* initiated by the theologians. For them, and, indeed, for the philosophers too, *jadal* was *question* and *answer*. In order for a statement to be allowed into the debate, it had to be put into one of these categories. This is why the objections were understood primarily as questions, and secondarily as objections. When al-Bājī, for example, introduces objections to analogical reasoning he will often say by way of introduction, "And this is a sound question (*su'āl saḥīḥ*)."[159] As we have seen not all of the techniques of objection were universally accepted, but the determining factor was often whether or not "x" is a question or not. If we turn to the "proponent's" side, we see that properly speaking the proponent is almost always in the position of a respondent. The debate is initiated by the "questioner." Thus, anything that the other party says is a response, be it a statement of his position, proof, or refutation of Q's objections. In the face of such evidence, Makdisi's position is no longer tenable.

al-ʿAmīdī's Irshād

A short theoretical work of al-ʿAmīdī on juristic disputation has survived, the *Irshād*. It is an orderly account of juristic argumentation of the *uṣūl al-fiqh*:

> The proponent (*muʿallil*) must base his argument on Scripture, *ḥadīth* (*athar*), analogical reasoning, implication, incompatibility, method of agreement and difference (*dawarān*), proof (*burhān*), unobjectionable evidence, praesumptio, and so forth.[160]

He then proceeds to consider the arguments of P and Q with respect to the various types of evidence displaying a concern for the evidence at the expense of the traditional chapters on politeness. In this respect, it is very much reminiscent of al-Shīrāzī's short work on juristic *jadal*. But there is a tremendous gap between these two works in respect to style and technique.

As we saw earlier, the *kalām* method of discussion is already present in the *ṭarīqa* of al-Sarakhsī who lived a good fifty years before al-ʿAmīdī's *Irshād* – the *kalām*-method is again in force.

---

[158] Makdisi, "Scholasticism," p. 653.

[159] al-Bājī, *Minhāj*, p. 173, lines 5–6; 174, line –1; cf. 191, line 3: "al-kasr suʾāl ḥasan."

[160] Rukn al-Dīn al-ʿAmīdī, "al-Irshād," fol.15b:2 ff., MS.650 Escurial. Copies of his "Ṭarīqa" reveal it to be a work on the *furūʿ* written in the style of the other *ṭarīqas* that we mentioned. On *dawarān* see van Ess, *Īcī*, pp. 384 ff. J. Mill, *A System of Logic*, ed. J. Robson, *Collected Works of John Stuart Mill*, vol. 7–8 (Toronto: University of Toronto Press, 1973–4), vol. 7, p. 388. ʿA. al-Nashshār, *Manāhij al-baḥth ʿinda mufakkirī l-islām* 4th ed.(Cairo: Dār al-Maʿārif, 1978), p. 95. L. Jacobs, *Studies in Talmudic Logic and Methodology* (London: Valentine, 1961), p.12, where he relates this method to Rabbinic *binyan ab*.

But before turning to instances of style, I wish to discuss the appearance of three new techniques in the arsenal of debate: implication, incompatibility, and method of agreement and difference (*dawarān*).

These terms crop up in juristic and theological texts written after the time of al-Ghazzālī. It was al-Ghazzālī, indeed, who attempted to bring jurisprudence and logic together. And a century after his death, both the fields of jurisprudence and theology were alive with logical concepts. al-ʿAmīdī does not bother to define what he means by *talāzum* and *tanāfin*; but from his examples we get a fairly good idea of what he meant. An example of "implication" would be "P says: If the *zakāt* tax were incumbent upon debtors, it would also be incumbent upon beggars"—in logical terms, if P then Q. Now in modern logic, there need not be any relationship between "P" and "Q" in order for the statement to be true or for the material implication to work. The statement would be false only in the case where P is true and Q is false. In our case, the proponent is confident that Q is false and, thus, P must be false so that the statement be true in the *modus tollens*. But not only that; he assumes a correlation between the case of the beggar and that of the debtor. He assumes that in an essential way they are similar, and that similar juristic qualifications should apply to them. In other words, the proponent makes an analogy which he clothes in the form of an entailment.[161]

A generation or two after al-ʿAmīdī, we find logical explanations of implication in the corpus of books on juristic dialectic:

> Implication (*talāzum*) is an expression of the impossibility of the realization (*taḥaqquq*) of the implicans (*malzūm*) unless the implicate (*lāzim*) is also realized. The meaning of "impossibility" is absolute impossibility. The existence of mutual implication does not *per se* require the actual existence of either the implicans or the implicate.[162]

The author of this statement, Burhān al-Dīn al-Nasafī,[163] then proceeds to consider the various possible relations between the implicans and the implicate. He identifies two sorts: one in which the implicate is more general than the implicans as "animal" to "man," and another where both terms are "equal" as in the case of "rational" and "man."[164] He then goes on to consider the "truth tables" which result from the "absence" and "existence" of the two terms:

---

161 See *The Cambridge History of Later Medieval Philosophy (CHMP)*, ed. N. Kretzmann, A. Kenny, J. Pinborg (Cambridge, England: Cambridge University Press, 1982), p. 300. In the vocabulary of Abelard, these are called *consequentia*. W. and M. Kneale, *The Development of Logic* (Oxford: Clarendon Press, 1962), pp. 216, 290, 292.

162 Burhān al-Dīn al-Nasafī, "al-Muqaddima al-Burhānīya," fol.44b:8 ff. MS.5168 (Lbg. 72), Staatsbibliothek, Berlin.

163 See below.

164 The example is taken from Aristotle *APr*. 25a14 ff. Cf. al-Fārābī, *Kitāb al-qiyās al-saghīr*, ed. M. Türker, in Ankara Üniversitesi Dil ve Tarih-Cografya Dergisi 16 (1958), p. 271, line 11 ff. Avicenna, *K. al-Maqūlāt*, ed. G. Anawati et al., *al-Shifā':al-Manṭiq* gen. ed. I. Madkour, vol. 2 (Cairo: Organisation Generale des Imprimeries Gouvermentales, 1959) p. 150, line 17. Idem, *K. al-Qiyās*, ed. S. Zāʿyid, *al-Shifā': al-Manṭiq* vol. 4 (Cairo: Imprimerie Nationale, 1958), pp. 361 ff.

Case	Implicans P	Implicate Q	Equal	Not equal
(I)	*0*	*X*	*0*	–
(II)	*X*	*0*	*0*	–
(III)	*X*	*X*	*X*	*?*
(IV)	*0*	*0*	*X*	*?*

0 = FALSE X = TRUE

In cases (III) and (IV), the correlate implicans and implicate result in true statements; but when the implicate is more general than the implicans it is true to say "if P then Q" but not "if Q then P;" again it would be true to say "not-Q, therefore not-P"[165] but not "not-P therefore not-Q." In a logical material-implication, the only statement that would be false would be the one of case (II).[166]

al-Nasafī gives a formula for expressing implication and explains the meaning of the implication:

> ...When you say in a disputation (*munāẓara*) "Were this so, it would have been so" you should know that this is a claim about reality (*fī nafs al-amr*); except that the implicate may be "necessary" (*ḍarūrī*) in accord with what you know through signs of the intellect...or it could be demonstrative as when we say "Were the *zakāt* tax incumbent upon debtor it would also be incumbent upon beggars" for this statement is not realized in reality unless the obligation upon beggars is realized *when* the obligation upon debtors is realized (to pay the *zakāt* tax).[167]

al-Nasafī's statement indicates that he sees that the relation between debtors and beggars is that of equals, so that what applies to the one must apply to the other.

al-Nasafī's account of implication did not go uncriticized. Shams al-Dīn al-Samarqandī, the author of a commentary to al-Nasafī's "Muqaddima," remarks that his definition of *talāzum* is unsound because it amounts to defining a thing by itself:

> He defined *talāzum* as the "impossibility of the realization of the implicans (*malzūm*) unless the implicate (*lāzim*)[168] is also realized" ...There are several objections (to this definition):

---

[165] I. Boh, "Consequences," *CHMP*, p. 312 note 48, "In omni consequentia bona, quae non est syllogistica, ex opposito consequentis contradictorie sequitur oppositum antecedentis," from Walter Burley.

[166] Nuʿmān al-Khwārizmī, "Sharḥ fuṣūl al-Nasafī," fol.10b: 5 ff., MS.5167 (Mq.55), Staatsbibliothek, Berlin "know that an implication may be true in reality if it is between two true propositions or two false ones, or two propositions whose truth and falsehood is not known (i.e., future contingents) or between a false implicans and a true implicate; but not *vice versa* for this is impossible (*muḥāl*) due to the impossibility of what is false attaching itself as an implicate to what is true since it would necessarily follow from the "truth of what is false" the "falsity of what is true" (i.e., P –> Q and Q is false; therefore -Q –> -P). Since the truth of the implicans implicates the truth of the 'implicate that is false,' and the falsehood of the implicate implicates the falsehood of the 'implicans that is true'."

[167] al-Nasafī, "al-Muqaddima," 45b: 6 ff.

[168] In logic, the normal terms for antecedent and consequent are *al-muqaddam* and *al-tālī*.

(1) the implicans is that with which a thing's inherence (*luzūm shai'*) is connected, while the implicate is that in which the inherence subsists; thus, the gist of this definition is that *talāzum* is the impossibility (of the existence) of that with which a thing's inherence is connected except when that in which the inherence subsists is realized.

But no one disputes that the meaning of *luzūm* and *talāzum* is the same in the usage of the experts (*ahl al-'ilm*), since they use both of them in place of the other. Thus, it follows that we have the definition of a thing through itself, and this is not allowed....

The proper definition of *talāzum* is that it is (when) the realization of a thing necessarily requires the realization of another (thing); the first is (called) the implicans and the second the implicate.

Or we say that it is the necessary realization of a thing on the assumption of the realization of (another) thing which requires it. N.B., we said "which requires it", that is which necessarily requires it in order to exclude incidental (implication)... and the word thing (*shai'*) is used to include both existent and non-existent things for non-existent things when objects of knowledge exist in the mind....[169]

al-Samarqandī's criticism subtly shows the errors of al-Nasafī's definition. But it also shows that al-Nasafī was trying to make logical distinctions, even if he did not make them well. al-Samarqandī also indicates that our authors understood these implications as being non-incidental.

al-Samarqandī then goes on to identify three types of implication: one in reality (*khārijī/realis*); another in the mind (*dhihnī/rationis*); and a final one being a combination of the two.[170] An example of the second type would be "If (the concept of) blindness exists in the mind, then (the concept of) sight must exist in the mind."[171] An example of the first type would be "if man exists, then animal exists." He then goes on to examine the relation between implicans and implicate. He notes that it could be either universal or particular. Unlike al-Nasafī, he treats the case where the implicans is more general than the implicate and this, indeed, is his example of "particular" implication: "It may be the case that if animal exists, then man exists."[172] As an example of implication between equals, he suggests that if you do not accept that "man" is "equal" to "rational" because the angels, *jinn*, and parrots are also "rational," then you should substitute whatever examples you like such as "If the sun is rising it is day." This last instance is the classic example of implication as known to the Arab logicians.

In an independent treatise on the subject of logic in juristic *jadal*, al-Samarqandī gives six rules of implication:

1. If p, then q.
2. If not-q, then not-p.

---

[169] Shams al-Dīn al-Samarqandī, "Sharḥ al-Muqaddima al-Burhānīya," fol.5b: 1 ff, MS.4396 Chester Beatty Library, Dublin. [For the proper identification of this MS, see below Chapter IV. Nu'mān al-Khwārizmī offers another definition: implication expresses the impossibility of the realization of a thing except when another thing is realized and the first is called the implicans and the second the implicate (in al-Khwārizmī, "Sharḥ," fol.9a: 11–12).

[170] On *dhihnī* cf. van Ess, *Īcī*, pp. 87,202.

[171] Shams al-Dīn al-Samarqandī, "Sharḥ," fol.6a: 12 ff.

[172] Ibid., fol.6b: 15, "*qad yakūnu idhā kāna al-ḥayawān maujūdan fal-insān maujūd.*"

3. If q, then p. (Only when p and q are equipollent)
4. If (If p, then q), then q.
5. If not (If p, then q), then not-p.
6. If (If p_1, then p), then q. [that is, the antecedent of the antecedent is also antecedent of the conclusion].[173]

Turning back to al-ʿAmīdī's original example of the beggar and the debtor, we see that the proponent in the example is counting on al-Samarqandī's second rule to prove his point. Even when not stated, the logic of implication lies at the fundament of this new device.

Incompatibility is like the other side of the coin in respect to implication. While the latter involves the association or compatibility of two propositions, the former specifically excludes it. In incompatibility, it is denied that the two propositions can be both true at one and the same time. Again, for lack of definition in al-ʿAmīdī's account, we turn to al-Nasafī's explanation:

> Two things are incompatible if it is not possible for them to be true together in one and the same substrate (*maḥall*), time, and respect: this is as in the case of two contradictories or two contraries and the like. (An example is) Someone says the legal qualification (*ḥukm*) in this case cannot be true along with the legal qualification in that case.... (Another example) The obligation upon the debtor and the absence of obligation upon the person who possesses less than the minimum amount of property (*niṣāb*) are two things which cannot be both true, and the second is established by consensus; therefore, not the first."[174]

In implication, the proponent counts on the second part of the implication's being false, and from that to the assumption that the implicans is false: otherwise, the implication would be false. But in incompatibility, the proponent counts on precisely one statement being true and the other being false. al-ʿAmīdī actually assumes that his audience is very familiar with it:

> The thing to which the opposite of the claim is annexed exists either through consensus or through some preponderant piece of evidence (*dalīl*); or, it is equally possible that it exist or not....[175]

Our authors talk about incompatibility as if the opponents were making exclusive alterations or exclusive disjunctions. If the proponent follows the advice that al-ʿAmīdī is apparently offering, then one merely has to annex the opposite of one's claim to a true proposition in order to prove it. Would that it were so simple. Naturally the opponent is given the option of showing that the disjunction is not exclusive—that both parts are false. But before looking at a few of techniques that

[173] Shams al-Dīn al-Samarqandī, "ʿAin al-naẓar fī al-manṭiq fī ʿilm al-jadal," fol. 1b: 15 ff. MS.1124 V (Or. 3730), British Museum Supplement, London. Another copy of this MS is probably contained in MS.6 (majmūʿ), al-Maktaba al-Gharbīya bil-Jāmiʿ al-Kabīr, Sana, Yemen. There the title is listed as "Ghaib al-naẓar," which is obviously a misprint. Cf. ʿĪsawī and Mālīḥ, *Fihris*, s.v. *Ghaib al-naẓar*.

[174] al-Nasafī, "al-Muqaddima," fol.51a: 11 ff.

[175] al-ʿAmīdī, "al-Irshād," fol.19b: 11 ff.

the opponent uses to destroy these proofs, let us turn to the final new technique, method of agreement and difference (*dawarān*).

Dawarān is an argument in which the proponent argues that a given thing might be the *ratio legis* of the juristic qualification or the cause of a given phenomenon. Thus, al-Nasafī defines it:

> It is the basing of the "effect" (*athar*) upon that thing which could possibly have been its cause. It is also said: "It is the basing of the existence of the effect upon the existence of the thing time after time." *Dawarān* does not require the (actual) existence of either the "effect" (*dā'ir*) nor of the "possible cause" (*madār*).[176]

al-Nasafī gives some rather interesting examples of how this phenomenon works. He notes that there are three possible combinations with respect to actual existence and absence of the *dā'ir* and *madār:*

	Dā'ir	Madār	Dā'ir/Madār
(1)	Exists	Exists	Day/Sunrise
(2)	Not-Exist	Not-Exist	Not-Day/Not-Sunrise
(3)	Not-Exist	Exists	Not-Night/Day
(4)	Exists	Not-Exist	Day/Not-Night

After using these logical examples to establish the four categories, he gives examples applicable to jurisprudence:

I. Adultery stemming from a married (*muḥṣan*) person and the stoning penalty are like cases (1) and (2): For if adultery exists, then the stoning penalty is necessitated (and exists); but if adultery did not exist, then the penalty would not be necessary (and not exist).
II. A bequest (*hiba*) and possession are related as cases (1) and (4): for, if the bequest occurs, then possession exists; but possession can exist on account of something else.
III. Ritual purity and prayer are related as cases (2) and (3): for if that ritual purity that is made a pre-condition for the validity for prayer is absent, then the prayer (is not valid and) does not exist: but if ritual purity does exist, prayer could be voided by the absence of some other pre-condition such as facing the *qibla* or covering privates, and so forth.[177]

Dawarān as we see is the latest version of the old question of applying the cause to its *causata*. It is interesting to see al-Nasafī give logical examples for *dawarān*; for to my knowledge it is not treated in any of the later handbooks of logic.

Now all three of these "new" techniques—implication, incompatibility, and "method of agreement and difference" are treated exactly in that order by al-ʿAmīdī, al-Nasafī, and al-Samarqandī in their works.

In al-ʿAmīdī's account, the questions of the previous period not to mention their order are no longer treated.[178] Like al-Shīrāzī, he was interested primarily in

[176] al-Nasafī, "al-Muqaddima," fol.54a: 11 ff.

[177] Ibid., fol.54b: 1 ff.

[178] This fact could be equally derived from the *Irshād*'s being a short treatise on juristic *jadal*. We know from a short report from Ḥājjī Khalīfa that al-ʿAmīdī produced another work on *jadal*—*al-Nafā'is (fī al-jadal)*, *Kashf al-ẓunūn*, Sh. Yaltkaya and R. Bilge, eds., 2 vols. (Istanbul: Maarif

questions vis-à-vis the evidence of the *uṣūl al-fiqh*. The determinate factor in most cases is, thus, whether the evidence is "specific or not" (*mu'aiyan*). If it is specific, then Q can use some of the old techniques such as "inconsistency" (*naqḍ*). But a great part of the evidence has that quasi-logical style of the *kalām*: endless divisions and alterations. Thus, even in the case of arguments against a proponent (*mu'allil*) who uses Qur'ānic evidence, al-'Amīdī says:

> To sum up, if you claim one of two things, and if both of them are non-specific (*munkar*), then you will certainly be successful whether you claim it to be actual or not; the same is true if one is non-specific and the other specific, where both are possibly incompatible, you will succeed...[179]

In the tradition that comes after al-'Amīdī and that is perhaps best exemplified by the work of al-Nasafī, the questions of juristic dialectic such as inconsistency and false construction are either neglected or reconstituted to be used against the new logical evidence. To give but a brief example from al-Nasafī, he says that "the implication between the contradictory of the implicans and the same implicate is called reversal (*qalb*), and so, too, that between the same implicans and contradictory of the implicate (that is, –p –> q; and p –> -q)...."[180] In al-Nasafī, the concept of reversal is expanded to include all those possibilities that are logically possible.

Let me close by turning back to al-'Amīdī's style. It is replete with the terminology of *kalām* and formal debate and is, thus, unlike its predecessors. Here are six random examples of what I mean:

1. As for the first we do not grant that...as for the second, we do not grant.[181]
2. He said "x"...we say: we do not grant that "x"...[182]
3. Should he say, "Why do you say that this is another proof," we would then say...[183]
4. There are many sorts of reply to it.[184]
5. The proper sort of response is for us to say...[185]
6. Should he disallow...[186]
7. If he behaves peevishly and disallows...[187]

Matbaasi, 1941–3) vol. 2, p. 1966. A commentary on this work has survived. Cf. Brockelmann *GAL* S I p. 786, and Saiyid, *Fihris*, p. 332, no. 36.

[179] al-'Amīdī, "al-Irshād," fol.16a: 30 ff; al-Nasafī, ibid., also discusses the non-specific *madār*.

[180] al-Nasafī, "al-Muqaddima," fol.50b: 13 ff.

[181] al-'Amīdī, "al-Irshād," fol.16a: 30 ff.

[182] Ibid., fol.16a: 5.

[183] Ibid., fol.17b: 3.

[184] Ibid., fol.17b: 9, "*Lahu wujūh min al-taujīh.*" *Taujīh* is a technical term for "formulating a reply or objection in debate."

[185] Ibid., fol.20b: 6,32-3, "*wa-wajhuhū an naqūla.*" *Wajhuhū* is here synonymous with *taujīhuhū*.

[186] Ibid., fol.18a: 1 "*in mana'a.*" 18 a 11, "*lau mana'a.*"

[187] Ibid., fol.20b: 18, "*lau kābara wa-mana'a.*" On *mukābara* see our chapter on the signs of defeat in theological *jadal*.

8. Although the evidence that you mentioned indicates the existence of the two combinations, we have another piece of evidence that indicates....[188]

The first three formulas are typical of the early style of the *kalām* while the rest are typical of or reminiscent of formal disputation. We have, indeed, encountered most of these examples in our random perusal of the *ṭarīqa* literature. There, the purpose was to give instruction in practical cases; here, however, the purpose is to give theoretical instruction applicable to any case. The last example (8) which we previously found in citing al-Sarakhsī's work was to become the classic formulation of the objection called *muʿāraḍa* in the *ādāb al-baḥth*.[189]

To sum up, al-ʿAmīdī's work when considered in the light of theoretical works of the previous period shows the extent that juristic *jadal* has developed. While its subject matter clearly binds it to the earlier works, its style and method show novelty. Gone are the discussions of the types of questions and their order. The relation between it and the *jadal* of the theologians is no longer transparent. And yet when we consider it with respect to the styles of the *ṭarīqas* that we discussed above, or the evidence-oriented approach of al-Shīrāzī, or even with respect to the problems discussed, those of the *uṣūl al-fiqh*, we cannot doubt that this work belongs to the genre that we identified as juristic *jadal*. The most important new characteristic found in al-ʿAmīdī's work is the use of logical terms and techniques, side by side the traditional ones.[190] It is a characteristic shared by another work of an author slightly earlier than al-ʿAmīdī.

al-Barawī's Muqtaraḥ fī l-Muṣṭalaḥ

In another work of an author slightly earlier than al-ʿAmīdī the old tradition lives on: there are the questions which we encountered in the first period, as well as discussion of the new logical techniques which have now been subjected to some of the questions of the earlier period. The author, al-Barawī, was a Shāfiʿite jurist (d. 1172) and his work *al-Muqtaraḥ fi l-muṣṭalaḥ* exists (in part) in the body of a commentary written by Taqī al-Dīn Muẓaffar b. Abī al-ʿIzz the Shāfiʿite, who was known under the nick-name of al-Muqtaraḥ on account of his commentary to al-Barawī's work.[191] We have already mentioned al-Barawī's discussion of the new techniques: implication and incompatibility. There is mention of *dawarān*.

[188] al-ʿAmīdī, "al-Irshād," fol.17a: 28ff: "*mā dhakartum min al-dalīl wa-in dalla ʿalā mā dhakartum min al-ḥukm fī ṣūrat al-nizāʿ, fa-hāhunā dalīl ākhar yadullu ʿalā mā dhakarnā min al-ḥukm fi ṣūrat al-nizaʿ; fol.21a: 27, "mā dhakartum min al-dalīl in dalla ʿalā thubūt aḥad al-majmuʿain, fa-maʿanā dalīl ākhar yadullu ʿalā ghair...*" Cf. fol.17b: 2, 25; 18a: 21.

[189] See above.

[190] See above.

[191] Taqī al-Dīn Abū al-ʿIzz al-Muqtaraḥ, "al-Muqtaraḥ fī al-muṣṭalaḥ," MS.693 Escurial. For more details, see van Ess, *Īcī*, pp. 51–2.

al-Barawī describes two sorts of demonstration that are the "fruit of the *qiyās al-'illa*"—analogical reasoning based on the *ratio legis*:

> There are two sorts of proof by way of negation (*nafy*). The first is the removal (*intifā'*) of the effect (*athar*) due to the removal of the effector (*mu'aththir*); and from the removal of the of effector to the removal of the effect.
>
> The latter is (only true) when the status (*ḥukmuhū*) of both is one. But if it is several, then there results two sorts of demonstration: (1) from the existence of the one to the existence of the other; and (2) from the absence of one to the absence of the other. But in all this, one must take a close look at the "cause" (*sabab*) and its status (*ḥukm*) ....[192]

al-Barawī's account is not written in precise logical prose but the meaning is clear. In the first case, one argues according to the *modus tollens* from -q to -p; and vice versa if they are equipollent. But if the antecedent or consequent is complex, then one can only argue from p to q or from -q to -p and one must take a long hard look at the implication involved.

The commentator, al-Muqtaraḥ, discusses this section with respect to the "grammar" of the conditional. Of the four ways of expressing it, we offer the first two:

> The expression "if" (*in/realis*) expresses the connection and binding (*al-ta'līq wal-irtibāṭ*) of the protasis (*sharṭ*) to the apodosis (*jazā'*); the condition (*sharṭ*) for its being conclusive (*intājihī*) is the exclusion of the denial of the apodosis when the protasis exists [that is, –(p –>-q)].

The expression "if" (*lau/irrealis*) expresses the removal (*imtinā'*) of a thing due to the removal of another thing.[193]The terminology seems to be influenced by Avicenna's discussion of conditionals in the *Shifā'*.[194] But this is not the only instance where logical terminology or thinking has invaded his treatise. At one point he talks about the "canon of dialectic" (*qānūn al-jadal*) that requires "that each (party) have a specific opinion so that (the discussion) not lead to contentiousness (*'inād*) and the disputation (*munāẓara*) become imprecise."[195] We encountered this rule in the earliest works on theological dialectic; but, it is not described as being part of the "canon" of dialectic. Both al-Barawī and al-Muqtaraḥ were aware of logic's incursion into juristic dialectics and were apparently doing their best to prevent further assaults:

> He (al-Barawī) said: "What we have mentioned is sufficient; there is no need for using the technical language of the non-jurists, since every art (*fann*) has its own (type of) speculation (proper to it) and every group of people (*qaum*) has its own technical language."
>
> [al-Muqtaraḥ comments:] He means the technical language of the logicians (*ahl al-manṭiq*). For (their conventions) have become widely used by the people of our time: (indeed,) the use of logical terminology has become frequent in jurisprudence (although

[192] al-Muqtaraḥ, ""al-Muṣṭalaḥ,"" fol.62b: 12 ff.

[193] Ibid., fol.64a: 9 ff.

[194] Avicenna, *K. al-Qiyās*, p. 234, line 18 ff., and N. Shehaby, *The Propositional Logic of Avicenna* (Dordrecht: D. Reidel, 1973), pp. 226–28.

[195] al-Muqtaraḥ, "al-Muṣṭalaḥ," fol.60a: 12 ff.

> many of the terms have different meanings in jurisprudence as in the case of *burhān al-khulf*); for, the logicians' concept of *burhān al-khulf* differs from that of the jurists.
>
> They call *burhān al-khulf* what the logicians call hypothetical disjunctive [propositions] (*al-sharṭī al-munfaṣil*) and the latter is [also called] *al-sibr wal-taqsīm* by the jurists. But the philosophers mean by *burhān al-khulf* that you take the claim of the opponent and make it a premise in the proof: you add to it a true proposition in order to obtain a false conclusion; the opponent says "the falsity [of the conclusion] cannot result from the construction (*tarkīb*) of the [other] proof because it is valid. Therefore, there must be some other source for the falsity; but all that is left is your opinion which was made as a second premise to the other true one ...."[196]

In the technique of *al-sibr wal-taqsīm*, which al-Barawī discussed earlier in his treatise, the proponent lists all the possible causes of a thing and then eliminates all but one.[197] Apparently he understood this process of elimination, normally called *sibr*, as *burhān al-khulf*. The point that both al-Barawī and al-Muqtaraḥ are trying to make is that logic is unwelcome in juristic dialectics. Fakhr al-Din al-Rāzī who composed several books on logic notes in his epistle on juristic dialectics that the structures of logic carry no sway here.[198]

al-Muqtaraḥ's commentary ends with a curious chapter on the participants in a disputation. There are five positions (*marātib*) which may be filled by the speaker (*mutakallim*) in a disputation (*munāẓara*):

1. The first is the questioner. He can ask many questions about the proof bringing them all at once...
2. When Q has finished putting his questions and P begins answering them, then those present may *interrupt* and this is the second position, interruption (*mudākhala*). It is a precondition of this technique that the interrupter keep to the subject that is being discussed...and so if P has already answered Q's questions (on one subject) and begins answering another, then the interrupter is not allowed to bring an objection to P's answer to the previous question because the opportunity has passed him by. This is a necessary rule since otherwise the dispute cannot endure... The interrupter is allowed to speak at every stage [of the debate] unlike the questioner who can only speak at the first stage!
3. The third position is the appender (*al-mudhdhanib*). This is the person who, after P has finished answering Q's questions, explains Q's questions, and, as it were, gives them a tail (*dhanab*) and feathers (*rīsh*) after they had been stripped of explanation.
4. The fourth position is objection (*i'tirāḍ*) ....

---

196 Ibid., fol.73a: 9 ff.

197 al-Muqtaraḥ, "al-Muṣṭalaḥ," fol.21b: 4 ff. On the vocalization *sibr*, cf. 'Abd al-Nabī al-Ahmadnagarī, *Dustūr al-'ulūm*, ed. M. al-Haidarābādī, 4 vols. (Hyderabad: Dā'irat al-ma'ārif al-Niẓāmīya, 1911–13), vol. 2, p. 161, line 3.

198 Fakhr al-Dīn al-Rāzī, "K. al-Jadal," fol.125b: 1 ff. [= 3b: 5 ff., Arab League]. For details on this work see text related to note 87, *infra*.

5. The fifth position is the objection of some noble person (*sharīf*), and this is precisely the fourth position; except that here, the criticism comes from the more exalted to the less....[199]

The above translation is a preliminary one. The text appears to be corrupt in crucial places. Even so, the reasoning seems to be clear. There are more than two disputants in a juristic disputation. In the previous stages, disputation was understood as occurring between precisely two opponents, something like a boxing match.[200] Now it has become something like a "tag-team" match. Part of the change in perspective had been signaled by the vocabulary of debate. Authors of the middle period tend to speak exclusively about the questioner and proponent (*mustadill/mu'allil*). The latter term occurs in the earlier stage of dialectical jurisprudence, but it is there understood in respect to its being a sub-category of "answerer" or "respondent." From this evidence we must conclude that a change has occurred in our author's understanding of *jadal*. *Jadal* is no longer understood as just question and answer; no, now it is also understood as equivalent to *munāẓara*, speculation, or as al-Muqtaraḥ notes, "helping one another speculate" (*al-ma'ūna 'alā al-naẓar*).[201] *Jadal* has lost its adversary character and now there seems room for spectators noble and ignoble alike to butt in and have their say.

al-Muqtaraḥ's account is rather short on explanation. But several things are clear. First of all, he has abandoned the old four questions schema and apparently allows the proponent to start out with his proof. This may or may not be part of the disputation. Secondly, at the first stage, Q asks all of his questions and then P must answer them. Then the interrupter may have his say. After this, the questioner probably now takes on the role of objector, and the proponent must either defend his thesis or lose the debate. If this interpretation of al-Barawī's account is correct, then what we have is the same basic method which we found in the *ṭarīqas*: (1) problem; (2) proof; (3) objection; (4) response; (5) objection; (6) response. The only difference is that al-Muqtaraḥ allows for audience participation—something ruled out by previous handbooks on *jadal*.[202]

The question naturally arises as to whether this text of al-Muqtaraḥ is descriptive of the reality of juristic debate or prescriptive as to how a debate should be carried on. In as much as al-Muqtaraḥ's discussion represents a clean break with the previous

[199] al-Muqtaraḥ, "al-Muṣṭalaḥ," fol.74b: 15 ff. See supra, p. at note 4.

[200] Cf. van Ess, "Disputationspraxis," p. 25, where he compares it to a modern political debate.

[201] al-Muqtaraḥ, "al-Muṣṭalaḥ," fol.3b: 1. Although a similar remark is made by al-Juwaynī the idea has little effect upon his understanding of *jadal* and his formulation of its rules. *Jadal* is as it ever was an encounter between precisely two people. The increase in the number on participants in a debate indicates a rethinking about the meaning of debate and a consequent emphasis on its truth-theoretical (*naẓarī*) goals as opposed to practical-dialectical (*jadalī*) considerations.

[202] Eg., al-Juwaynī, *al-Kāfiya*, p. 547, par. 813.

discussions of juristic dialectic, it would seem likely that he is describing how debates were being carried on in his time.[203]

Three Other Texts

We have three other texts that provide evidence as to how deep logical terminology penetrated into jurisprudence:

1. Muḥyī al-Dīn Jamāl al-Islām A. M.'s *al-Mukhtaṣar fī 'ilm al-naẓar.*[204]
2. b. Mi'mār, *al-Mukhtaṣar fī al-jadal.*[205]
3. Fakhr al-Dīn al-Razī, *Kitāb al-jadal.*[206]

The second work is b. Mi'mār's summary of this longer work, *Nihāyat al-'amal fī 'ilm al-jadal.* He tells us he made this summary of it "in order to make it easier for the student to learn and memorize." The summary runs 163 folios! The work begins with an introduction treating the nature of *jadal* and disputation (*munāẓara*), its benefits, its parts and its rules (*aḥkāmuhu*).[207] This procedure is also followed by al-Rāzī.[208] It is similar to the procedure of Avicenna in his commentary in the Shifā,[209] al-Rāzī and b. Mi'mār give definitions of *jadal* in its proper sense—"tying or twisting together of rope"—and then go on to consider its technical meaning. Thus, b. Mi'mār writes:

[203] We have indirect confirmation from Fakhr al-Dīn al-Rāzī's disputations in F. Kholeif, *A Study on Fakhr al-Dīn al-Rāzī and His Controversies in Transoxiana* (Beirut: Dar el-Machreq, 1966) where he says, "fa-qāla ba'ḍu al-ḥadirīn 'alā sabīl al-dakhl" (p. 11, line 5).

[204] Muhyī al-Dīn Jamāl al-Islām A. M.'s "al-Mukhtaṣar fī 'ilm al-naẓar," MS.1864 Feyzullah Efendi, Istanbul. Cf. R. Sheshen, *Nawādir al-makhṭūṭāt al-'arabīya fī maktabāt Turkiyā*, 2 vols. at present (Beirut: Dār al-Kitāb al-Jadīd, 1975-), p. 408, Number 1328.

[205] Ibn Mi'mār, "al-Mukhtaṣar fī 'ilm al-jadal," MS.2421, Atif Efendi, Istanbul. Cf. Sheshen, *Nawādir*, p. 183.

[206] Fakhr al-Dīn al-Rāzī, "Kitāb al-jadal," MS.519 Köprülü. Cf. Sheshen, *Nawādir*, p. 283, Number 1132. Brockelmann, GAL I pp. 666–9, SI pp. 920–4. Saiyid, *Fihris*, p. 135. F. Kholeif, *Disputations of al-Rāzī*, p. 9 and p. 203 Number 111 where he cites from al-Qifṭī a work entitled *al-Ṭarīqa fī al-jadal.*

[207] Ibn Mi'mār, "al-Mukhtaṣar," fol.1b, "*ammā al-muqaddima, fa-tashtamilu 'alā qismain, al-auwal fī ḥaqīqat al-jadal wal-munāẓara wa-fā'idat dhālika wa-aqsāmihī wa-aḥkāmihī.*"

[208] Fakhr al-Dīn al-Rāzī, "Kitāb al-jadal," fol.1b: 4. "al-faṣl al-auwal fī bayān ma'nā al-jadal;" 2b: 14 ff, "*al-faṣl al-thānī fī bayān fā'idat al-jadal wa-ādābihī.*"

[209] Avicenna, *al-Jadal*, p. 7. *K. al-Jadal*, ed. F. al- Ahwānī, *al-Shifā': al-Manṭiq*, gen. ed. I. Madkour, vol. 6 (Cairo, Organisme General des Imprimeries Gouvermentales, 1965) "*al-faṣal al-auwal fī ma'rifat al-qiyās al-jadalī wa-manfa'atihī;*" p. 15, "*al-faṣl al-thānī fī al-sabab alladhī yusammā lahū hādha al-ḍarb min al-maqāyīs jadalīya.*"

1. Someone said: "It is a conference between two *or more* contending parties in order to establish the truth or destroy the false, or to show which opinion is more probable."[210]
2. But the preferred definition is: Contention between two *or more* opponents to make plain where the truth (*ʿilm*) or probability of the matter debated lies.
3. As for *munāẓara*, it is used in the technical sense of disputation (*mujādala*); the difference between this *naẓar* and the *naẓar* that we call "speculation," is that speculation can be on the part of the individual while *munāẓara* is grammatically a form expressing something mutual (*mufāʿala*), and cannot come about unless two or more people participate.
4. The difference between *jadal* and eristic (*mirāʾ*) is that eristic aims at finding out the opponent's opinion and refuting it by dissimulation; but, *jadal* is finding out the opponent's opinion in order to establish a proof against it. *Jadal* is *praiseworthy* while eristic is *blameworthy*. [The difference between the two is sometimes obscured since] *mirāʾ*, eristic, is sometimes used in the meaning of *jadal*.[211]

In al-Rāzī's book, he quotes the first opinion above (1) as the definition that al-Ghazzālī gives in *al-Muntakhal*.[212] al-Rāzī explains that Ghazzālī's reference to "establishing the truth and destroying the false" refers to questions of the *uṣūl al-fiqh*, while the last part of the question refers to the *furūʿ*.[213] al-Ghazzālī, however, only speaks of two opponents (*mutanāziʿāni*). The additional opponents were added by b. Miʿmār's source, who no doubt understood *jadal* as b. Miʿmār and al-Muqtaraḥ did, that is, as synonymous with *munāẓara*. The contrast between *jadal* and *munāẓara* no longer holds for our author. *Jadal* itself seems to have lost its razor's edge. Now, just as in philosophy, *jadal* is contrasted with eristic. Nevertheless the remarks must still be understood in their "Islamic" context, as al-Rāzī's comment on the same subject illustrates:

> As for the praiseworthy and blameworthy sort of dialectic, that dialectic is praiseworthy that seeks to reveal the truth and to return the opponent to the truth (*ṣawāb*). And this is, indeed, the sort commanded in Qurʾān 16/125...but the blameworthy sort is any whose purpose is to silence the opponent by behaving contentiously or peevishly and seeking to hide the truth.[214]

[210] Ibn Miʿmār, "al-Mukhtaṣar," fol.3b: 1. "*fa-qīla huwa tafāwuḍ baina mutanāziʿain fa-ṣāʿidan li-taḥqīq ḥaqq au li-ibṭāl bāṭil au li-taghlīb ẓann.*"

[211] Ibn Miʿmār, "al-Mukhtaṣar," fol.3b: -1 ff.

[212] Fakhr al-Dīn al-Rāzī, "Kitāb al-jadal," fol.1b: 10–11 [= 123b:10–11 Arab League], "*fa-qad aurada al-Ghazzālī fī al-Muntakhal annahū tafāwuḍ yajrī baina mutanāziʿain li-taḥqīq ḥaqq au li-ibṭāl bāṭil au li-taghlīb ẓann*;" for other uses of the root, cf. F. Jabre, *Essai sur le lexique de Ghazali* (Beirut: Imprimerie Catholique, 1970), pp. 47–9.

[213] Fakhr al-Dīn al-Rāzī, "Kitāb al-jadal," fol.1b: 14–15 [= 123b:14–15 Arab League].

[214] Fakhr al-Dīn al-Rāzī, "Kitāb al-jadal," fol.124a: 12 [= 2a: 12 Arab League], "*...min haithu al-nakar wal-ʿinād wa-ikhfāʾ al-ḥaqq.* al-Rāzī previously gave the meaning of *jadal* as "*tabyīn mā yustaqbaḥ min al-mutanāẓirain fī sharīʿat al-jadal min haithu al-īrād*" at fol.124a: 6–7 [= 2a: 6–7 Arab League].

The discussion of good and bad *jadal* here is oddly reminiscent of Aristotle's discussion in the *Topics*:

> Now in business, he who hinders the common task is a bad partner and the same is true in argument....It makes no difference whether a man acts like this in his answers or in his questions: for he who asks questions in a contentious spirit (*eristikos*) and he who in replying refuses to admit what is apparent and to accept whatever question the questioner wishes to put, are both of them bad dialecticians.[215]

While b. Mi'mār's discussion of the dialectic and eristic is related to that of al-Rāzī, the similarity to Aristotle's division is striking. It is worthy of note that in making this contrast, b. Mi'mār makes no mention of *jadal*'s goal of obtaining the truth and opposing it with the goal of eristic—hiding the truth. If we are not dealing with a *lapsus calami*, we are entitled to conclude that for b. Mi'mār *jadal* is wholly praiseworthy. And *jadal* has come a long way, indeed, since its humble origins as a method for obtaining truth. Now all three authors understand *jadal* as the "logic of thought." Thus, Muḥyī al-Dīn in his introduction:

> You should know...that the knowledge of this science is indispensable to the investigator (*nāẓir*) and that the speech of the disputant (*munāẓir*) does not progress without it; for, *through it* the *soundness* (*ṣiḥḥa*) of the evidence becomes clearly distinguished from *falsity* (*fasād*), and so too the questions which occur in debate, be they particular or general, are explained.
>
> Were it not for it, the establishment of the truth would be confounded by peevishness (*mukābara*)...and there would be much confusion and uncertainty in debate.
>
> For only the rules of dialectic (*marāsim al-jadal*) separate the *true* from the *false*, and distinguish the *sound* (*al-mustaqīm*) from the *unsound* (*al-saqīm*) ....[216]

Ibn Mi'mār writes in the same vein:

> You should know every juristconsult (*mujtahid*), jurist (*mutafaqqih*) and theologian must know the science of dialectic in as much as each one seeks to hold discussions (*mufāwaḍa*); and his debates (*muḥāwara*) do not reach their intended benefits (except through it).
>
> For, it is the measure (*mizān*) of all expressions (*'ibārāt*) and through it, the proper way to use evidence, bring objections and replies, becomes known...and it prevents the discussion, by its "good method of bringing questions and responses," from becoming pointless.
>
> For its is to science (*'ilm*) what *prosody* is to *poetry*, for through it the *sound* (*ṣaḥīḥ*) is known from the *unsound* (*fāsid*); just as *grammar* is to *speech*, for it is the foundation of every science![217]

al-Rāzī notes that it prevents error in discussion and keeps *both* disputants on the lookout against error:

> It is as if it were a measure (*qānūn*) to which the *sound* and *unsound* were referred back. In addition, it distinguishes between the two, for dialectic is in respect to the science of debate (*fann al-munāẓara*) like prosody with respect to poetry; for prosody is the measure (*mizān*) of poetry, and through it is known the *sound* (*ṣaḥīḥ*) and the *unsound* (*saqīm*).[218]

---

[215] Aristotle *Top.* 161a37 ff. (trans. from Loeb).

[216] Muḥyī al-Dīn, "Mukhtaṣar," fol.2b ff.

[217] Ibn Mi'mār, "al-Mukhtaṣar," fol.4a ff.

[218] Fakhr al-Dīn al-Rāzī, "Kitāb al-jadal," fol.124b: 17 ff. [= 2b: 17 ff. Arab League].

The above three accounts of dialectic describe it in terms that were once the haughty preserve of logic. Thus, did Mattā b. Yūnus arouse the wrath of the Muslim scholars by his "extravagant claim" that:

> Logic is the only instrument through which we know truth from falsehood veracity from lying, good from bad and doubt from certainty...[he said] I understand by logic an "instrument" of speech, by which correct speech is known from incorrect and unsound meaning from sound: like a balance, for by it I know the overweight from underweight and what rises from what sinks.[219]

A century later, Avicenna noted in his introduction to the logic of the *Shifā'*:

> This art (logic) is indispensable for human perfection..its relation to internal deliberation, which is called *al-nuṭq al-dākhilī*, is like...the relation of prosody to poetry. Except that prosody is not of much use in writing poetry; a person of sound taste (*dhauq*) does not need to know it...but no human being who wishes to attain scientific knowledge by speculation and reflection can do so without it, unless he be supported by God himself![220]

It would be difficult to say exactly when these metaphors and epithets used in connection with logic came to be used about *jadal*. What is clear is that by the thirteenth century this identification had become commonplace.

In the works of Muḥyī al-Dīn and b. Mi'mār, there are initial chapters on "words and terms" used in disputation. Thus, Muḥyī al-Dīn says in a manner similar to that of al-Barawī:

> The second chapter concerns the introduction to the rules of disputation and it has an introduction....As for the introduction, you should know that the masters of every art have certain expressions that they use among themselves in their discussions; for, they posited them vis-à-vis the referents that they needed in their debates, so that other people do not understand what these words mean unless helped by the experts.[221]

He then goes on to give definitions of certain terms used in the *uṣūl al-fiqh* such as *dalīl, naqḍ, maḥall al-nizā', khāṣṣ, 'āmm, etc.*; in addition certain "philosophical" definitions turn up—the three types of signification are mentioned, namely, correspondence (*muṭābaqa*), containment (*taḍammun*), and implication (*iltizām*).[222] Likewise, b. Mi'mār defines terms of *uṣūl al-fiqh* such as *dalīl, amāra, i'tirāḍ*, but he also defines philosophical terms such as tri-partite and quadripartite propositions, indefinite propositions (*ma'dūla*), and so forth.[223] Only al-Rāzī walks the

[219] M. Mahdi, "Language and Logic in Classical Islam," G. von Grunebaum, ed., *Logic in Classical Islamic Culture* (Wiesbaden: Harrasowitz, 1970), pp. 62, 64.

[220] Avicenna, *al-Madkhal*, ed. G. Anawati, *al-Shifā': al-Manṭiq*, gen ed. I. Madkour, vol. 1 (Cairo: Imprimerie Nationale, 1956), p. 20, line 13 ff.

[221] Muḥyī al-Dīn, "Mukhtaṣar," fol.5a: 3 ff.

[222] Ibid., fol.5b ff. Cf. Vajda, "Autour de la théorie de la connaissance chez Saadia," *REJ* 126 (1967): 286 ff.

[223] Ibn Mi'mār, "al-Mukhtaṣar," fol.5a ff, 37a ff., 51b ff.

straight line and gives only juristic definitions of terms like *qiyās*, *amāra*, *dalīl*—for philosophy has no business telling the jurisconsult what to do in the field of his expertise.[224]

The tradition of providing introductory chapters on definitions of the terms used in the work at hand is not peculiar to the writings of Muḥyī al-Dīn and b. Miʿmār. In the *jadal*-books of Bājī and al-Juwaynī, there were also introductory chapters on definitions and one could give a long list of other works in jurisprudence and philosophy which began with definitions of the terms used. That said, we shall soon see that this tradition of providing an initial chapter on definitions was to play a role in the first treatise on general disputation.

All three works contain chapters on the *adab al-jadal*. Muḥyī al-Dīn warns that the debaters should have good intentions and seek to display the truth on account of their seeking God's will. "They should avoid cursing and railing at one another since these are two things that decrease their rank and increase their sin...."[225] He then goes on to define what is questioner, question, respondent and answer. And lo and behold, we are in the old-world of the "four questions:"

> The questioner is the one who says "What is God's statute (*ḥukm*) in this case?" After R mentions the "statute," Q asks, "What is the proof (*dalīl*) for this?" Q must not interrupt R by bringing anything extraneous that refutes R's evidence in the manner of reversal (*qalb*) or counter-objection (*muʿāraḍa*), since that is the obligation (*waẓīfa*) of the objectioner (*muʿṭarid*)!
>
> "Question" is Q's saying, "What is the status of that?" or, "What is the evidence for that?" and so forth. R is, in our subject, the one who is obliged to demonstrate his opinion; it is preferred that he begin giving evidence as soon as the question is asked, but if he delays a bit, he does not lose unless he was totally unable to answer it.
>
> As for "answer", "it is the juristic status about which the *fatwā* is given."[226]

Muḥyī al-Dīn's distinction between the questioner and the objectioner reminds us of al-Barawī's distinction between the first and fourth "positions" of debate. Perhaps in both cases we are dealing with the tradition that there are two types of question, one about the opinion and another about its verification. In Muḥyī al-Dīn's account it seems that both roles would be filled by the same person, while in al-Barawī, the issue is left open.

Ibn Miʿmār's chapter on the *adab al-jadal* is the most extensive treatment of the subject since that of al-Juwaynī. But it is nothing more than a rehashing of the old admonitions that we discussed in our chapter on the theologians. The most interesting thing found in his account is its division into different chapters:

1. The intentions of the debate (*maqāṣid*).
2. The expressions used (*aqwāl*).
3. The deeds (*afʿāl*).
4. The conditions of the debates (*aḥwāl*).

---

[224] Fakhr al-Dīn al-Rāzī, "Kitāb al-jadal," fol.126b: 12 ff [= 4b: 12 ff. Arab League].

[225] Muḥyī al-Dīn, "Mukhtaṣar," fol.16a: 3 ff.

[226] Ibid., fol.16b ff.

5. When to debate.
6. Where to debate.
7. The qualities of the good debater (*auṣāf al-shaikh*).[227]

Chapters five and six are, indeed, new, but they deal with matters that lie on the periphery of this study.

Ibn Mi'mār's last chapter concerns the *adab al-jadal* but at the beginning of his work he has a chapter on sophistic and playing fair in debate (*al-mughālaṭa wal-inṣāf*).[228] It is perhaps the best example of direct logical influence on the development of juristic dialectics. Ibn Mi'mār writes:

> Sophistic is (1) when you make the opponent appear to be wrong in a case where he is right, or (2) when you make consequent what is not consequent, or (3) or when you bring (an) eristic (proof) in place of one that affords certainty or (4) taking as cause what is not the cause....
>
> But fairness is avoiding all this...and holding fast to the canon of religion and good manners (*al-tamassuk bi-qānūn al-dīn wal-adab*). One should not suppose that Abraham's disputation (*munāẓara*) with Nimrod was sophistic. Rather he followed the method of dialectic (*jadal*) so when he saw that his opponent did not understand what he meant by "bringing back to life" and "causing to die" he turned to (language) which was easier for him to understand.[229]

His second and fourth examples are taken directly from Aristotle's Sophistic Elenchi, and the other points that he makes clearly derive from the philosophical tradition.[230]

The Final Period of Juristic Dialectics

In the final period, logical content and style practically took over juristic dialectic. The author of the key work of this period was Burhān al-Din al-Nasafī. al-Nasafī was a Ḥanafite jurist who also commented upon logical works such as Avicenna's *al-Ishārāt wal-tanbīhāt*, as well as on al-Urmawī's *Asās al-kiyāsa*.[231] But his treatise on juristic dialectic, the so-called "Muqaddima al-Burhānīya" or "al-Fuṣūl lil-Nasafī,"[232] played a key role in the evolution of the general theory of debate known

[227] Ibn Mi'mār, "al-Mukhtaṣar," fol.156b: 3 ff.

[228] Ibid., fol.69a ff.

[229] Ibid., fol.69a: 3 ff.

[230] Aristotle *SE* 166a24-6.

[231] On al-Nasafī's biography cf. Brockelmann GAL I p. 467 SI p. 849; Kh. Kaḥḥāla, *Mu'jam al-mu'allifīn*,15 vols. (Damascus: Maṭba'at al-Taraqqī, 1957–61), vol. 11, p. 297. Hājji Khalīfa, *Kashf*, p. 1798, line -1; p. 1272, line 5; cf. Saiyid, *Fihris* p. 222, no. 223. R. Sellheim, *Arabische Handschriften. Materialen zur arabischen Literatturgeschichte*, vol. 1 (Wiesbaden: Steiner, 1976), p. 163. al-Nasafī's importance for the history of dialectic has been noted by G. Makdisi in "Le Livre de Dialectique," p. 109; and "The Tanbīh of Ibn Taimīya on Dialectic," *Medieval and Middle Eastern Studies in Honor of A. S. Atiya*, ed. S. Hanna (Leiden: E. J. Brill, 1972).

[232] As Ḥājji Khalīfa points out, they are the same work, cf. preceding note.

as the *ādāb al-baḥth*; for, the founder of this new science, Shams al-Dīn al-Samarqandī, was a student of al-Nasafī's and commented upon his text on juristic *jadal*.[233]

The Muqaddima of al-Nasafī

This work contains over twenty-five chapters on the types of argumentation used in juristic dialectics. We have already mentioned three of those chapters in our discussion of al-ʿAmīdī's "Irshād." Now, however, we would like to concentrate on his introductory chapter, for there, he is the first author to spell out exactly what the rules of dialectic are.

The introduction is divided into two parts, one in which the rules of dialectic are treated, and another where definitions of key technical terms are given.

In what follows, we will first discuss the rules of debate and then consider technical terms.

al-Nasafī's "Muqaddimma" seems to have been available in two forms, a short one and a longer commentary (*sharḥ*) on the former. In the shorter version the text runs as follows:

> It is incumbent upon the disputant (*al-munāẓir*) (1) to explain the subjects of dispute (*al-mabāḥith*) and (2) to give precedence to pointing out (what they are), as when he determines precisely questions, the first principles, or establishes what the various opinions (about the subject of dispute) are before (bringing their) proofs (*dalāʾil*). This is all done in the manner of citation (*ḥikāya*)—there can be no interruption here (on the part of the questioner).
>
> (3) But when he (P) starts to establish a proof (*dalīl*) for his claim, then his opponent (*al-khaṣm*) can (either): [a] refrain from helping him. Indeed he can (i) proffer objections to his premises; this is done in the manner of refutation (*munāqaḍa*).
>
> But should Q (ii) object to a premise by establishing (a proof of) the point of dispute, then it is said that he usurped (*ghaṣaba*) (P's position) and no attention is given to him, in accord with the conventions of the experts, even if a few people permitted it.
>
> Or, [b] Q can help him to establish his evidence (*dalīl*) without committing himself to accepting the *demonstrandum* (*madlūl*); indeed, he can go on to use P's evidence in order to demonstrate the opposite of what P said. If so, he has done this in the manner of counter-objection (*muʿāraḍa*); for counter-objection is opposition in the manner of disallowing something.[234]

Let us reverse the order of al-Nasafī's discussion by first talking about the participants in a disputation (*munāẓara*) and then about disputation in general.

---

[233] That he was at one time al-Nasafī's student becomes clear from the remark which he makes in the commentary "*wa-samiʿtu al-muṣannif ajāba ʿan hādha bi-wajhain*" (Shams al-Dīn al-Samarqandī, "Sharḥ," fol.5b: 10–11). If we are right in presuming that al-Samarqandī was born and raised in Samarqand, it would not be surprising that he studied in Nasaf, a town not so distant from Samarqand.

[234] Shams al-Dīn al-Samarqandī, "Sharḥ," fol.1b ff.

al-Nasafī is the first author to formulate explicit rules of debate, to say exactly who starts the debate. Although the formulation of the rules is unprecedented when considered in the light of previous works in the genre, the rules obviously derive from the tradition of the "four questions" or rather from the tradition that there are really two sorts of questions, one about the opinion and the other about its verification.[235] But now there is no more pretense made about the proponent's being a respondent. al-Nasafī calls him the "disputant." It is perhaps not accidental that the word *jadal* does not appear in al-Nasafī's text. It has been replaced by *munāẓara* a word which no longer has such a close association with question and answer. Indeed, Q is no longer merely a questioner—he brings objections and even counter-evidence, *mu'āraḍa*. al-Nasafī calls him "the opponent." Here it is interesting to note that the old problem about whether *mu'āraḍa* is a question or not is no longer of importance. What counts is whether it is used before or after P has brought his evidence. In the first case it would be "usurpation," while in the latter it is permitted.

Should we compare the rules that al-Nasafī gives with the system used in the *ṭarīqa*s of the middle-period, we would see that they could easily be applied to them. But there is an essential difference. In the *ṭarīqas*, question and answer predominate, while in al-Nasafī's system we have P's thesis and also Q's objections and anti-thesis. In the periods previous to al-Nasafī, it was disputed whether Q could set out to prove his opposing thesis; this was considered by some to be a digression (*intiqāl*) from the subject-matter of the debate.[236] But this no longer appears to be the case. A change in perspective with respect to the nature of the discussion occurred and brought with it a change in the conception of the roles of the opponents.

Q has basically two weapons that he can wield against P—refutation and counter-evidence. al-Nasafī seems to understand all *objection per se* as falling under the category of *man'*, disallowance. Objection that occurs before P finishes his proof is called refutation, while that which occurs afterwards is called counter-objection. al-Nasafī gives formulae for both types of objection in his commentary. Thus, speaking about refutation (*munāqaḍa*), he says:

Just as when you use it against an explicit text (*naṣṣ*) (a) "*Why do you say that* (*lima qultum*) the wording of the text includes the disputed point?

(b) *Even if it does* include it, *why do you say that* it is intended or a part of the intention?

(c) *How could this be when* there exists something that prevents (*al-māni'*) it in this case?[237]

Parts (a) and (b) are standard parts of *munāqaḍa*; part (c) is optional. In the first two parts, Q asks P to provide backing or support for his statement that "x" is the case. In part (c), Q makes explicit that in a certain case, C_0, "x" is not the case, and

[235] See our discussion in the beginning of this Chapter on "Question and Answer".

[236] Cf. above on theological *mu'āraḍa*.

[237] al-Nasafī, "al-Muqaddima," fol.43a: 10 ff.

therefore, P's argument is refuted or needs further supporting evidence. The technique itself we encountered in the writings of the first period, where it went under the name of *naqḍ* incommensurability. al-Nasafī, however, gives it a more general definition: "It is the destruction of one of the two statements by the other." This definition would bring it close to the meaning of refutation or *elenchus*.[238] al-Nu'mān al-Khwārizmī objects to al-Nasafī's definition, since it does not exclude reversal, *qalb*, nor counter-objection. "It is more appropriate to say that *munāqaḍa* is the disallowing of some premise of the evidence (*al-dalīl*) or all of the evidence."[239] Centuries later, al-Aḥmadnagarī cites al-Nasafī's definition as the "literal" meaning of *munāqaḍa*, while al-Nu'mān's is the technical definition, whose "detailed explanation occurs in the writings on the *ādāb al-baḥth wal-munāẓara*."[240]

In his commentary, al-Nasafī also provides a formula and definition of counter-objection (*mu'āraḍa*):

> ...as when Q says (in demonstrating the contrary of P's claim) "Although the text (*naṣṣ*) *that you mentioned indicated that, however, we have* other texts that are incompatible with yours and that render it void."
>
> This is done in the manner of counter-objection since *mu'āraḍa* is opposition in the manner of denying. (N.B.) There is no *mu'āraḍa* between the two proofs (*dalīlāni*) unless one of them is potentially contained in the other or nearly so.[241]

While the formula itself is again taken from the *ṭarīqa* literature it is novel in that al-Nasafī understands it as a formula.

al-Nasafī also informs the reader what Q is not allowed to do: he may not bring counter-evidence before P is finished presenting his evidence, since this is usurpation. Again, his commentary provides more detail:

> You should know that disallowing a premise by establishing the disputed legal qualification is called usurpation, *ghaṣb*. For example, if Q says, "If 'x', then the point of dispute would be as P claims; but this is not so due to the following contrary evidence...."
>
> The word *ghaṣb* is used, because Q is involved in objecting to the premise (at that time) and not in counter-objecting; for, counter-objection (*mu'āraḍa*) is the position of the other person (P), and Q has usurped his position. This is not allowed according to the conventions of the jurists and theoreticians (of our time) just as it was disallowed by the *ulamā'* of old; because, it contains a digression from one speech to another before P has completely presented his argument. Some of the moderns allowed it on the grounds that disallowing it does him (P) no good....[242]

The commentators inform us that the person who did allow. *Ghaṣb* was none other than Rukn al-Dīn al-'Amīdī, the author of the famous *ṭarīqa*. Indeed, in the "Irshād" we get a hint at this position. There, al-'Amīdī allows that not all (*intiqāl*) are bad (*qabīḥ/mustadrak*), since if P wants to prove "y" and sees that he needs to prove "x"

---

[238] Aristotle *Topics* 163b6; *SE* 169b27.

[239] al-Khwārizmī, "Sharḥ," fol.5a: 12–14.

[240] al-Aḥmadnagarī, *Dustūr*, vol. 3, pp. 337–8.

[241] al-Nasafī, "al-Muqaddima," 43b: 17 ff.

[242] al-Nasafī, "al-Muqaddima," fol.43a: 17 ff.

in order to prove "y," then this digression is useful and should not be disallowed.[243] al-Nasafī most certainly had al-ʿAmīdī in mind since they were both Ḥanafite jurists. al-Nasafī argues that *ghaṣb* is *per se* false (*bāṭil*) and therefore, does not merit a reply. al-Samarqandī–ˉ does not agree with al-Nasafī's position. *Ghaṣb* is not disallowed, he says, because Q has no right to use *muʿāraḍa*, or because that is P's right. Rather it is because before the establishment of the proposition, it is P's right to bring evidence (*taʿlīl*); at this point, Q is only allowed to object or ask for verification. The most Q can do, indeed, is to bring an objection with backing (that is, not a proof), since anything else would be usurping P's position and lead to randomness in debate. *Muʿāraḍa* is Q's rightful instrument, however, he may only use it after P has finished giving his proof.[244]

In al-Nasafī's account, the role of the proponent is less complex than that of the questioner. His first duty is to explain exactly what the debate will consider. al-Nasafī chooses as his example a *topos* from the literature of juristic dialectics:

> If P says in the beginning: "Intention is not a precondition for the *wuḍūʾ* ablution in the opinion of Abū Ḥanīfa and his companions but it is in the opinion of al-Shāfiʿī," then you cannot object and say, "Why don't you say it is not a precondition?" or "It is a precondition in this respect but not in that one," because he did not relate that it is in his own opinion a precondition or not; he only related that Abū Ḥanīfa said this and al-Shāfiʿī said that.[245]

al-Nasafī notes that if the positions which P cites are well-known (*umūr mashhūra*) then he does not have to bother explaining them but may proceed directly to his proof.[246] al-Samarqandī disagrees again with al-Nasafī's account. Q may object even when P is explaining what is the point of dispute (*maḥall al-nizāʿ*). For P might very well substitute something else in its stead, and, thus, Q is entitled to object and ask for a "verification of the report" (*taṣḥiḥ al-naql*).[247] In the next part of the debate, P gives his proof, and answers any objections that Q may bring to bear against his premises. Perhaps this is what al-Nasafī means when he says that it is P who has the right to make counter-objection at the time when he is setting forth his proof. Unfortunately, al-Nasafī's is not very explicit here about the course of the debate after P has given his proof and Q has countered with counter-proof. In this respect, al-Nasafī's account is incomplete.

Let us now return to al-Nasafī's definition of disputation. He gives it in his commentary in explaining who is the disputant (*munāẓir*):

1. The disputant is the person who disputes someone else in a disputation.
2. The word *munāẓara*, disputation, has several possible derivations.
   (a) It could derive from the word "equal"(*naẓīr*) in the sense that the two opponents become equals in debate.

---

[243] al-ʿAmīdī, "Irshād," fol.19a: 28–9.

[244] Shams al-Dīn al-Samarqandī, "Sharḥ," fol.3b: 1, al-Khwārizmī, "Sharḥ," fol.6a: 14 ff.

[245] Shams al-Dīn al-Samarqandī, "Sharḥ," fol.3a: 5 ff.

[246] al-Nasafī, "al-Muqaddima," fol.42b: 12 ff.

[247] Ibid., fol.43a: 4 ff.

(b) It could derive from the word "speculation" (*naẓar*) as when you say, "He speculated about it (*naẓara fīhī*)," if it is done with "insight" (*baṣīra*).

(c) ...But the technical definition of the ulamāʿ says that it is (1) speculation (*naẓar*) from the two sides about (2) the relation between the two things with (3) the goal of making plain which one is true.[248]

al-Nasafī chooses that last definition (2,c) as the correct definition of *munāẓara*. It was not a happy choice. al-Samarqandī criticizes it: "This is a definition of cogitation (*mufākara*) and not disputation. The correct definition is 'the bandying back and forth of the discussion (*mudāfaʿat al-kalām*) between the two sides in order to reveal the truth;ʿ if it is *not* done to reveal then it is dialectic (*mujādala*)!"[249] al-Samarqandī's criticism is aimed at al-Nasafī's use of the word *naẓar*, that we translated above as speculation. It is of course possible that al-Nasafī intended to use it in the sense of disputation or argumentation. If so, he was guilty of using an equivocal word in his definition as well as of defining a thing by itself. That being said, if we consider the definition itself along with al-Nasafī's explanation, we see the great inroads that logic has made in juristic dialectics. The two disputants, P and Q, are now called "the two sides" (*al-jānibāni*); the two opinions, thesis and antithesis, are called "the two things (*al-shaiʾāni*). But the goal of disputation is still the same: to reveal the truth (*al-ṣawāb* [lit. what is correct]). Let us, however, take a closer look at al-Nasafī's explanation about "the relation between the two things:"

> There is no doubt that the knowledge of that relation is based upon the knowledge of the two terms (*ṭarāfaihī*) e.g., the "world" in our statement "the world is eternal, *a parte ante*." For the former (the word "world") is the subject (of the proposition) (*al-maḥkūm ʿalaihī*) while the latter ("is eternal *a parte ante*") is the predicate (*al-maḥkūm bihī*).[250]

al-Nasafī's example is the same example that Aristotle uses in the *Topics* as an example of a dialectical question. Its use in a book on juristic dialectics is unprecedented. We must keep in mind, however, that although these terms are logical, they do have a juristic flavor. For "*ḥukm*" in juristic contexts means legal qualification, so that the terms that we just translated as subject and predicate might equally be translated as "the thing which is given a legal qualification" and "the legal qualification" respectively. That al-Nasafī intends these words in their logical meanings without any reference to jurisprudence becomes clear when we consider that al-Nasafī attaches to his account a section on contradictory relations (*tanāquḍ*): "Contradiction between two propositions is their essential incompatibility with respect to existence and non-existence in the sense that they cannot both be true or both false at the same time; this cannot occur unless there is one subject (in both propositions)."[251] al-Nasafī then goes on to list the various types of contradictory relations such as those with respect to the part, the whole, place, time, relation, potentiality, actuality,

---

[248] Burhān al-Dīn al-Nasafī, "al-Muqaddima al-Burhānīya," fol.1b, MS.2246 (Yahuda Collection), Princeton University Library, Princeton, N.J. (Henceforth, "al-Muqaddima [Yahuda].)"

[249] Shams al-Dīn al-Samarqandī, "Sharḥ," fol.2b: 3–4.

[250] Burhān al-Dīn al-Nasafī, "al-Muqaddima [Yahuda]," fol.1b.

[251] Burhān al-Dīn al-Nasafī, "al-Muqaddima [Yahuda]," fol.1b: 8 ff.

quality, and quantity. There is, therefore, no room to doubt that he intends to use the terms "subject" and "predicate" in their logical meanings.

As a sort of appendix to his discussion of the rules of debate, and more particularly as an expansion upon his definition of counter-objection, al-Nasafī brings definitions of three key terms: *dalīl* (evidence), *istidlāl* (demonstration) and *ta'līl* (argument/*aitiologia*).

al-Nasafī's definition of *dalīl* is crucial to his explanation of counter-objection, since otherwise, it would not be clear what he means by saying, "one of the two *dalīls* is potentially contained in the other or nearly so." Thus, al-Nasafī defines *dalīl* as follows:

1. "*Dalīl* (evidence) is that thing the knowledge of which results in the knowledge of the existence of the thing indicated (*madlūl*) whether it be traditional (*naqlī*), intellectual (*'aqlī*), or a combination of the two.
   (a) Intellectual (evidence) is such that the existence of the thing indicated follows (necessarily) from it. This (relation of) "following" (*luzūm*) must either result from the two terms (*ṭarafainī*) (i) as in demonstration (*istidlāl*) of the specific *causatum* (*mu'aiyan*) by means of the absolute cause (*al-'illa al-muṭlaqa*), or (ii) of the latter by means of the former, or (iii) from one of the causes to the other and not *vice versa* as when we demonstrate from the stipulated (*mashrūṭ*) to the stipulation (*sharṭ*)....
   (b) Evidence wholly based upon tradition is impossible (*muḥāl*), for reports that come to us from others do not benefit us unless we know that they are true: but that only comes about by using the intellect (*bil-'aql*). Therefore, this evidence must be (c) combined with evidence of the intellect.
2. It could be said that the meaning of *dalīl* is that it is that thing which were it the sole object of consideration (*lau jurrida al-naẓar ilaihī*), there would result the overwhelming opinion that the thing indicated (*madlūl*) exists.[252]

al-Samarqandī notes that al-Nasafī's first definition is the current definition among the experts (*al-mashhūr baina ahl al-'ilm*); however, he finds fault with it on two grounds: (1) it uses correlative terms (*dalīl/madlūl*) and this is not permissible in definitions and (2) it stipulates the "existence" (*wujūd*) of the thing indicated although the latter might well be something non-existent:

> The proper definition is to say *dalīl* is that thing the knowledge of which results in the knowledge of another thing. This is a definition of stringent evidence and not of evidence absolutely, for that is more general and, thus, neither (exclusively) probable *ẓannī* nor stringent (*qat'ī*)....[253]

As a comprehensive definition of (absolute) *dalīl*, al-Samarqandī offers this definition: "It is that thing, the knowledge or opinion of which results in the knowledge or opinion about the realization (*taḥaqquq*) of something else."[254]

---

[252] Ibid., fol.1b: 11 ff.

[253] Shams al-Dīn al-Samarqandī, "Sharḥ," fol.4a. Cf. al-Nasafī, "al-Muqaddima," fol.44a: 6 ff. "*huwa alladhī yalzam min al-'ilm bihī al-'ilm bi-wujūd al-madlūl.*"

[254] Shams al-Dīn al-Samarqandī, *Sharḥ*, fol.4a: 18 ff, "*huwa alladhī yalzam min al-'ilm bihī al-'ilm bi-shai'in ākhar.*"

al-Nasafī's definition of *dalīl* is taken from the *Muḥaṣṣal* of al-Rāzī.[255] Neither al-Rāzī nor his commentator, Naṣīr al-Dīn al-Ṭūsī, saw the errors that al-Samarqandī pointed out, although it was al-Samarqandī's definition that was eventually chosen as the definition of *dalīl* by al-Jurjānī.[256]

al-Nasafī's final definitions are of *istidlāl* and *ta'līl*. "Argument from the evidence (*istidlāl*) is the movement of the mind from the effect to the effector", while "argument by means of the cause (*ta'līl*) is the movement of the mind from the effector to the effect."2[257] He gives as examples of the two the relation between smoke and fire for the former, and its reverse for the latter. The Aristotelian commentators know two similar concepts: *analysis*, which goes from the effects to the causes, and *apodeixis* which goes from the causes to the effects.[258] There, as perhaps here, the distinction derives from Aristotle's division of proof *that* something is so, and proof *why* something is so.[259]

These last three definitions are not very well integrated into the text, and this gives the chapter an amorphous appearance. al-Nu'mān notes, for example, that al-Nasafī really ought to define *dalīl* before he defines *munāqaḍa* (refutation) since the understanding of the latter also rests upon it.[260]

But this does not detract much from the importance of the introduction, for it is one of the clearest elucidations of the rules of juristic debate that we have in respect to writings of his period and those of his predecessors. The old rules of the *adab al-jadal*, the code of conduct, have been set aside while the four questions have been reformulated and set down as rules. Though not all the rules are set down—absent are rules about how to end the debate and what the signs of defeat are—an important start has been made.

---

[255] Fakhr al-Dīn al-Rāzī, *Muḥaṣṣal afkār al-mutaqaddimīn wal-muta'akhkhirīn*, ed. T. Sa'ad (Cairo, Maktabat al-Kulliyāt al-Azharīya, n.d.), p. 50, line 12 ff.

[256] 'Alī b. Muḥammad al-Jurjānī, *Ta'rīfāt* (Istanbul: Maṭba'at Aḥmad Kāmil, 1327), s.v. *dalīl*.

[257] al-Nasafī, "al-Muqaddima," fol.44b: 1 ff; cf. *Īcī*, p. 359.

[258] Eustratius, *In Analyticorum posteriorum librum secundum commentarium*, ed. M. Hayduck, *CAG*, vol. 21,1 (Berlin: G. Reimer, 1907), p. 3, line 34. John Philoponus, *In Analytica posteriora commentaria*, ed. M. Wallies, *CAG*, vol. 13,3 (Berlin,: G. Reimer, 1909), p. 334, line 20.

[259] Aristotle *APo*. Book II.1.

[260] al-Khwārizmī, "Sharḥ," fol.7b: 9 f.

Chapter 5
The Ādāb Al-Baḥth

Out of the traditions of juristic and philosophical dialectics there arose a new theory of dialectics or disputation, the *ādāb al-baḥth* or general theory of disputation. In this chapter, we shall discuss the *ādāb al-baḥth* and relate it to the traditions from which it took its inspiration. In this chapter, I try to show how *ādāb al-baḥth* emerged as an independent intellectual discipline and literary genre by adopting concepts from Aristotelean logic and philosophy as well as rules formulated in the context of both juridical and theological dialectics. Al-Samarqandī combined these traditions principally by his application of Aristotle's epistemology to the rules of debate.

When discussing the *ādāb al-baḥth*, we find that one name appears at the head of the list of authors who wrote on this subject, that of Shams al-Dīn Muḥammad b. Ashraf al-Ḥussainī al-Samarqandī. We would therefore do well to examine his work since it is the earliest surviving work on the subject, and because he claims to have discovered it himself. But before turning to his work, let us briefly look at his biography.

About the life-span of al-Samarqandī we know little. A manuscript of the Ṣahā'if al-Ilāhīya indicates he died in 722/1322.[1] Other evidence shows he was at some time a student of Burhān al-Dīn al-Nasafī (d. 1286). He was an expert in both the Islamic

Special thanks to the late David Eisenberg and Walter Edward Young for assistance in adding additional references and assisting me with updating the chapter. I am responsible for whatever faults have crept in or remain in this newer version. Recent literature discussing Samarqandī and the *ādāb al-baḥth* include: Dominique "Scientific Controversies; the foregoing is a translation "Al-Samarqandī. Un précurseur de l'analyse des controverse scientifiques"; Karabela, "The Development of Dialectic and Argumentation Theory in Post-Classical Islamic Intellectual History" (Karabela argues for a more substantial contribution to the genre by Samarqandī's successors); it also contains an edition of Samarqandī's *Risāla*; Pehlivan and Ceylan, "Ādābu'l-Baḥs Devrimine Doğru Son Evrim: Burhānuddīn en-Nesefī'nin el-Fuṣūl'ü" (this article includes an edition of Nasafī's Fuṣūl).

[1] The correct date is provided in Sheshen, "Tawqīʿāt Athīr al-Dīn al-Abharī wa-Shams al-Dīn al-Samarqandī", in Yūsuf Zaydān (ed.), al-Makhṭūṭāt al-Muwaqqaʿa (al-Iskandariyya, 2008), 151 correcting Miller, "al-Samarḳandī, Shams al-Dīn," EI[2].

L. B. Miller, *Islamic Disputation Theory*, Logic, Argumentation & Reasoning 21,
https://doi.org/10.1007/978-3-030-45012-0_5

and ancient sciences, composing works on astronomy, geometry, logic, theology, and juristic dialectics.[2] But of utmost importance for our study is a short epistle that he wrote—the so-called *al-Risāla al-Samarqandīya fī ādāb al-baḥth.*[3] According to Ḥājjī Khalīfa, it was the most famous treatment of the subject, its only rival being the epistle of Aḍud al-Dīn al-Ījī.[4] al-Samarqandī set down his opinions about the *ādāb al-baḥth* in several of his works. In perhaps his last work, his commentary on al-Nasafī's *Muqaddima*, he says, "… but we have discussed these things in detail in our *Qusṭās, al-Muʿtaqadāt* and *al-Anwār*."[5] The "things" that he refers to are definitions of the techniques and rules of disputation. Of the works to which he refers, only the *Qusṭās al-afkār*, his *Summae Logicales*, is available to us.[6]

---

[2]For other information about his biography and dates, see Sellheim, *Arabische Handschriften: Materialen zur Arabischen Literaturgeschichte*, 162–3. Ismail Pasha Baghdatli claims that he saw a copy of al-Samarqandī's commentary on al-Nasafī's *Muqaddima* that was finished in the year 690 [A.H] in Baghdatli, *Hadīyat al-Ārifīn*, ed. Bilge and Inal, 106. For further bibliographical information, cf.: Al-Sāwī, *al-Tabṣira ya-dū risāla-i dīgar dar manṭiq*, 14–15 and Dilgan, "Shams al-Dīn al-Samarqandī," *Encyclopedia of Men of Science*. Anawati, *Muʿallafāt Ibn Sīnā*, 11. Ḥājji Khalīfa, *Kashf al-Zunūn*, 2:1803, line 16 ff. claims that al-Samarqandī taught in Mārdin. See also Al-Kaḥḥāla, *Muʿjam al-muʾallifīn*, 9:63. ʿAbd al-Razzāq, *Talkhīṣ majma' al-ādāb fī mu'jam al-alqāb*, 4, pt. 2: 719 mentions the dedicatee of al-Samarqandī's *Sharḥ al-Qusṭās*, ʿImād al-Dīn al-Khidr b. Ibrāhīm al-Mu'minī as the dedicatee of Sirāj al-Dīn al-Urmawī's *Sharḥ k. al—Qusṭās*[!]. For information on al-Samarqandī's scientific activity, cf. Sezgin, *Geschichte des arabischen Schrifttums*, 5: 99, 114 and 6: 94.

[3]Al-Samarqandī, *al-Risāla al-Samarqandīya fī ādāb al–baḥth.* It is uncertain whether this was the title that al-Samarqandī gave to this treatise. There exists a copy of another treatise that is probably the same as this one in the MS collection in Sana'a, Yemen. Cf. ʿ Isawī and al-M āliḥ, eds., *Fihris al-makhṭūṭāt al-Maktaba al-Gharbīya bil-Jāmiʿ al-Kabīr bil-Ṣanʿā'* s.v. "*al-Munya wal-amal*."

[4]Ḥājji Khalīfa, *Kashf*, 1:39, line 12 ff.

[5]Al-Samarqandī, *Sharḥ al-Muqadimma al-Burhānīya*, fol.4a: 17. Although Arberry lists this as an anonymous commentary in *The Chester Beatty Library: A Handlist of the Arabic Manuscripts*, 5 q.v. no. 4396, the internal evidence shows that it was written by al-Samarqandī. At fol.9a: 3–4, he refers to his treatment of *talāzum* in the *Qusṭās*. So, too, the commentators on the *Risāla*, such as at-Bihishtī al-Isfarā'inī (d. ca, 1494), cite al-Samarqandī's definition from his commentary on al-Nasafī's *Muqaddima* and it is the same as in our text. He also repeats his teaching on *ādāb al-baḥth* within the commentary, fol.4a: 5 ff. Further confirmation for this attribution comes from MS.438 (*Fiqh Taimūr*), Dār al-Kutub al-Miṣrīya, which contains another slightly mutilated copy of al-Samarqandī's commentary with the same *incipit*: "*Basmala al-ḥamdu lil-lāh rabb al-ʿālamīn…wa-baʿdu, fa-inna al-saʿādāt l-ʿājila wal-karāmāt al-ājila manūṭa bi-iktisāb al-ʿilm wa-huwa immā taṣauwur au ḥukm wal-taṣauwur….*" As for the works he cites, all but the last can be identified and survive. For the *Muʿtaqadāt*, there is one copy from the year 743 in the ʿĀrif Ḥikmat library in Medina, Majāmīʿ, no.206, 35 fols. Cf. *RIMA* 23, fasc. 2 (1977) p. 21 entry 254.

[6]Al-Samarqandī, *Qusṭās* al-Afkār, MS.3399. Cf. Fihris al-Makhṭūṭāt al-Muṣauwara, ed. F. Saiyid, vol. 1. Incipit: "*wa-ba'du fa-hādhā al-kitāb jāmi' li-qawānin al-manṭiq auradnā fīhī jumalan wāfiyatan wa-uṣūlan kāfiyatan…wa-samaināhū Qusṭās al-afkār fī taḥrīr al-asrār.*" This MS is the earliest copy of the *Qusṭās* that I know of. It was written in Ramaḍān of the year 690 A.H. The 0"*wa-baʿdu fa-inna ḥuṣūl al-saʿādāt al-abadīya wal-ladhāt al-sarmadīya innamā yatawaqqaʿu bi-iktisāb al-kāmālāt al-ʿilmīya wa-iqtinā' al-faḍā'il al-ʿamalīya wa-dhālika mauqūf ʿalā saḥīḥ al-naẓar ….wa-qad ṣanaftu fīmā maḍḍā kitāb al-Qusṭās fī al-manṭiq mushtamilan ʿalā khulāṣat arā' al-mutaqaddimīn wal-muta'akhkhirīn maʿa abḥāth badīʿa wa-shukūk manīʿa lā maḥīṣa li-ṭālib al-ḥaqq ʿan taʿallumihā. …*"; a downloadable copy of the *Sharḥ al-Qusṭās,* Landberg 1035,

In what follows we will base ourselves upon the accounts of disputation found in al-Samarqandī's *Qusṭās*, his commentary on the *Qusṭās*, his epistle on the *ādāb al-baḥth* and his commentary on al-Nasafī's *Muqaddima*.

al-Qusṭās

The twelfth section of al-Samarqandī's *Qusṭās* is devoted to disputation (*al-baḥth wal-munāẓara*). The section is organized in the following manner:

Section XII: On disputation (with a short justification of its place in a handbook on logic).

A. On the [proper] conduct of a disputation (*fī tamhīd baḥth*).

1. Introduction: On the divisions of the sciences and the types of investigation proper to them.
2. First section: On the order of debate and the proper formulation of questions and answers.
   (a) On definitions.
   (b) On propositions (*masā'il*).
3. Second section: on the parts of disputation (*baḥth*) and how they prevent randomness.[7]

B. On paralogism and its causes.

This chapter is unique: it is virtually the only treatment of disputation found in a handbook of logic. We will consider first al-Samarqandī's account of disputation in his *Qusṭās* and then turn to the account in his *Risāla*.

The Introduction

al-Samarqandī justifies the novel enterprise of treating disputation in a book on logic in the following manner:

Ahlwardt 5166 [Digitalisierte Sammlungen der Staatsbibliothek zu Berlin (Preußischer Kulturbesizt): Werkansicht - PPN741370395] is now available online at http:// digital.staatsbibliothek-berlin.de. The section on the *ādāb al-baḥth* begins at 40v 11 lines from the bottom of the page. For a list of the commentaries on al-Samarqandī's work see Wisnovsky, "The nature and scope of Arabic philosophical commentary in post-classical (ca. 1100–1900 AD) Islamic intellectual history: Some preliminary observations," 169–70.

[7] al-Samarqandī, *Qusṭās*, fol.59a: 1 ff

1. It has been the custom of our predecessors to place a chapter on dialectics (*jadal*) in their logical works.
2. But since the science of juristic dialectics (*khilāf*) of our times does not need it, I have brought in its stead a canon (*qānūn*) for the art of disputation and its order, the proper formulation of speech (in disputation) and its rectification.
3. This (art) is vis-à-vis establishing (a thesis) and explaining it just like logic with respect to deliberation and thought [i.e. it plays a similar role in debate to that of logic with respect to deliberation and thinking]; for through it we are kept on the desired path and are saved from the recalcitrance of speech.
4. Although it is observed by the experts, no one has yet gathered its scattered parts. This is, indeed, what I intend to do in what follows.[8]

Al-Samarqandī starts out by referring to the tradition of logical writings on "dialectics" (*jadal*). This tradition is an ancient one. It finds its roots in the practice of the Alexandrian school, within which commentaries were written on the eight books comprising Aristotle's *Organon*, starting out with the *Categories* and closing with the *Poetics*.[9] In Arabic logic, this was the order in which the great commentators al-Fārābī, Avicenna, and Averroes ordered their writings, and the authors of handbooks on logic followed closely in their footsteps. In these handbooks of logic, which became prevalent in the thirteenth century, the subject matter of the *Topics* (*Kitāb al-Jadal*) is perfunctorily mentioned; it was given little space when compared to that devoted to the teachings of the *Categories*, *De Interpretatione* and the *Prior* and *Posterior Analytics*. The order followed was, to repeat, the traditional order of Aristotle's *Organon*, but the model seems to have been that of Avicenna's *al-Ishārāt wal-tanbīhāt*. The predecessors to whom he refers are people whom he mentions in the first part of his treatise on logic: al-Ghazzālī (d. 1111), Avicenna (d. 1037), al-Khunajī (d. 1249), Fakhr al-Dīn al-Rāzī (d. 1209), al-Urmawī (d. 1283) and Naṣīr al-Dīn al-Ṭūsī (d. 1274).[10] These authors mention the dialectical syllogism, usually in the company of sophistic, poetical rhetorical syllogisms, enthymeme and induction.[11] But al-Samarqandī is taking a new path because "the science of *khilāf* has no need for it." He apparently is claiming that the points of dispute or *topoi* and the method for arguing for or against them are known. Although there was no dearth of material on juristic dialectics, the *rules* of disputation were not at all

[8] Ibid, fol.59a: 2 ff.

[9] Walzer, Greek into Arabic, 239 ff. *Al-Farabi's Commentary and Short Treatise on Aristotle's De Interpretatione*, xxii. While the tradition was Aristotelian, the model seems to have been Avicenna's *al-Ish ārāt wal-tanbīhāt*, an extremely popular and much commented upon summary of the whole of Aristotle's logic. For commentaries, cf. Anawati, *Mu'allafāt*, 9 ff.

[10] M. b. Namwār Al-Khunajī, *Kashf al-asrār ʿan ghawāmiḍ al-afkār*, cf. *GAL* I 607; *SI*, 838. His dates are 1194–1249. Al- Samarqandī refers to al-Khunajī's work throughout his *Sharh al-Qusṭās*. He also refers to al-Rāzī's *Mulakhkhaṣ fī al-manṭiq wal-ḥikma*, Arab League MS.376 (*manṭiq*). For al-Urmawī, ċf. *GAL* I 614; *Sl*, 848: Al-Urmawī wrote a treatise on juristic dialectics, *al-Wasā'il ilā taḥqīq al-dalā'il*, MS.2304/1, fol.lb-45b. Cf. Sheshen, *Nawādir al-makhṭūṭāt al-ʿarabīya fī maktabāt Turkiyā*, 84, Number 830.

[11] Avicenna, *al-Ishārāt wal-tanbīhāt*, 1: 510 ff. Al-Urmawī, *Maṭāliʿ al-Anwār*, 349.

precisely stated.[12] In order to repair this fault al-Samarqandī includes in his book on logic a final chapter on the rules of disputation.

Al-Samarqandī was not the first person to treat the rules of disputation in a work on logic. He had been preceded in this by Ibn Ḥazm (d. 1064), who included a chapter on disputation in his work on logic.[13] In truth, however, we may consider al-Samarqandī the first Arab logician to have devoted himself, *qua* logician, to the logic of debate. He coined a term for this new "science": *ādāb al-baḥth*. Literally, this means the arts or rules of investigation. *Baḥth*, which means investigation, has a relatively early association with Aristotelian dialectic; for it appears on the margins of the Paris manuscript of the *Organon* with the word *naẓar* as an alternative appellation for the science of dialectic, there called the science of logic (*ṣināʿat al-manṭiq*).[14] Ibn Ḥazm, again in his book on logic, says that the only way to arrive at truth is through demonstration (*istidlāl*) and investigation (*baḥth*). He notes that "this can result either from the thinking (*fikr*) of one person or a discussion (*tadhākur*) between two people..."[15] This second meaning of *baḥth* is not peculiar to Ibn Ḥazm, for we often read in commentaries on theological and logical works from that period "*wa-fīhī baḥth*" or "*wa-fīhī naẓar*," meaning "there is some debate about this point" or "this opinion is open to objection."[16] The word *ādāb*, which means rules, reminds us of the word *adab*, "politesse," and the first treatises on systematic disputation. The expression *ādāb al-baḥth* is used synonymously with the expression *ʿilm al-munāẓara* as a formal designation of the new science of disputation.

According to al-Samarqandī, the science of *khilāf* was sorely in need of rules for disputation so that debate runs a proper course and all objections and replies are properly formulated. Now, al-Samarqandī does not claim any originality in discovering these rules but rather in putting them together in a single treatment. The rules to which he is referring are perhaps the *marāsim al-jadal* that were often referred to by authors on juristic dialectic but never formulated systematically.

---

[12] See preceding chapter on juristic dialectics.

[13] Ibn Ḥazm, *al-Taqrīb li-ḥadd al-manṭiq wal-madkhal ilaihī*, ed. I. ʿAbbās (Beirut: Dār al-ʿIbād, 1959), p. 185, line 20 ff.

[14] Badawi, *Manṭiq Arisṭū*, 2: 492, note 7; Arist. Top.101b2-3.

[15] Ibn Ḥazm, *Taqrīb* 182, line 9; cf. 198, lines 15–17. At 182, line 10, I read *tadhākur* instead of *tadhakkur* of the text relying on Makdisi, *The Rise of Colleges*, 103–4, where he explains the practice of *mudhākara*. Whatever the reading, the meaning is clear. The passage that Makdisi cites indicates that the practice of *mudhākara* derives from or is parallel to a Jewish traditional practice—recalling the exodus from Egypt (*sipūr bi-yeẓi'at Miẓrayim*). In the Passover Haggadah we learn that four Rabbis were so deeply engaged in this "recalling" that they passed the entire night doing so until someone came reminding them that it was already time for the morning prayer (zeman li-qirī'at ha-Shema). In al-Khaṭīb al-Baghdādī's account, people discuss problems of the law until someone calls and reminds them that it is time for the morning prayer (*al-fajr*): Kasher, ed., *Israel Passover Haggadah*, 54. Al-Khaṭīb al-Baghdādī, *K. al-Faqīh wal-muṭafaqqih*, 2: 128–9.

[16] Van Ess, *Die Erkenntnislehre des 'Aḍudaddīn al-Īcī*, 239 and index s.v. *naẓar*. Cf. Lane, *Arabic-English Lexicon*, 2812b.

It is again from juristic dialectics that al-Samarqandī inherits his metaphor about the relation of logic and the new science to thought and speech. The words *taḥrīr* and *taqrīr* that appear in the beginning of al-Nasafī's shorter version of the *Muqaddima* have now been picked out by al-Samarqandī as exemplary of the field in which the new science is operative: the articulation of a thesis and its resolution (through disputation).

Before considering rules of debate applicable to all fields of investigation, al-Samarqandī informs us what the various fields of inquiry are and what sort of evidence they require. Every field of knowledge subject to investigation, he says, is either concerned with expressions (*alfāẓ*), their referents (*maʿānin*) or both:

> To the first category belong lexicography, prosody, grammar, and so forth; to the second belong metaphysics, physics, mathematics, medicine, ethics, and generally speaking, whatever has no connection whatsoever with words; to the third belong Qur'ānic exegesis (*tafsīr*), the science of the *ḥadīth*, the *uṣūl al-fiqh*, *fiqh* (itself), and so forth."[17]

That being established, al-Samarqandī divides these investigations into exact and inexact sciences. All the sciences have their own technical language and axioms (*musallamāt*), but since they have different intentions, they use evidence (*adilla*) with varying degrees of exactitude. These circumstances make difficult the application of principles or proofs (*adilla*) from one science to another. He lists the sciences according to their degrees of exactitude: (1) grammar, (2) *fiqh*, (3) *uṣūl al-fiqh*, (4) philosophy (*ḥikma*), (5) logic, (6) astronomy, and (7) geometry. In this list the Islamic sciences are at a distinct disadvantage.[18] Islamic theology, *kalām*, is not even mentioned, although al-Samarqandī wrote a long treatise with commentary on Islamic theology.[19] However, at the top of the list are astronomy and geometry, two fields in which we know al-Samarqandī was active.[20] The evidence of this list would seem to indicate that al-Samarqandī preferred the ancient sciences to the religious or traditional ones.

Section One: Definitions

Having given us a classification of the sciences and ordered them according to their degree of exactitude, al-Samarqandī turns in his "first section" to the order of the disputation and the proper formulation of questions and responses. Here

---

[17] al-Samarqandī, *Qusṭās*, fol.59a: 8 ff. Cf. Aristotle, De Int.16al-4 with Zimmermann, Farabi, 10ff.

[18] al-Samarqandī, *Qusṭās*, fol.59a: 12 ff. Aristotle, *Topics* 101a5. The order of this classification is unique. The only list that resembles it is that of Ibn Khaldūn (d. 1406). Cf. Anawati and Gardet, *Introduction à la théologie musulmane*, 94 ff. and 123 as well as Anawati, "Classification des sciences et structure des *summae* chez les auteurs musulmans," 61 ff.

[19] *al-Ṣaḥā'if al-ilāhīya*, ed. al-Sharīf.; *al-Maʿārif fī al-Ṣaḥā'if*." Cf: *GAL* 1: 850.

[20] Cf. n. 2, 3

al-Samarqandī makes explicit what he understands as the objects of investigation (*baḥth*):

> It only occurs with respect to that [thing] about which assertion or denial is made. It is divided into [two sorts: one concerning] definitions and [another] concerning propositions (*masā'il*); because if the "statement" (*ḥukm*) about the relation between the two things (i.e., the subject and predicate) is such that one of them defines the other, then it is the first sort; otherwise, it is the second sort. Each one of them has methods of explanation and questioning (*muṭālaba*) peculiar to it.[21]

The subjects of inquiry are statements "that x is the case" or "that x is y"; and whether these statements are subject to demonstration or not. The division derives from Aristotle's *Posterior Analytics*, for there Aristotle tries to prove that definitions are not subject to demonstration.[22]

In his discussion of definition, al-Samarqandī considers four types of definition: complete and deficient definition (*ḥadd tāmm/nāqiṣa*) as well as complete and deficient descriptive definition (*rasm*).[23] There are two sorts of objections that can be brought by a Questioner ("Q"): objection (*man'*) and the charge of the incommensurability of the *definiens* and the defined (*naqḍ*). The latter is "the most perspicuous and compelling weapon that Q can use, while the former is controversial since it is generally accepted (*al-mashhūr*) that this is not allowed; you should either charge incommensurability (*naqḍ*) or explain its falsity."[24] The opponents of *man'* oppose its use because in the technical language of the *ādāb al-baḥth*, *man'* means something more specific than "objections." It means "asking for evidence (*dalīl*) to support a statement."[25] To ask for evidence here is understood as "asking for a proof." But it is well-known that definitions are not subject to proof and, therefore, *man'* cannot be used against a definition. Against this sort of argument al-Samarqandī argues as follows:

> When the Proponent ("P") says: "This thing is of this sort," as if the statement were a definition, then he is stating a thesis (*da'wā*) and so it is possible that the matter could be otherwise. Should he, for instance, claim to give a complete definition, then he claims to base it on the proximate genus and proximate specific difference. (In such a case) Q can use *man'*, so that P is to clarify that the genus and specific difference are both proximate.
>
> If P claims that this definition derives from the conventions (of some group), then Q can use man, so that P is forced to verify the source of his claim (*taṣḥīḥ al-naql*).[26]

---

[21] Al-Samarqandī, *Qusṭās*, fol.59a21 ff.

[22] Aristotle, *APo*. 90a6 ff.

[23] On these terms cf. Van Ess, *Īcī*, 371. Al-Fārābī, *Kitāb al-Alfāẓ al-musta'mala fī al-manṭiq*, 78, lines 23 ff.

[24] Al-Samarqandī, *Qusṭās*, fol.59b: 6 ff. Al-Samarqandī refers to other defects in definition "that are detailed in (our) logic," but they are apparently brought in one of the two "types" of objection: Ibid., fol.59b:1 ff.

[25] This definition is found in the earliest commentary on the *al-Risāla al-Samarqandīya* by M. b. A. al-Bihishtī al-Isfarā'inī (d. 1348). Cf. Mach, *Catalogue of Arabic Manuscripts (Yahuda Section) in the Garrett Collection*, MS.3482, fol.25a: 25 "*li-anna al-man' ṭalab al-dalīl wa-kull mā lam yakun 'alaihī dalīl lā yatawajjah 'alaihī al-man'*."

[26] Al-Samarqandī, *Sharḥ al-Qusṭās*, fol.165a: 3 ff., MS.4767

P, on the other hand, is obliged, according to al-Samarqandī, to respond to every objection that Q brings.[27]

al-Samarqandī's treatment of the first type of disputation is replete with observations about defending technical as opposed to literal definitions, observations that have been culled from the Aristotelian teaching found in the *Topics* and the *Posterior Analytics*. But the *terms* that are used for types of objections that Q can bring are not taken from the Aristotelian tradition. They derive most immediately from the juristic tradition of dialectics. We recall that about two hundred years before al-Samarqandī, al-Juwaynī (d. 1085) declared that "asking for verification that such and such is the case" (*muṭālaba bi-taṣḥīḥ*) is sometimes used synonymously with disallowance (*man' /mumānaʿa*).[28] So, too, the objection of incommensurability was a standard part of all treatises on juristic dialectics.[29]

Propositions

In the second part of the first section, al-Samarqandī turns to propositions or problems (*masāʾil*):

> They are statements (*qadāyā*) that are in need of some form of proof (*dalīl*) since otherwise they would not be subject to investigation (*baḥth*). Indeed, it is either the matter itself or Q who requires this proof. (You should be aware that) every proof (*dalīl*) requires at least two premises, although there is no upper boundary.[30]

Here again, al-Samarqandī begins his discussion with a general remark about proof that is culled from traditional Aristotelian logic. But when he embarks upon his discussion about the order of debate, we find ourselves back in the world of juristic dialectics:

> When P begins the disputation, it is incumbent upon him, before he establishes the proof for his claim (*mā iddaʿāhū*) that he (a) explain the objects of his investigation (*taḥrīr al-mabāḥith*) and (b) establish (*taqrīr*) the opinions and beliefs [*madhāhib*][31], so that the point of dispute (*ṣūrat al-nizāʿ*) becomes perfectly clear.
>
> Q may here demand a verification of the attribution (*taṣḥīḥ al-naql*) of the opinions and beliefs; for often defects occur in the debate, since P might pretend to be arguing with someone other than his actual opponent and use premises granted by this other person as if they were granted by his actual opponent. This, however, leads to randomness in debate (*khabṭ*).
>
> But when P begins to establish a proof for his claim, then Q may either (a) object or (b) not object. If he does not object, then it is clear. If he does, he may do so either (a) before P is finished bringing his proof or (b) afterwards. If the former (a), then Q may merely object

---

[27] Ibid., fol.165a: 7 ff.

[28] al-Juwainī, *al-Kāfīya fī al-jadal*, 67, line 15. Cf. Chap. 4, *supra*, on *manʿ* in juristic dialectics.

[29] Cf. Chap. 4, *supra*, on *naqḍ* in juristic dialectics.

[30] al-Samarqandī, *Qusṭās*, fo1.59b: 15ff.

[31] *Madhāhib* can refer to the opinions of any school of thought; but it is generally used to refer to the interpretations of the Shariʿa of any of the legal schools.

(*yaqtaṣiru ʿalā mujarrad al-manʿ*) or not. If not, he may do so with "backing" (*mustanad*)[32] or not....

But if (b) Q objects after P is finished bringing his proof, he may either grant P's proof or not... But if he accepts the proof, then he must reject that it proves P's point (*al-madlūl*), basing himself on some other piece of evidence or not... All this advice is for Q.

As for P, he must ward off any objection by bringing evidence (*dalīl*) or alerting Q to something which is known *a priori* (*tanbīh*) ....

The debate continues until P is silenced (*ifḥām*) or Q is forced to accept his argument (*ilzām*).[33]

al-Samarqandī's account of the rules of disputation is a familiar one, since in the main it is a repetition of the account that al-Nasafī gives in his *Muqaddima*. But there is a fundamental difference between these works, because the latter is a treatise on juristic dialectics, while the former is an exposition of a general theory of disputation applicable to any discussion between two parties where statement-making statements[34] are used to prove or disprove something. Rabelaisan debates through signs are ruled out. But before expanding upon this theme, let us return to al-Samarqandī's account of the debate and examine to what extent it is but a repetition of al-Nasafī's teaching.

In paragraphs (1) and (2) al-Samarqandī only deviates slightly from the rules set down by al-Nasafī. He maintains that Q may "ask P to verify his attribution of some opinion or belief (*wa-lil-sā'il an yaṭlub siḥḥat mā naqala min al-aqwāl wal-madhāhib*)."[35] We find this same teaching in his commentary to al-Nasafī's *Muqaddima*, although in the *Risāla* it is absent.[36] There, he says explicitly "Q cannot object since this is done in the manner of a citation (of a source)."[37] This is, indeed, precisely what al-Nasafī said in his *Muqaddima*.[38] This fact would seem to indicate that the *Risāla* was written before the *Qusṭās*.

In paragraph (3) al-Samarqandī makes more additions to al-Nasafī's account. He brings in the concept of "backing" that he defines as "what strengthens an objection" or "it is that upon which the objection is based."[39] Al-Samarqandī gives three sample formulations of an objection with backing:

1. We do not grant (that it is so); why could it not be otherwise?
2. We do not grant that this is implicated; this implication would hold were that the case.

[32] See *infra*.

[33] Ibid., fol. 59b: 22 ff.

[34] That is, statements that are either true or false.

[35] Ibid., fol. 59b: 20.

[36] al-Samarqandī, *Sharḥ al-Muqaddima*, fol.2b: 3 ff.

[37] al-Samarqandī, *Risāla*, p. 126, lines 8–9.

[38] al-Nasafī, *al-Muqaddima al-Burhāniya*, MS.4396 at the top of al-Samarqandī's commentary, fol. 2a: 2.

[39] al-Samarqandī: *Qusṭās*, fol.60a: 6 ff.; *al-Risāla*, 126, line 14; *Sharḥ al-Muqaddima*, fol,4a: 8–9. The terms *mustanad* and *sanad* were both used. Cf. Al-Ahmadnagarī, *Dustūr al- ʿulūm*, 2:187, line 1.

3. We do not grant that this is so; how could it, when the situation is of this sort?[40]

Al-Samarqandī does not give a formulation for "objection *per se*" (*mujarrad al-man*ʿ), but it is clear from the three examples above that the phrase "we do not grant 'x'" is the objection. Al-Samarqandī calls these two types of objection "disagreement" or "contradiction" (*munāqaḍa*).[41]

At this juncture of the debate there is a third possible sort of objection: that with something other than backing:

> This is usurpation (*ghaṣb*); for it amounts to arguing for a thesis (*taʿlīl*) and this is P's role. Q has usurped P's role and this is not allowed by the experts, since as long as P is presenting his argument, all Q (*al-māniʿ*) can do is agree (*taslīm*) or object; indeed, the most he can do is object with backing (at this time) ... But should he object using something else, proof (*dalīl*) or otherwise, to disprove a specific premise, then the disputation (*baḥth*) becomes random, the discussion (*kalām*) drawn out, and the *quaesitum* (*maṭlūb*) is not reached.[42]

Al-Samarqandī here gives roughly the same account of usurpation that he gives in his commentary on al-Nasafī's *Muqaddima*, which was perhaps his last formulation of his theory of disputation. In the version of the *Risāla*, al-Samarqandī gives a much briefer explanation that differs little in substance from al-Nasafī's account.[43]

In paragraph (4), al-Samarqandī makes further refinements to al-Nasafī's account. Q has two basic options after P has finished presenting his proof. In the first, he may object to the proof on the grounds that "the qualification (*ḥukm*) is absent in some cases."[44] He calls this technique general refutation (*naqḍ ijmālī*), "since it refutes the premises of P's proof in a general manner."[45] We assume that if Q does not raise any objections to any one of P's premises, then he has granted them. But should Q not show cause in objecting to P's proof, "this is called peevishness (*mukābara*) and eristic behavior (*ʿinād*), and his objection does not merit a reply."[46] The terms that al-Samarqandī uses are not those used in the philosophical tradition, even though Aristotle discusses a similar phenomenon in the *Topics*.[47] The

---

[40] al-Samarqandī: *Qusṭās*, fol.60a: 7; *Sharḥ al-Qusṭās*, fol.166a: 10–12; *al-Risāla*, p. 126, line 15–17.

[41] al-Samarqandī: *Qusṭās*, fol.59b: −1 ff.; *Sharḥ al-Muqaddima*, fol.4a: p. 126, line 17.

[42] al-Samarqandī: *Qusṭās*, fol.60a: 1 ff.; *Sharḥ al-Qusṭās*, fol.166a: 5 'ff.; *Sharḥ al-Muqaddima*, fol.4a: 8; 2b: 16 ff.; *al-Risāla*, p. 126, lines 18–19. On the concept of randomness (*khabṭ*) cf. van Ess, *Īcī*, pp. 37, 40.

[43] Cf. note 37.

[44] *Ḥukm* is a notoriously difficult word to translate. In logic it means "judgment" or in the terminology of modern logic "statement." But in our case it appears that he is using *ḥukm* in its juristic sense, legal qualification. The matter is made even more difficult because in theology it is often used in the sense of quality or attribute: cf. Frank, *Beings and their Attributes*, index s.v. *ḥukm*.

[45] al-Samarqandī: *Qusṭās*," fol. 608: 9–11; *Sharḥ al–Qusṭās*, fol.166a 13–15; *al-Risāla*, p. 126, lines 21–2; *Sharḥ al-Muqaddima*, fol,4a: 10–1.

[46] Cf. n. 40.

[47] Aristotle *Topics* 161a25 ff. The usual word to express this in Greek is *duskolainein* or *duskolia* (literally dyspeptic or ill-temperedness), which in Aristotle describes "a psychological state arising in oral dialectic, and results from the humiliation of being publicly trapped in absurdity," on which

term *mukābara* is used by authors of handbooks on theological *jadal* to describe people who reject evidence of the senses or *a priori* evidence.[48] So, too, the technique of *naqḍ* has a long history in the writings on juristic dialectics.

Q has another option: he can bring counter-evidence (*muʿāraḍa*). Al-Samarqandī identifies three different types of counter-evidence. The first type, reversal (*qalb*), occurs when Q uses P's evidence to draw a different conclusion. If the evidence that Q uses is only similar to P's, it is called "counter-proof through the similar" (*muʿāraḍa bil-mithl*); otherwise it is counter-proof by means of something different (*bil-ghair*). When Q uses this device, says al-Samarqandī, he effects a role-reversal: P becomes like Q and must use his techniques to prevent his opponent from establishing his counter-proof.[49] The technique of *muʿāraḍa* is also a familiar one. We encountered it in this meaning in al-Bājī's (d. 1081) long treatise on juristic dialectics.[50] Al-Samarqandī provides sample formulations of these techniques:

> (General Refutation:) The evidence that you mentioned is, along with all its premises, not correct because of the absence (*takhāluf*) of the qualification (*ḥukm*) in this case.
>
> (Counter-proof:) Although your evidence (*dalīl*) indicates your point (*al-madlūl*), we have something that is incompatible with it (*mā yunāfīhī*) and it is so-and-so.[51]

Although similar formulations are found in al-Nasafī's *Muqaddima*, they are not expressed in general terms.[52] By divesting these techniques of their juristic garb and expressing them in general terms, al-Samarqandī makes them appropriate components of his general theory of disputation.

In paragraph (6) al-Samarqandī delineates P's obligations. P is required to respond to all of Q's objections either by giving further evidence to provide the disputed premise or by "alerting" him to something he has forgotten or overlooked. An example of the latter would be, "(P says) 'The world is subject to change (*mutaghaiyir*) since we *observe* (*nushāhid*) various changes in it, recent and non-recent.'" The appeal to evidence of the senses is called *tanbīh*.

A little later, al-Samarqandī gives two pieces of advice to P, one of which derives from the tradition of chapters of the *adab al-jadal*:

see Allen, "Zeno, Aristotle, the Racetrack and Achilles: A Historical Philosophical Investigation," 29. The word is translated into Arabic as follows: *ṣaʿʿaba Top.* 112a12; *taṣaʿʿaba SE* 174a33, 175b35 (Y.); *ṣaʿūba SE* 180b5; *iʿtāṣa Top.* 156b34–6, 161 b 9; *maḥaka Top.* 160b4, 11; *mumāḥaka Top.* 160b6; *taʿassafa Top.* 160b3; *taʿassara SE* 174a33, 175b35 (bZ); *mushākasa Top.* 161a23; *shaghab SE* 174a33, 175b35.

48 See our discussion in Chap. 2 on the "signs of defeat" of the theologians.

49 al-Samarqandī: *Qusṭās*, fol.60a: 11 ff.; *Sharḥ al-Qusṭās*, fol. 166a: 16 ff.; *Sharḥ al-Samarqandī*, fol. 4a: 11 ff.; *al-Risāla*, p. 126, line 22 ff. al-Samarqandī: *Qusṭās*, fol.60a: 11 ff.; *Sharḥ al-Qusṭās*, fol. 166a: 16 ff.; *Sharḥ al-Samarqandī*, fol. 4a: 11 ff.; *al-Risāla*, p. 126, line 22 ff. al-Samarqandī: *Qusṭās*, fol.60a: 11 ff.; *Sharḥ al-Qusṭās*, fol. 166a: 16 ff.; *Sharḥ al-Samarqandī*, fol. 4a: 11 ff.; *al-Risāla*, p. 126, line 22 ff.

50 See our discussion in Chap. 4.

51 al-Samarqandī: *Qusṭās*, fol.60a: 15 ff.; *Sharḥ al-Qusṭās*, fol.166a: 20 ff.; *al-Risāla*, p. 126, line-1 ff.

52 See our discussion on al-Nasafī's *Muqaddima, supra.*

> If Q asks a question, then it is a good move (*tadbīr*) on P's part not to rush into answering it; rather, he should make Q formulate it properly and precisely; for often he is not up to it and he loses; or the falsity of his position becomes clear; or P thinks up the answer (while Q reformulates the question).[53]

al-Samarqandī also advises P to make distinctions (*tafṣīl*) when responding to Q's objections, since it may occur that the contrary of the objectionable premise proves the *quaesitum* (*madlūl*), or that the removal of the premise does not harm P's proof.[54]

These considerations of strategy lead him to consider how P should respond to an "objection *per se*" or rather an objection with backing. He notes that if P refutes the backing of Q's objection, this does not entail the removal of the objection, "since the removal of the implicans, does not necessitate the removal of the implicate."[55] And he acknowledges that this state of affairs troubled some of the experts (*al-muḥaṣṣilūn*); since it was taken as a rule that one was not required to respond to the backing of Q's objection but he goes on to observe that "if Q's backing were not rebutted (*yundafaʿ*) nor even open to discussion (*baḥth*), how could the response to Q's objection be valid, when its backing remains (unrefuted)?"[56] To this problem al-Samarqandī offers a rather unsatisfactory solution.[57] He suggests that P make an exhaustive division between Q's backing and its alternatives and uses a process of elimination to exclude Q's backing.[58] The solution is unsatisfactory since, as al-Samarqandī himself admits, it is extremely difficult to make an exhaustive division.[59]

There is one other solution—*taqrīb*.[60] al-Samarqandī neglects to define this device but he does give an example of how it works. Q's backing is made the alternative of an exclusive disjunction, and is shown to lead to absurd consequences. In later treatises on *ādāb al-baḥth, taqrīb* is defined as "interpreting the evidence in such a way that the *quaesitum* necessarily follows from it." It is noteworthy that al-Nasafī gives no advice to P about how he should counter Q's objections. Al-Samarqandī's account of the rules of disputation is thus more rigorous.

In paragraph (7) al-Samarqandī explains why a debate is necessarily finite. He argues in the following way. If P and Q each make use of the techniques at their disposal, Q making objections and P countering them with further evidence in support of his thesis, then there must necessarily come a point in the debate where P is unable to answer Q's objections or Q must accept P's thesis, whether it be true or false. In the first case Q wins whereas in the second P wins. If an opponent should

[53] al-Samarqandī: *Qusṭās*, fol.60b: 5 ff.; *Sharḥ al-Qusṭās*, fol.166b: 11 ff. Cf. al-Baghdādī, *K. al-Faqīh,* 2: 32, line 9.

[54] al-Samarqandī: *Qusṭās*," fol.60a: 21. *Sharḥ al-Qusṭās*, fol.166b: 1 ff.; *al-Risāla*, p.127, line 18 ff.

[55] al-Samarqandī: *Qusṭās*, fol.60b: 15; *Sharḥ al-Qusṭās*, fol.166b: 21 ff.

[56] al-Samarqandī: *Qusṭās*, fol.60b: 18 ff.; *Sharḥ al-Qusṭās*, fol.166b: 2 ff.

[57] al-Samarqandī: *Qusṭās*, fol.60b: 18 ff.; *Sharḥ al-Qusṭās*, fol.166b: 2 ff.

[58] Cf. note 52 Cf. note 52.

[59] al-Samarqandī: *Qusṭās*, fol.61a: 4 ff.; *Sharḥ al-Qusṭās*, fol.167a: 7 ff.

[60] Al-Jurjānī, *Taʿrīfāt*, 44.

deny the second alternative, al-Samarqandī argues that either P would be forced to bring an infinite number of proofs or he would be unable to respond (*ʿajz*). But the first possibility is excluded because it would entail an infinite chain of reasoning from a single beginning (*mabda'*) or cause (*ʿilla*). This is because al-Samarqandī understands the relation of the "proof" (*dalīl*) to the "proven" (*madlūl*) as that of the cause to its effect. An infinite chain of reasoning is absurd, and, therefore, it follows that P has been refuted since he cannot establish an infinite number of things.[61]

The above proof establishes al-Samarqandī's position as a pioneer of disputation theory. In all the previous periods of writings on dialectic, the best that our authors could do was to give nothing more than a list of the "signs of defeat." Aristotle, himself, gives certain *ad hoc* criticisms of a disputation, one of which [is] the claim that it has taken up too much time, without, however, bothering to delve into the theoretical conditions.[62] This is, indeed, on account of Aristotle's lower opinion of dialectic. It is true that authors on theological *jadal* claimed that its inquiries must reach the truth, but they did not relate this assertion to the "signs of defeat." Furthermore, al-Samarqandī has expanded the field of inquiry. Disputation can be applied to the exact and inexact sciences. It must necessarily conclude with Q accepting P's argument or P's inability to continue.

The Second Section

In the second section of his account, al-Samarqandī expands upon the rules and advice he gave concerning disputation about "questions," and also reveals the theoretical underpinning for his general theory of disputation:

> Know, that disputation is comprised of three components (*ajzā'*): "beginnings" (*mabādi'*), "means" (*ausāṭ [or "middle"]*), and "ends" (*maqāṭiʿ* [or "that which cuts off the disputation"]).

1. The "beginnings" are [a] the theses (*daʿāwā*), [b] explaining the objects of debate (*mabāḥith*) and [c] establishing the opinions and beliefs.
2. The "means" are the evidence (*dalīl*) and proofs (*ḥujaj*) that are used to demonstrate the theses.
3. The "ends" are the premises that the evidence and proofs lead to, whether they be a *priori* or probable as in accord with the stringency of the less-exact sciences (*al-ʿulūm al-ẓannīya*). [I mean] circular reasoning, infinite chain of reasoning (*tasalsul*) or the simultaneous truth of contradictories, or predicating a thing and its contrary or contradictory, or making the greater equal to the lesser, or allowing preponderance without a preponderator... So, too, in respect of language,

[61] al-Samarqandī: *Qusṭās*, fol.60a: 1 ff.; *Sharḥ al-Qusṭās*, fol.166b: 4 ff.; *al-Risāla*, p.127, line 11 ff. On the equivalence of *mabda'* and *ʿilla* here, see below our discussion of the *maqāṭiʿ*. On the confusion of ontology and causation associated with *dalīl*, see S. van den Bergh, *EI*[2], s.v. "Dalīl".
[62] Aristotle *Topics* 161a9–11.

> such things as the implication of metaphor or the use of equivocal words, suppression of the subject, particularization of the meaning (*takhṣiṣ*), abrogation, tropical usage, and so forth. In every one of these components, ambiguities and defects arise that engender error.[63]

In the previous section, al-Samarqandī considered disputation from the perspective of P and Q. Now he considers it with respect to its three components, "beginnings," "means", and "ends." Let us look at his argument.

"Beginnings"

A precise explanation of the thesis is necessary for several reasons. P may use expressions, be they technical or not, which are ambiguous. In that case P himself might be confused and grant something incompatible with his thesis or with a consequent of his thesis; or P might suppose that his proof is conclusive although it is not.[64] "But if the thesis is properly formulated … it is easier to rebut (*daf*ʿ) the opponent (*al-khaṣm*), be he questioner or respondent."[65] This is why it is recommended that Q ask P to explain the expressions he uses (*istifsār ʿan al-alfāẓ*), in case P means something other than the meaning that Q understands from the same expression. Afterwards Q must determine whether the *quaesitum* results from it or from P's explanation of the thesis.[66] Thus, in al-Samarqandī's opinion, both P and Q have an interest in keeping the thesis of the disputation clear and unambiguous.

"Means"

The means, according to al-Samarqandī, are the proofs used to establish the theses:

> There are many types, as we have shown in our *Logic*, but they all derive from hypothetical syllogisms in which the antecedent is made the subject of the hypothesis. The proof (*dalīl*) must be the implicate of the *quaesitum* since otherwise it would not be a proof at all.[67]

Al-Samarqandī is thinking about statements like, "if the sun is rising, then the stars are hidden; but the first, therefore, the second."[68] Because all proofs derive from hypothetical syllogisms, the focus of the debate is on the antecedent and the explanation of the consequence. P may use any sort of evidence to establish the antecedent hypothetical or categorical syllogisms, induction, enthymeme, and so forth. But

---

[63] al-Samarqandī: *Qusṭās*, fol.61a: ff. Cf. *Sharḥ al-Qusṭās*, fol.167a: −2 ff.

[64] al-Samarqandī, *Qusṭās*, fol.61a: 19 ff.

[65] Ibid., fol.61a: 22–3. Ibid., fol.61a: 22–3.

[66] Ibid., fol.61a: 23 ff.

[67] Ibid., fol.61b: 3–5.

[68] Avicenna, *al-Ishārāt wal-tanbīhāt*, 78, line 10 ff. Citation from Goichon, *Lexique de la langue philosophique d'ibn Sina*, 32 ff.

he must explain each premise in detail "so that the *quaesitum*'s following (*luzūm al-maṭlūb*) as a consequence of the premise(s) becomes conspicuous."[69] It is up to Q, on the other hand, to make sure that P gives detailed accounts, so that Q might immediately grasp any falsehood that arises from P's proof and demand evidence for it in order to expose it.[70] Al-Samarqandī uses this occasion again to borrow a rule from the authors on the *ādāb al-jadal*. He notes that neither of the parties should give to the other too much leeway since "many errors can derive from one little thing."[71]

Al-Samarqandī also gives advice about proving something by means of its contradictory. Since, as we have seen, every demonstration (*dalīl*) derives from a hypothetical syllogism, one might try to prove "x", by showing that "-x therefore q; and -q, therefore, x." Although, in theory, this is clear enough, in practice, trouble arises when the opponent uses the contrary instead of the contradictory or a consequence that does not follow, or posits as cause what is not a cause. He mentions in his *Sharḥ al-Qusṭās* examples that he has selected from the writings of Fakhr al-Dīn al-Rāzī (d. 1209) and Themistius.[72]

Al-Samarqandī concludes this section with advice for Q that illustrates, again, the general character of his theory of disputation:

> After the complete presentation of each proof, be it of a premise or of the thesis (as a whole), it is necessary that Q inspect whether his thesis follows as a consequence or not.
>
> For sometimes a completed proof does not implicate the alleged thesis: since P may have used *ad hominem* (*ilzāmīya*) premises, I mean those that are established in the opinion of the opponent alone. This is permissible in probable and dialectical matters (*fī al-zannīyāt wal-jadalīyāt*) since their goal is plausibility (*ghalabat al-ẓann*). This is not true in scientific matters (*al-ʿaqlīyāt*) since there the thesis is about whether something exists in reality, and not whether it exists in the opinion of the opponent or anyone else.[73]

In this paragraph, al-Samarqandī shows the applicability of disputation to any learned subject, whether it be subject to stringent or non-stringent proof. As in Aristotle's theory, it is the methods of proof or axioms of each field that determine what arguments are permissible. But unlike Aristotle, he widens the field to which disputation or dialectic is applicable and grounds the entire system on a firm epistemological foundation.

---

[69] al-Samarqandī, *Qusṭās*, fol.61b: 6 ff.

[70] Ibid., fol,61b: 9 ff.

[71] Ibid., fol.61b: 10–11.

[72] al-Samarqandī, *Sharḥ al-Qusṭās*, fol.168a: 4ff. Cf; Avicenna, *K. al-Jadal*, 6:313, line 15 ff.

[73] al-Samarqandī, *Qusṭās*, fol.61b: 22 ff.

"Ends"

The *maqāṭiʿ* or "ends" of debate are the ultimate grounds of proof or the "warrants" of a system that is fundamentally Aristotelian in conception, even though much of its terminology is of Islamic provenance."[74] The "ends" are the indemonstrable principles of the various sciences that make proof possible. Al-Samarqandī gives the long list that we translated above. He warns against supposing that these rules are broken when they are actually not.[75] He also provides an example connected to his proof of the finitude of debate.

An infinite chain of reasoning (*tasalsul*) is not always absurd:

> For there, the infinite chain stems from the side of the effect (*maʿlūl*): that is, that some cause has an effect and its effect has an effect *ad infinitum*. However, the proof that shows that an infinite chain of reasoning is impossible only proves it for that chain which originates from the side of the principle (*mabda'*): that is, that a thing has a cause and its cause has a cause *ad infinitum*.[76]

The argument against an infinite chain of reasoning from the side of the cause was used by Aristotle to prove the possibility of demonstrative knowledge.[77] Al-Samarqandī uses this same proof to show that the debate must be finite. Its application to the field of disputation is unique. Aristotle did not bother to apply it to dialectic since, as we have seen, dialectic was accorded a rather lower place in his theory of knowledge. He does mention that one could criticize on the grounds that it takes too much time, but Aristotle considers this a weak objection. Inasmuch as the argument is based upon plausible premises and the respondent's admission, Aristotle must have seen no reason why it should come to some point and conclude. It is here that we most clearly observe al-Samarqandī's innovation of applying Aristotle's epistemology to the *rules* of debate.

Now, we saw already in the earliest theoretical handbooks that theologians appropriated Aristotle's arguments about knowledge in order to show that *jadal* must arrive at the truth.[78] But they did not consider the relation between the epistemological suppositions of their system and the "signs of defeat." In other words, they did not translate their theory into practical rules. The rules that they do give are *ad hoc* and derive more from practice than theory. Although there can be little doubt that al-Samarqandī draws upon this Islamic tradition of debate, equally there can be little doubt that he grounds his theory of debate on a firmer logical foundation, so that his theory can be considered a logic of rational discussion or disputation.

We noted earlier the sharp antithesis between theological and philosophical dialectic, where the former sought truth and the latter probability.[79] In al-Samarqandī's

---

[74] On the term "warrants" see Toulmin, *The Uses of Argument*, 98 ff.

[75] al-Samarqandī, *Qusṭās*, fol.62a: 1 ff.

[76] Ibid., fol.62a: 12 ff. Cf. *Sharḥ al-Qusṭās*, fol.169a: 10 ff.

[77] Aristotle *APo*. 72b18 ff.

[78] See Chap. 2, *supra*.

[79] See Chap. 3, *supra*.

work, we encounter a synthesis of the two approaches. He allows that debate can use either strict or lenient rules of evidence (*dalīl*), for "'evidence' is that thing the knowledge of or opinion of which leads to the knowledge of or opinion about something else."[80] His definition accommodates the dialectics of jurisprudence and theology. He tells us in commenting upon al-Nasafī's *Muqaddima*:

> You should know that the evidence (*dalā'il*) of the Law is of five sorts: Qur'ān, tradition (*sunna*), consensus, analogy, and the purely intellectual ones such as implication, incompatibility, and method of agreement and disagreement, and so forth. The first three are traditional (*naqlīya*) while the other two are intellectual (*ʿaqlīya*). If the evidence is composed of apodictic premises, then the thing indicated (*madlūl*) is only plausible since its existence is a ramification of the evidence, and the ramification (*farʿ*) is never stronger than its source. In that case it is called persuasive (*iqnāʿī*) or "hint" (*amāra*).[81]

That this was no meager achievement is perhaps best indicated by the course that modern logic has taken. In this past century, logicians began to occupy themselves with the logic of debate and discussion. One of the main problems in this field is the Münchausen trilemma, the problem of finding the meta-rules applicable to debate.

There are according to this thesis three basic problems in constructing rules for argumentation:

1. The rules lead to other ones and so the reasoning is circular.
2. The rules lead to an infinite regress.
3. The problem of the "breaking-off" lemma: P refuses to answer O's question because he claims that it involves a fundamental axiom. But how are we, as impartial observers, to judge P's denial?[82]

One solution is to limit the "proof-field" while another is to base the rules on a "prediscursive agreement" that finds its expression in "Protologic."[83] The latter is based upon usage and not on any other system of rules.[84] In a study of the logic of discussion, where discussion is understood as a game, Kuno Lorenz notes that if the argument arrives at no conclusion, then by definition one player has lost, namely, the one who must prove his thesis.[85] The problem of rules of argumentation and the closing off of debate also attracted the attention of modern jurists.[86]

Al-Samarqandī closes his *Qusṭās* with a consideration of the causes of paralogism.[87]

This subject, however, lies beyond the scope of our study. Let us, therefore, turn to al-Samarqandī's *Risāla* and consider what it says about the *ādāb al-baḥth*.

---

[80] al-Samarqandī, *Sharḥ al-Muqaddima*, fol.4b: 16–17.

[81] Ibid., fol.5a: 4ff.

[82] Gethmann, *Protologik*, 34–5; O stands for Opponent.

[83] Ibid., p. 37–38.

[84] Ibid., pp. 40–1. Ibid., pp. 40–1.

[85] Lorenz, "Arithmetik and Logik als Spiele," 28.

[86] Alexy, *Theorie der juristischen Argumentation*.

[87] Al-Samarqandī, *Qusṭās*, fol.63a: 10 ff.

al-Risāla

The *Risāla* was the most famous version of al-Samarqandī's rules of disputation. We have already suggested that it is probably the earliest version of al-Samarqandī's treatment of the subject. In it he follows a different procedure from the one used in the *Qusṭās*. He divides his epistle into three parts: on definitions; on the order of debate; on several problems (*masā'il*)[88] that al-Samarqandī invented.[89] The second part of the *Risāla* is virtually the same as the first section of the *Qusṭās* where al-Samarqandī treats the order of the debate with respect to propositions (*masā'il*).[90] Let us therefore focus our attention on the first and third parts of the *Risāla*.

On Definitions

The definitions that al-Samarqandī gives are almost all terms used in the dialectics of *uṣūl al-fiqh*. His first three definitions, indeed, are treated by al-Nasafī in his *Muqaddima*: disputation (*munāẓara*); proof (*dalīl*); and hint (*amāra)*.[91] His first definition is practically the same as the one chosen by al-Nasafī in his *Muqaddima*: "It is insightful speculation from the two sides about the relation between two things in order to show which one of them is the correct one." He has merely added the word "insightful" (baṣīra) to al-Nasafī's definition. To us, this close correspondence of the two definitions appears to be another sign that the *Risāla* was one of al-Samarqandī's early works written under the influence of his study with al-Nasafī. To commentators on al-Samarqandī's *Risāla*, however, the definition has wide-ranging "philosophical" import. So one of the earliest commentators explains:

> Know, that this definition contains the four causes... For "speculation" points to the *formal* cause: the "two sides" to the *efficient* cause, although you could say that "speculation" points to the disputant who is the actor and who is here the intellect (*'aql*); "the relation" points to the *material* cause; and finally, "to show which one of them is true" points to the *final* cause.[92]

Some of the commentators refer to the discrepancy between the definition that al-Samarqandī gives here and the one that he offered in the commentary on

---

[88] Literally, "questions" but it also takes on the meaning of questions or problems (Gr. *problemata)* about which there is no one generally accepted view; cf. Arist. Top. 101b28 ff.

[89] al-Samarqandī, *al-Risāla*, 125, lines 12–4.

[90] Cf. notes 32–35 for details.

[91] al-Samarqandī, *al-Risāla*, p. 125, lines 16–9. On al-Nasafī see the discussion in the chapter on juristic dialectics, *supra*.

[92] Al-Shirwānī al-Rūmī, *Sharḥ 'alā al-Risāla al-Samarqandīya*, fol.3a: 8 ff., MS.4253. Cf. al-Bihishtī al-Isfarā'īnī, *Sharh 'alā al-Risāla al-Samarqandīya*, fol.16a: 21ff., MS.3482. Al-Kīlānī, *Sharh 'alā al-Risāla al-Samarqandīya*, fol.4a: 4 ff., MS.724.

al-Nasafī's *Muqaddima*. Al-Kīlānī (d. ca.1427) is the earliest writer to cite this discrepancy and offers the following explanation:

> But this (the definition of disputation as "the bandying about of the discussion between the two sides in order to reveal the truth") is not exclusive (*māniʿ*) since it includes that sort of bandying about (*mudāfaʿa*) that occurs with respect to *the subject or* the predicate of the statement (but the *subject* of dispute is not disputed).[93]

al-Kīlānī is not interested in the order in which al-Samarqandī composed his works and, therefore, does not speculate any further about why al-Samarqandī chose one definition instead of the other. A much later commentator remarks that "he is following the author of the Commentary on the *Muqaddima* (that is, al-Nasafī's *Muqaddima*) in his definition."[94] None of the authors of commentaries is, however, concerned with the genesis of al-Samarqandī's thought.

When in the *Risāla* al-Samarqandī defines the terms *dalīl* and *amāra,* he gives virtually the same definitions that appear in his commentary to al-Nasafī's *Muqaddima.* However, there is in al-Samarqandī's arrangement an improvement upon the order chosen by al-Nasafī. Al-Kīlānī shrewdly observes that al-Samarqandī defines these two things before defining *munāqaḍa* and *muʿāraḍa* because the latter are based upon them.[95]

The next three definitions given by al-Samarqandī are connected with the juristic concept of cause:

> That upon which the existence of a thing is based is called basis (*rukn*) if it be internal (*dākhil*) and condition (*sharṭ*) if it be external yet effecting (*muʾaththir*) its existence. Perfect cause (*ʿilla tāmma*) is everything upon which the existence of a thing rests.[96]

Some of the commentators are quick to spot Aristotelian logic and, more particularly, Aristotelian causes (the well-known four causes):

> There are two types of basis (*rukn*): (1) *material* as when the thing is potentially in it (e.g., wood with respect to a bed) and (2) *formal* if it is potentially in it (e.g., as in the form of the bed).[97]

al-Kīlānī mentions these things, too, but notes that actually al-Samarqandī's definitions are according to the conventions of the theoreticians and authors of *uṣūl al-fiqh* works (*iṣṭilāḥ ahl al-naẓar wal-uṣuliyīn*), and that these conventions are different from those of the philosophers.[98] Al-Kīlānī offers examples of *rukn* and *sharṭ* that are not unfamiliar to those familiar with *uṣūl al-fiqh* and that are often mentioned by other commentators: standing up or sitting down with respect to prayer [= *rukn*] and ritual ablution or cleanliness with respect to prayer [= *sharṭ*].[99]

---

[93] Ibid., fol.4b: 7 ff.

[94] Al-Kāshī, *Qara Ḥāshīya*, fol.46b: 9–10, MS.3482.

[95] Al-Kīlānī, *Sharḥ*, fol.5a: 2 ff.

[96] al-Samarqandī, *al-Risāla*, p. 126, lines 3–6.

[97] Al-Samarqandī, *Sharḥ*, fol. 19 b ff.

[98] Al-Kīlānī, *Sharḥ*, fol. 9b: 13 ff.; cf. 9a: 8–10.

[99] Ibid., fol. 8b: 12–3; –2 ff.

These three definitions are followed by another three that also appear in al-Nasafī's *Muqaddima*: explanation (*taʿlīl*), implication (*mulāzama*) and method of agreement and disagreement (*dawarān*).[100] In his commentary to the *Muqaddima*[101] al-Samarqandī remarks that the proper definition of *taʿlīl* is "the establishment of the existence (*thubūt*) of the effector (*muʾaththir*) on account of the existence (*ithbāt*) of the effect."[102] Here, however, he gives another definition: "an explanation *(tabyīn)* of the cause (*ʿilla*) of a thing." His definitions of implication and method of agreement and disagreement are the same as those discussed earlier in connection with their use by al-Nasafī, and so it is unnecessary to repeat them here.[103]

A remark that he makes in his *Commentary* on the *Muqaddima* reveals, however, the reason for his setting forth the previous six definitions in the order that he has chosen. There, he remarks on the definition of *dawarān* as "the basing of the effect upon that thing which could possibly be its cause (*alladhī lahū ṣulūḥīya*)." That the last phrase means "possible explanation" (*ṣiḥḥat al-taʿlīl*) of that effect through that cause is shown by the example he brings of how one "explains that someone has diarrhea through adducing that he has drunk sacomony."[104] Thus, from his viewpoint, he needs to define *taʿlīl* before he defines *dawarān* and *ʿilla* before he defines *taʿlīl*.

Al-Samarqandī closes his section on definition with the definitions of four "weapons" at Q's disposal:

1. *Munāqaḍa* disallowing a premise of the proof.
2. *Muʿāraḍa* setting up a proof contrary to the one set up by the opponent.
3. *Naqḍ* the absence of the juristic quality (*ḥukm*) from the evidence (*dalīl*).
4. *Mustanad* that upon which the objection is based.[105]

These terms all occur in the second part of the *Risāla* where the order and rules of debate are delineated. All save the last are mentioned by al-Nasafī in his *Muqaddima*, and are, indeed, present in the earliest works on juristic dialectics. However, *here* they are envisaged as *the* sorts of objection possible against *any* piece of evidence. At this point in the *Risāla* it is not at all clear to the reader that the work is anything more than a short work on juristic dialectics. The definitions almost to a one are from jurisprudence and there was, indeed, a tradition of prefacing chapters on definition to works on jurisprudence.

---

[100] Al-Samarqandī, *al-Risāla*, p. 125, line −1 ff. At 126, line 2 read *tarattub* for *tartīb*.

[101] See section in Chap. 4 on Nasafī, *supra*.

[102] al-Samarqandī, *Sharḥ al-Muqadimma*, fol.5a: −3.

[103] See text accompanying footnote 82, *supra*.

[104] Ibid., fol. 17a: 13 ff.; cf. al-Isfarāʾīnī, *Sharḥ*, fol.22a: 10–11.

[105] al-Samarqandī, *al-Risāla*, p. 126, lines 3–6.

The Questions/Problems (masā'il)

al-Samarqandī illustrates how his rules of disputation work by giving sample theses from various "sciences:"

1. The world needs an "effector" because it is contingent.[106]
2. The necessary existent is one (theology).[107]
3. The necessary existent does not exercise free will (philosophy).[108]
4. al-Shāfiʿī says: The father has power to force a virgin daughter of age to marry, contrary to what Abū Ḥanīfa says… (jurisprudence).[109]

The questions are given in the form of reports that are similar to those that one finds in the *ṭarīqa* literature: explication of the thesis along with its proof, followed by objections and replies.[110] What is important and surprising is that this method is now applied to philosophy and theology. The choice of examples shows that even in its earliest formulation, assuming that the *Risāla* was the first treatise on the subject, the *ādāb al-baḥth* was thought of as a universal or general theory of disputation.

---

[106] Ibid., p. 127, line 21 ff.

[107] Ibid., p. 130, line 7.

[108] Ibid., p. 130, line 22 ff.

[109] 110 Ibid., p. 131, line 16 ff.

[110] See Chap. 4.

Conclusion

Al-Samarqandī's new science the *ādāb al-baḥth* is to a great extent the product of a long tradition of juristic dialectics. The definitions that he gives and the order of debate that he proposes are best understood in the light of this tradition. At times, we have seen, he draws upon rules from the *ādāb al-jadal* of theological dialectics. But we have also seen that he is not wholly dependent upon this tradition. If his technical terminology and rules are a product of the juristic tradition of dialectics, they are, nevertheless, informed by concepts that derive from Aristotelian logic and philosophy. One result of this influence is the new designation for the old "science." We observed that even in the middle period of juristic dialectics, the word *jadal* was being replaced by *naẓar* or *munāẓara* as the title for the discipline. In the writings of al-Samarqandī, *mujādala* retains its Aristotelian meaning of a conversation that aims at persuasion or conviction and not at truth. The title of the new discipline is the science of disputation or the rules of investigation. The change in designation brought with it a change in subject matter. Logic now becomes the final arbiter since the subject matter is no longer theses taken from jurisprudence or theology but rather *statements per se*, whether they be formulated as definitions or "problems" (*masā'il*). Aristotle's epistemology is then called in to guarantee the foundations of the new science and to prove that disputation must be finite.

Al-Samarqandī's *Risāla* is, thus, the first treatise that we have of an entirely new genre of literature, the *ādāb al-baḥth*. Following his lead, great Muslim scholars such as Aḍud al-Dīn al Ījī (d. 1355), al-[Saiyid] al-Sharīf al-Jurjānī (d. 1413), al-Marʿashī (d. (1732)), al-Kalanbawī (d. 1790/1) and Tashköprüzāde (d. 1529) all wrote treatises in this new genre.[1]

[1] The works of al-Kalanbawī and al-Jurjānī were printed in the same *majmu'a* as al-Samarqandī's *Risāla*. Al-Ījī's work has been printed several times in *majmu' muhimmat al-mutun*: cf. *GAL*. Tashköprüzāde's work has also been printed several times. For evidence of al-Samarqandī's influence, see Āmulī, *Kitāb Nafāyis al-Funūn fī gharā'ib al-'uyūn,* 1: 521 ff. In this curious Persian encyclopedia, the author devotes a chapter to the science of juristic dialectics (*'ilm al-khilāf*). It has two parts, one called dialectic (*jadal*), which deals with syllogisms fashioned from *endoxa*; the

L. B. Miller, *Islamic Disputation Theory*, Logic, Argumentation & Reasoning 21,
https://doi.org/10.1007/978-3-030-45012-0

None of these writings went much beyond the rules that al-Samarqandī set forth in the *Risāla* and the *Qusṭās*. There were, of course, refinements. The new science was called *ādāb al-baḥth*, the art of disputation (*fann al-munāẓara*) and the art of formulation.[2]

Some of the authors chose as a definition of disputation the one that al-Samarqandī offers in the *Commentary* to al-Nasafī's *Muqaddima*, while others adopted the traditional definition. Some had short chapters or brief mentions of rules of politeness (*adab al-munāẓara*) and strategy. But, on the whole, the order of the debate, the definitions of the technical terms and the understanding of the duties (*waẓā'if*) of the disputants did not change.

In his learned study on the rise of colleges, Makdisi argues that the scholastic method derives from Islamic methods of disputation. However, the theoretical literature that has been the object of this study, when compared to what little we actually know about scholastic disputation does not support Makdisi's thesis. In scholastic debates, there were one or more respondents who defended a thesis against the objections of one or more opponents who in turn tried to refute it within a given time limit. Then there was a master who arbitrated the debate and gave a determination at its end. However, in our theoretical works, there is no mention of an arbiter, a determination, or even a time limit on debate. What is more, in the ideal case, disputation was between precisely two opponents, a questioner and a respondent. The respondent is always pictured as someone who first of all proposes a thesis that he supports, and second of all, as someone who responds to the questioner's objections. What technical terms that coincide in the two traditions derive primarily from their understanding of disputation as question and answer, an understanding that could be traced to a common intellectual forefather, Aristotle. So, too, the *ars obligatoria*, the body of literature that evolved in the West in the fourteenth century, has practically no connection whatsoever to Islamic disputation theory. If parallels are to be sought, we must instead look to modern theories of rational argumentation.[3]

---

other is called the science of disputation (*'ilm-i naẓar*). The entire treatment derives from the writings of al-Nasafī and al-Samarqandī. The first part contains Persian translations of al-Nasafī's and al-Samarqandī's definitions; a second chapter concerns the order of the debate where we read "*bi-dān kih baḥth dar chīzī vāqi' shavad kih dar ū ḥukmi bāshad bi-nafy yā ithbāt va ū-rā sih juz ast: mabādī' u-avsāṭ u-maqāṭi'*" (p. 526, lines 18–9). Cf. nn. 19 and 58. A third chapter contains the *ādāb-i munāẓara*, which contains the old admonitions of chapters on the *ādāb al-jadal*. Practically all of his examples are taken from jurisprudence.

[2] Al-Jaunpūrī, *al-Rashīdīya* (Commentary to al-Sayyid al-Sharīf 'Alī ibn Maḥmūd al-Jurjānī's *al-Risāla al-Sharīfīya fī ādāb al-baḥth al-munāẓara*, 11, line 3.

[3] Cf. Makdisi, *Colleges*, 281 ff.; Kenny, "Medieval philosophical literature" and Strump and Spade, "Obligations," 315–341 and 24 ff.

Selected Bibliography

A. Manuscripts

Berlin. Staatsbibliothek. MS.5167 (Mq. 55). Nuʿmān al-Khwārizmī. "Sharḥ fuṣūl lil-Nasafī."
________. MS.5168 (Lbg. 72). Burhān al-Dīn al-Nasafī. "al-Muqaddima al-Burhānīya."
Bratislava. MS.231 TE41. al-Fārābī. "Kitāb al-Jadal." [Type script of M. Galston].
Cairo. Dār al-Kutub al-Miṣrīya. MS.236 (Fiqh Ḥanafī). Rukn al-Dīn al-ʿAmīdī. "al-Ṭarīqa al-ʿAmīdīya fī al-khilāf wal-jadal."
________. MS.804 (Lugha). Abū Hilāl al-ʿAskarī. "al-Furūq."
________. MS.258 (Taimūr). Abū Hilāl al-ʿAskarī. "al-Furūq."
________. MS.1523 (Fiqh Shāfiʿī). al-Ḥasan b. Shuʿaib al-Marwazī. "Ṭarīqat al-khilāf baina al-Shāfiʿīya wal-Ḥanafīya maʿa dhikr al-adilla li kull minhumā."
________. MS.239 (Fiqh Ḥanafī). Raḍī al-Dīn al-Nisabūrī. "al-Ṭarīqa al-Raḍawīya."
________. MS.438 (Fiqh Taimūr). Shams al-Dīn al-Samarqandī. "Sharḥ al-Muqaddima al-Burhānīya."
Dublin. The Chester Beatty Library. MS.4396. Shams al-Dīn Muḥammad b. Ashraf al-Samarqandī. "Sharḥ al-Muqaddima al-Burhānīya."
________. MS.4767. Shams al-Dīn Muḥammad b. Ashraf al-Samarqandī. "Sharḥ al-Qusṭās."
Escurial. MS.650. Rukn al-Dīn al-ʿAmīdī. "al-Irshād."
________. MS.693. Taqī al-Dīn Muẓaffar b. a. l-ʿIzz al-Muqtaraḥ al-Shāfiʿī. "Sharḥ al-Muqtaraḥ fī al-muṣtalaḥ."
Istanbul. Atif Efendi Library. MS.2421. Ibn Miʿmār. "al-Mukhtaṣar fī al-jadal."
________. Feyzullah Efendi Library. MS.1864. Muḥyī al-Dīn Jamāl al-Islām a. Muḥammad. "al-Mukhtaṣar fī ʿilm al-naẓar."
________. Köprülü Library. MS.519/3. Fakhr al-Dīn al-Rāzī. "Kitāb al-Jadal."
________. Ahmet Thaleth Library. MS.3399. Shams al-Dīn Muḥammad b. Ashraf al-Samarqandī. "Qusṭās al-afkār."
________. MS.3399. Shams al-Dīn Muḥammad b. Ashraf al-Samarqandī. "Sharḥ al-Qusṭās."
London. British Museum. MS Supplement 1124 V (Or. 3730). Shams al-Dīn Muḥammad b. Ashraf al-Samarqandī. "ʿAin al-naẓar fī al-manṭiq fī ʿilm al-jadal."
Medina. Maktabat Shaikh al-Islām ʿĀrif Ḥikmat. MS.253 (Tauḥīd). Ibn Fūrak."Mujarrad maqālāt al-Shaikh Abī l-Ḥasan ... al-Ashʿarī."
Princeton. Princeton University Library. MS.867 (Garrett). Fīrūzabādī al-Shīrāzī, Abū Isḥāq Ibrāhīm ibn ʿAlī ibn Yūsuf. "Maʿūnat al-mubtadiʾīn wa-tadhkirat al-muntahīn fī al-jadal."

L. B. Miller, *Islamic Disputation Theory*, Logic, Argumentation & Reasoning 21,
https://doi.org/10.1007/978-3-030-45012-0

_______. MS.882 (Yahuda). Jalāl al-Dīn Muḥammad b. As'ad al-Dauwānī. "Ḥāshiya 'alā sharḥ Mas'ūd al-Rūmī."
_______. MS.882 (Yahuda). Aḥmad Dunquz. "Ḥāshiya sharḥ Mas'ūd al-Rūmī."
_______. MS.4319 (Yahuda). Muḥammad b. Aḥmad al-Bihishtī al-Isfarā'inī. "Sharḥ al-Samarqandīya fī ādāb al-baḥth."
_______. MS.3482 (Yahuda). 'Imād al-Dīn Yaḥyā b. Aḥmad al-Kāshī. "Qara Ḥāshiya."
_______. MS.724 (Yahuda). Quṭb al-Dīn al-Kīlānī. "Sharḥ al-Samarqandīya fī ādāb al-baḥth."
_______. MS.4319 (Yahuda). Ḥusain b. Mu'īn al-Dīn al-Maibudī. "Sharḥ al-Samarqandīya fī ādāb al-baḥth."
_______. MSS.187,2246. Burhān al-Dīn al-Nasafī. "al-Muqaddima al-Burhānīya fī al-khilāf."
_______. MS.2331. Mas'ūd al-Rūmī. "Sharḥ al-Samarqandīya fī ādāb al-baḥth."

B. Books

al-A'asam, A. *History of Ibn al-Rīwandī the Heretic*. Beirut: Dār al-Āfāq al-Jadīda, 1975.
_______. *Ibn al-Rīwandī in the Modern References*. 2 vols. Beirut: Dār al-Āfāq al-Jadīda, 1978a–9.
'Abd al-Jabbār, b. Aḥmad, al-Qāḍī. *Faḍl al-i'tizāl*. Ed. F. Saiyid. Tunis: al-Dār al-Tūnisīya lil-Nashr, 1974.
_______. *al-Naẓar wal-Ma'ārif. al-Mughnī fī abwāb al-tauḥīd*. Ed. I. Madkour. Cairo: Wizārat al-Thaqāfa wal-Irshād al-'Āmma, 1964.
Abū Ḥaiyān al-Tauḥīdī. *al-Muqābasāt*. Ed. T. Ḥusain. Baghdad: Maṭba'at al-Irshād, 1970.
Abū Isḥāq al-Shīrāzī. *al-Luma' fī uṣūl al-fiqh*. 3d ed. Cairo: Shirkat M. Ḥalabī, 1957.
_______. *K. Ṭabaqāt al-fugahā'*. Ed. I. 'Abbās. 2nd ed. Beirut: Dār al-Rā'id, 1981.
Abū l-Ḥusain al-Baṣrī. *al-Mu'tamad fī uṣūl al-fiqh*. Ed. M. Hamīdullāh. 2 vols. Damascus: Imprimerie Catholique 1964.
Afnan, S. *Philosophical Terminology in Arabic and Persian*. Leiden: E. J. Brill 1964.
Ahlwardt, W. *Die Handschriftenverzeichnisse der arabischen Handschriften der Kőniglichen Bibliothek in Berlin*. 10 vols. Berlin: A. W. Schade, 1887–99.
al-Aḥmadnagarī, 'Abd al-Nabī. *Dustūr al-'ulamā'*. Ed. M. al-Haidarābādī. 4 vols. Hyderabad: Dā'irat al-ma'ārif al-Niẓāmīya, 1911–13.
Alexander of Aphrodisias. *Alexandri quod fertur in Aristotelis Sophisticos Elenchos commentarium*. Ed. M. Wallies. *Commentaria in Aristotelem Graeca*. vol. 2, pt. 3. Berlin: G. Reimer, 1898.
———. *In Aristotelis Analyticorum priorum librum I commentarium*. Ed. M. Wallies. *Commentaria in Aristotelem Graeca*. vol. 2, pt. 1. Berlin: 1883.
———. *In Aristotelis Topicorum libros octo commentaria*. Ed. M. Wallies. *Commentaria in Aristotelem Graeca*. vol. 2, pt. 2. Berlin: G. Reimer, 1891.
Alexy, R. *Theorie der juristischen Argumentation*. Frankfurt: Suhrkamp, 1978.
Altmann, A. and S. Stern. *Isaac Israeli. A Neoplatonic Philosopher of the Early Tenth Century*. Oxford: Clarendon Press, 1958.
Ammonius. *In Aristotelis Analyticorum Priorum Librum I Commentarium*. Ed. M. Wallies. *Commentaria in Aristo-telem Graeca*. vol. 4, pt. 6. Berlin: G. Reimer, 1899.
———. *In Aristotelis De Interpretatione Commentarius*. Ed. A. Busse. *Commentaria in Aristotelem Graeca*. vol. 4, pt. 5. Berlin: G. Reimer, 1897.
al-Āmulī, Shams al-Dīn. *Kitāb Nafā'is al-funūn*. 3 vols. Tehran, 1957–59.
Anawati, G. and L. Gardet. *Introduction à la théologie musulmane*. Paris: J. Vrin, 1948.
Anawati, G. *Mu'allafāt Ibn Sīnā*. Cairo: Dār al-Ma'ārif, 1950.
An Anonymous Commentary on Aristotle's De Interpretatione. Ed. L. Taran. Meisenheim am Glan: A. Hain, 1978.
Arberry, J. *The Chester Beatty Library, A Handlist of the Arabic manuscripts*. 7 vols. Dublin: E. Walker et al., 1955–64.

Aristotle. *Aristotle's Prior and Posterior Analytics*. Ed. W. Ross. Oxford: Clarendon Press, 1949.
_______. *Categories and De Interpretatione*. Trans. J. Ackrill. Oxford: Clarendon Press, 1963a.
———. *Opera*. Ed. by I. Bekker. 5 vols. Berlin: 1831 ff.
———. *The Works of Aristotle Translated into English*. Ed. W. Ross. 11 vols. Oxford: Clarendon Press 1908–31.
al-Ash'arī, Abū l-Ḥasan. *Maqālāt al-Islāmīyīn*. Ed. H. Ritter. 2 vols. Constantinople: 1929–33.
_______. *Risāla fī istiḥsān al-khauḍ fī 'ilm al-kalām*. Ed. R. McCarthy. *The Theology of Al-Ash'arī*. Beirut: Imprimerie Catholique, 1953a.
al-'Askarī, Abū Hilāl. *al-Furūq fī al-lugha*. 2nd Ed. Beirut: Dār al-Āfāq al-Jadīda, 1977.
Averroes. See below under G. Jehamy.
_______. *Tafsīr mā ba'd al-ṭabī'a*. Ed. M. Bouyges. 2nd ed. 3 vols. Beirut: Dar el-Machreq, 1948–67.
———. *Tahāfut al-Tahāfut*. Ed. M. Bouyges. Beirut: Imprimerie Catholique, 1930.
———. *Tahāfut al-tahāfut*. Trans. S. van den Bergh. *Averroes 'Tahafut at-Tahafut*. 2 vols. London: Luzac, 1954.
———. *Talkhīṣ kitāb al-jadal*. Ed. C. Butterworth and A. Harīdī. Cairo: General Egyptian Book Organization, 1979a.
———. *Talkhīṣ kitāb al-qiyās*. Ed. C. Butterworth and A. Harīdī. Cairo: General Egyptian Book Organization, 1983a.
———. *Talkhīṣ kitāb al-safsaṭa*. Ed. M. Sālim. Cairo: Dār al-Kutub wal-Wathā'iq al-Qaumīya, 1972a.
———. *al-Ishārāt wal-tanbīhāt*. Ed. J. Forget. Leiden: E. J. Brill, 1892.
———. *al-Ishārāt wal-tanbīhāt*. Ed. S. Dunyā. 3d ed. vol. 1. Cairo: Dār al-Ma'ārif, 1983b.
Avicenna. *Kitāb al-Burhān*. Ed. A. 'Afīfī. *al-Shifā': al-Manṭiq*. vol. 5. Cairo: Government Press, 1956.
_______. *Kitāb al-'Ibāra*. Ed. M. al-Khudairī. *al-Shifā': al-Manṭiq*. vol. 3. Cairo: Dār al-Kātib al-'Arabī, 1970a.
———. *Kitāb al-Jadal*. Ed. F. al-Ahwānī. *al-Shifā': al-Manṭiq*. vol. 6. Cairo: Organisme Generale des Imprimeries Gouvermentales, 1965.
———. *Kitāb al-Madkhal*. Ed. G. Anawati et al. *al-Shifā': al-Manṭiq*. vol. 1. Cairo: Imprimerie Nationale, 1952.
———. *Kitāb al-Maqūlāt*. Ed. G. Anawati et al. *al-Shifā': al-Manṭiq*. vol. 2. Cairo: Organisation Generale des Imprimeries Gouvermentales, 1959a.
———. *Kitāb al-Qiyās*. Ed. S. Zāyid. *al-Shifā': al-Manṭiq*. vol. 4. Cairo: Organisme Generale des Imprimeries Gouvermentales, 1959b.
———. *Kitāb al-Safsaṭa*. Ed. F. al-Ahwānī. *al-Shifā': al-Manṭiq* Cairo: Imprimerie Nationale, 1958.
———. *al-Shifa'*. Ed. by I. Madkour. Cairo: al-Maṭba'a al-Amīrīya, 1953b ff.
Badawi, A. *Manṭiq Arisṭū*. 3 vols. Beirut: Dār al-Qalam, 1980.
al-Baghdādī, 'Abd al-Qāhir. *Uṣūl al-dīn*. Istanbul: Maṭba'at al-Daula, 1928.
Baghdatli, I. *Hadīyat al-'ārifīn*. Ed. R. Bilge and I. Inal. Istanbul: Maarif Basimevi, 1951–55.
al-Bājī, Abū l-Walīd. *al-Minhāj fī tartīb al-ḥijāj*. Ed. A. Turki. Paris: G. P. Maisonneuve et Larose, 1978.
Barnes, J. *Aristotle's Posterior Analytics*. trans. J. Barnes. Oxford: Oxford University Press, 1975.
Becker, C. H. *Islamstudien*. 2 vols. Leipzig: Quelle & Meyer, 1924–31.
Boethius. *Anicii Manlii Severini Boetii commentarii in librum Aristotelis peri hermeneias*. Ed. C. Meiser. 2nd ed., 2 vols. Leipzig, Teubner, 1880.
Brockelmann, C. *Geschichte der arabischen Litteratur*. 5 vols. Leiden: E. J. Brill, 1949.
Brunschvig, R. *Mélanges d'Islamologie*. Ed. A. Turki. Paris: G. P. Maisonneuve et Larose, 1976.
Commentaria in Aristotelem Graeca. Edita consilio et auctoritate Academiae litterarum Regiae Borussicae. 23 vols. Berlin: 1882–1909.
Cook, M. *Early Muslim Dogma*. Cambridge, England: Cambridge University Press, 1981.
Derenbourg, H. *Les Manuscrits arabes de l'Escurial*. vol. 1. Paris: 1884.
de Rijk, L. *Logica Modernorum*. 3 vols. Assen: Van Gorcum, 1962–67.

Diogenes Laertius. *Lives of the Eminent Philosophers*. Ed. and trans. R. Hicks. 2 vols. London: Heinemann, 1925.
Ebbenson, S. *Commentators and Commentaries on Aristotle's Sophistic Elenchi*. 3 vols. Leiden: E. J. Brill, 1981.
Elias, J. *The Haggadah*. New York: Mesorah Publications, 1977.
Encyclopedia Iranica. Ed. E. Yar-Shater. London: Keagan and Routledge, 1982.
Encyclopedia of Islam. 2d ed. 4 vols. at present. Leiden: E.J. Brill, 1960-.
Encyclopedia of Men of Science. Ed. C. Gillispie. New York: 1975.
Eustratius. In Analyticorum Posteriorum librum secundum commentarium. Ed. M. Hayduck. Commentaria in Aristotelem Graeca. vol. 21, pt. 1. Berlin: G. Reimer, 1907.
al-Fārābī. *K. al-Alfāẓ al-musta'mala fī al-manṭiq*. Ed. M. Mahdi. Beirut: Dar el-Machreq 1968.
———. *Kitāb al-Ḥurūf*. Ed. M. Mahdi. Beirut: Dar el-Machreq 1969.
———. *Kitāb al-Khaṭāba*. Ed. J. Langhade and M. Grignaschi. Beirut: Dar el-Machreq, 1971.
———. *Risalā fī al-'aql*. Ed. M. Bouyges. Beirut: Imprimerie Catholique, 1936.
———. *Sharḥ li-kitāb Arisṭū fī al-'ibāra*. Ed. W. Kutsch and S. Marrow. Beirut: Imprimerie Catholique, 1960.
Frank, R. *Beings and their Attributes*. Albany: State University of New York Press, 1978.
Gerber, U. *Disputatio als Sprache des Glaubens*. Zürich: EVZ Verlag, 1970.
Gethmann, C. Protologik. *Untersuchungen zur formalen Pragmatik von Begründungsdiskurse*. Frankfurt: Suhrkamp, 1979.
Goichon, A. *Lexique de la langue philosophique d'ibn Sina*. Paris: Desclee de Brouwer, 1938.
Grabmann, M. *Geschichte der scholastischen Methode*. 2 vols. Freiburg: Herder Verlag, 1909–11.
———. *Mittelalterliches Geistesleben*. 3 vols. Munich: M. Hueber, 1926–56.
Gräf, E. *Jagdbeute und Schlachttier im islamischen Recht*. Bonn: Selbstverlag des Orientalischen Seminars der Universität Bonn, 1959.
Ḥājjī Khalīfa. *Kash al-ẓunūn*. Ed. Sh. Yaltkaya and R. Bilge. 2 vols. Istanbul: Maarif Matbaasi, 1941–3.
Hamblin, C. *Fallacies*. London: Methuen, 1970.
Hitti, P., B. 'Abd al-Malik and N. Faris, eds. *Descriptive Catalogue of the Garrett Collection of Arabic Manuscripts in the Princeton University Library*. Princeton: Princeton University Press, 1938.
Hunger, H. *Die hochsprachliche profane Litteratur der Byzantiner*. Munich: Beck, 1978.
Ibn 'Abd al-Barr. *Jāmi' bayān al-'ilm wa-faḍlihī*. Ed. 'A 'Uthmān. Medina: al-Maktaba al-Salafīya, 1968.
Ibn 'Aqīl. *Kitāb al-jadal*. Ed. G. Makdisi. Bulletin d'Études Orientales 20 (1967).
Ibn al-Fuwaṭī. *Talkhīṣ majma' al-ādāb fī mu'jam al-alqāb*. Ed. M. Jawād. Damascus: Mudīrīyāt Iḥyā' al-Turāth al-Qadīm, 1963.
Ibn al-Ḥājib. *Muntahā al-wuṣūl wal-amal fī 'ilmai al-uṣūl wal-jadal*. Ed. M. Ḥalabī. Cairo: Maṭba'at al-Sa'āda, 1326.
Ibn Ḥazm, 'Ali. *Kitāb al-Taqrīb li-ḥadd al-manṭiq wal-madkhal ilaihī*. Ed. I. 'Abbās. Beirut: Dār al-'Ibād, 1959.
Ibn Khaldūn. *al-Muqaddima*. Ed. by M. Quatremère. 3 vols. Paris: Institut Imperial de France, 1858.
Ibn al-Muqaffa'. *al-Manṭiq*. Ed. M. Dānish Pazhūh. Tehran: Anjuman-i Shāhanshāhī-i Falsafah-i Īrān, 1357.
Ibn al-Nadīm. *al-Fihrist*. Ed. R. Tajaddud. Tehran: Maktabat al-Asadī, 1971.
'Īsawī, A. and M. al-Malih, eds. *Fihris al-Makhṭūṭāt al-Maktaba al-Gharbīya bil-Jāmi' al-Kabīr bi-San'ā'*. Cairo: Maṭba'at Aṭlas, 1978?.
Jacobs, L. *Studies in Talmudic Logic and Methodology*. London: Valentine, 1961.
Jabre, F. *Essai sur le lexique de Ghazali*. Beirut: Imprimerie Catholique 1970.
al-Jāhiẓ. *Kitāb al-Bayān wal-tabyīn*. Ed. 'A. Hārūn. 4 vols. Cairo: Maktabat al-Khānjī, 1960–1.
al-Jaunpūrī, 'Abd al-Rashīd. *al-Rashīdīya*. Cairo: n.p., 1941.
Jehamy, G. *Averroes Paraphrase de la Logique d'Aristote*. 3 vols. Beirut: Imprimerie Catholique, 1982.

John of Damascus. *Die Schriften des Joannes von Damaskus*. Ed. B. Kotter. 4 vols. Berlin: de Gruyter, 1969 ff.
John Philoponus. *In Aristotelis Analytica Posteriora Commentaria*. Ed. M. Wallies. *Commentaria in Aristotelem Graeca*. vol. 13, pt. 2. Berlin: G. Reimer, 1909.
al-Jurjānī, ʿAlī b. Muḥammad. *Taʿrīfāt*. Istanbul: Maṭbaʿat Aḥmad Kāmil, 1327.
al-Juwaynī, Imām al-Ḥaramain Abū Maʿāli ʿAbd al-Malik. *al-Burhān fī uṣūl al-fiqh*. Ed. ʿA. al-Dib. 2 vols. Cairo: Dār al-Anṣār, 1980.
________. *al-Kāfiya fī al-jadal*. Ed. F. Ḥusain Maḥmūd. Cairo: Maṭbaʿat ʿIsā Ḥalabī, 1979b.
Kaḥḥāla, ʿU. *Muʿjam al-muʾallifīn*. 15 vols. Damascus: Maṭbaʿat al-Tarraqī, 1957–61.
al-Karkhī. *al-Uṣūl allatī ʿalaihā madār kutub asḥābinā*. Cairo: al-Maṭbaʿa al-Adabīya, 1320.
al-Kātib, Isḥāq b. Ibrāhīm. *al-Burhān fī wujūh al-bayān*. Ed. A. Maṭlūb and Kh. Ḥadīthī. Baghdad: Jāmiʿat Baghdād, 1967.
al-Khaṭīb al-Baghdādī. *Kitāb al-faqīh wal-mutafaqqih*. Ed. M. al-Anṣārī. 2d ed. 2 vols. Beirut: Dār al-Kutub al-ʿIlmīya, 1981.
Kholeif, F. *A Study on Fakhr al-Dīn al-Rāzī and His Controversies in Transoxiana*. Beirut: Dar el-Machreq, 1966.
al-Khwārizmī. *Mafātīḥ al-ʿulūm*. Cairo: Maṭbaʿat al-Sharq 1342.
al-Kindī, Yaʿqūb b. Isḥāq. *Rasāʾil*. Ed. M. Abū Rīda. 2 vols. Cairo: Dār al-Fikr al-ʿArabī, 1950–3.
Kneale, W. and M. *The Development of Logic*. Oxford: Clarendon Press, 1962.
Kretzmann, N. J. Pinborg, and A. Kenny, eds. *The Cambridge History of Later Medieval Philosophy*. Cambridge, England: Cambridge University Press, 1982.
Lane, E. *Arabic-English Lexicon*. 8 pts. London: Williams and Norgate. 1863–93.
Lausberg, H. *Handbuch der literarischen Rhetorik*. 2 vols. Munich: M. Hueber, 1960.
Le Blond, J. *Logique et Méthode chez Aristote*. Paris: J. Vrin. 1938.
Lőschner, H. *Grundlagen des schiʿitischen Rechts*. Cologne: Heymann, 1971.
Lorenz, K. *Arithmetik und Logik als Spiele*. Kiel: Disser- tation of Christian-Albrechts-Universität Kiel, 1961.
Mach, R. *Catalogue of Arabic Manuscripts (Yahuda Section) in the Garrett Collection*, Princeton University Library. Princeton: Princeton Universtiy Press, 1977.
Makdisi, G. *The Rise of Colleges*. Edinburgh: Edinburgh University Press, 1981.
al-Maqdisī, Muṭahhar b. Ṭāhir. *Kitāb al-Badʾ wal-taʾrīkh*. Ed. and trans. C. Huart. 5 vols. Paris: Ernst Leroux, Editeur, 1899–1919.
Mates, B. *Stoic Logic*. Berkeley: University of California Press, 1961.
al-Māturīdī. *Kitāb al-Tauḥīd*. Ed. F. Kholeif. Beirut: Dar el-Machreq, 1970.
Migne, J. *Patrologia Graeco-Latina*. Paris: Garnier, 1857–66.
Mill, J. *A System of Logic*. Ed. J. Robson. *Collected Works of John Stuart Mill*. vols. 7–8. Toronto: University of Toronto Press, 1973–74.
Moraux, P. *Le Commentaire d'Alexandre d'Aphrodise aux "Secondes Analytiques" d'Aristote*. Berlin: de Gruyter, 1979.
al-Muḥāsibī, al-Ḥārith. *al-Masāʾil fī aʿamāl al-qulūb wal-jawariḥ wal-makāsib*. Ed. A. ʿAṭā. Cairo: ʿĀlam al-Kutub, 1969.
al-Nashshār, ʿA. *Manāhij al-baḥth ʿinda mufakkiri al-Islām*. 4th ed. Cairo: Dār al-Maʿārif, 1978
Nőldeke, T. *Kurzgefasste syrische Grammatik*. Leipzig: T. Weigel, 1898.
O'Meara, D. *Studies in Aristotle*. Washington, D.C.: Catholic University of America Press, 1981.
Philodemus, *On Signs*. Ed. and trans. P. and E. de Lacy. Revised ed. Naples: Bibliopolis, 1978.
Pohlenz, M. *Die Stoa*. 2 vols. Gőttingen: Vandenhoeck & Ruprecht, 1947–9.
Prantl, C. *Geschichte der Logik im Abendlande*. 4 vols. Leipzig: S. Hirzel, 1855–70.
al-Qirqisānī, Yaʿqūb b. Isḥāq. *K. al-Anwār wal-Marāqib*. Ed. L. Nemoy. New Haven: Alexander Kohut Memorial Foundation, 1939–43.
Quintilian. *Institutio Oratoria*. Ed. H. Butler. *The Institutio Oratoria of Quintilian*. 4 vols. London: Heinemann, 1920.
al-Rāzī, Fakhr al-Dīn. *Mafātīḥ al-ghaib*. 32 vols. Cairo: al-Maṭbaʿa al-Bahīya, 1934–62.

________. *Muḥaṣṣal afkār al-mutagaddimīn wal-muta'akhkhirīn*. Ed. T. Sa'ad. Cairo: Maktabat al-Kullīyāt al-Azharīya, n.d.-u
Rescher, N. *The Development of Arabic Logic*. Pittsburgh: University of Pittsburgh Press, 1964.
________. *Dialectics*. Albany: State University of New York Press, 1977.
Rosenthal, F. *The Muqaddimah*. 3 vols. New York: Pantheon Books, 1958.
Ryun, G. "*Ratio et Oratio*: Cicero, Rhetoric and the Sceptical Academy." Princeton University Ph.D. thesis, 1983.
Sachau, E. *Syrische Rechtsbücher*. 3 vols. Berlin: G. Reimer, 1907–14.
al-Samarqandī, Shams al-Dīn Muḥammad b. Ashraf. *al-Risāla al-Samarqandīya fī ādāb al-baḥth*. Ed.
al-'Alāma al-Shaikh Maḥmūd al-Imām al-Manṣūrī. *Majmū'a mushtamila 'alā al-ātī bayānuhū*. Cairo: n.p. 1353.
al-Sāwī, 'Umar b. Sahlān. *al-Tabṣira va-dū risāla-i dīgar dar manṭiq*. Ed. M. Dānishpazhūh. Tehran: 1337.
Saiyid, F. *Fihris al-Makhṭūṭāt al-muṣauwara*. vol. 1. Cairo: Dār al-Riyāḍ, 1954.
Schacht, J. *An Introduction to Islamic Law*. Oxford: Clarendon Press, 1964.
________. *The Origins of Muhammadan Jurisprudence*. Oxford: Clarendon Press, 1950.
Schofield, M., M. Burnyeat, and J. Barnes, eds. *Doubt and Dogmatism*. Oxford: Clarendon Press, 1980.
Sellheim, R. *Arabische Handschriften. Materialen zur arabischen Litteraturgeschichte*. Wiesbaden: Steiner 1976.
Sezgin, F. *Geschichte des arabischen Schrifttums*. 8 vols. at present Leiden: E. J. Brill, 1967-.
Shehaby, N. *The Propositional Logic of Avicenna*. Dordrecht: J. Reidel, 1973.
Sheshen, R. *Nawādir al-makhṭūṭāt al-'arabīya fī maktabāt Turkiyā*. 2 vols. at present Beirut: Dār al-Kitāb al-Jadīd, 1975-.
Strack, H. *Introduction to the Talmud and Midrash*. 4th ed. New York: Atheneum, 1978.
al-Ṭabarī, Muḥammad b. Jarīr. *Kitāb Ikhtilāf al-fuqahā'*. Ed. F. Kern. Cairo: Maṭba'at al-Mausū'āt wal-Taraqqī bi-Miṣr, 1902.
Themistius. *Themistii quae fertur in Analyticorum priorum librum I paraphrasis*. Ed. M. Hayduck. *Commentaria in Aristotelem Graeca*. vol. 23, pt. 3 Berlin: G. Reimer, 1884.
Throm, H. *Die Thesis. Rhetorische Studien* 17 (1932) Paderborn: F. Schöningh, 1932.
Toulmin, S. *The Uses of Argument*. Cambridge, England: Cambridge University Press, 1958.
Turki, A. *Polémiques entre Ibn Hazm et Bagi sur les principes de la loi musulmane. Essai sur le littéralisme zahirite et la finalité malikite*. Algiers: Société Nationale d'Édition et de Diffusion, 1976.
al-Ṭūsī, Naṣīr al-Dīn. *Āsās al-iqtibās*. Ed. M. Riẓavī. Tehran: Intishārāt-i Dānishgāh-i Tihrān, 1947.
al-Urmawī, Sirāj al-Dīn. *Maṭāli' al-anwār*. Istanbul: al-Maṭba'a al-Busnawīya, 1303.
van Ess, J. *Das Kitāb al-Nakt_ des Naẓẓām*. Gőttingen: Vandenhoeck & Ruprecht, 1971a.
———. *Der Wesir und seine Gelehrten*. Wiesbaden: Steiner, 1981.
———. *Die Erkenntnislehre des 'Aḍudaddīn al-Īcī*. Weisbaden: Steiner 1966.
———. *Die Gedankenwelt des Ḥārith al-Muḥāsibī*. Bonn: Selbstverlag des Orientalischen Seminars der Universität Bonn, 1961.
———. Frühe Mu'tazilitische Häresiographie: Zwei Werke des Nāshi' al-Akbar. Beirut: Steiner, 1971b.
Volkmann, R. *Die Rhetorik der Griechen und Rőmer*. 2d ed. Leipzig: B. G. Teubner, 1885.
von Grunebaum G., Ed. *Logic in Classical Islamic Culture*. Wiesbaden: Harrasowitz, 1970.
Voss, B. *Der* Dialog in der frühchristlichen Literatur. Munich: W. Fink, 1970.
Walzer, R. *Greek into Arabic*. Oxford: B. Cassirer, 1962.
Wansbrough, J. *The Sectarian Milieu*. Oxford: Oxford University Press, 1978.
Zimmermann, F. *al-Farabi's Commentary and Short Treatise on Aristotle's De Interpretatione*. London: Oxford University Press, 1981.
Ziriklī, Kh. *al-A'lām*. 10 vols. 2nd ed. Cairo: n.p. 1954–59.

C. Articles

Boh, I. "Consequences." *The Cambridge History of Later Medieval Philosophy*. Ed. N. Kretzmann, J. Pinborg, and A. Kenny. Cambridge, England: Cambridge University Press, 1982:

Bardy, J., ed. and trans. "Les trophées de Damas: controverse judéo-chrétienne du VIIe siècle." *Patrologia Orientalis* 15 (1920):

Brunschvig, R. "La théorie du *qiyās* juridique chez le Ḥanafite al-Dabūsī." *Orientalia Hispanica sive studia F. M. Pareja octogenaria dicata*. Ed. J. M. Barral. Lugduni Batavorum: E. J. Brill, 1974: 150–4.

Cook, M. "The origins of kalām." *Bulletin of the School of Oriental and African Studies* 43 (1980): 32–43.

al-Fārābī, "Kitāb al-qiyās al-ṣaghrīr." Ed. M. Türker. *Ankara Üniversitesi Dil ve Tarih-Cografya Fakültesi Dergisi* 16 (1958): 165–286.

________. "Sharā'iṭ al-yaqīn." Ed. M. Küyel-Türkcr. *Arashtirma* 1 (1963b): 151–228.

Gimaret, D. "Un document fondamental pour l'histoire de l'Asharisme." Unpublished paper delivered at Orientalist Congress in Japan, 1983.

Goldziher, I. "Bemerkungen zu Huarts Ausgabe des K. al-Bad' wal-ta'rīch von al-Balchī" *Zeitschrift der Deutschen Morgenländischen Gesellschaft* 54 (1900):

Kenny, A. "Medieval philosophical literature." *The Cambridge History of Later Medieval Philosophy*. Ed. N. Kretzmann, J. Pinborg, and A. Kenny. Cambridge, England: Cambridge University Press, 1982: 11–42.

Long, A. "Aristotle and the History of Greek Scepticism." *Studies in Aristotle*. Ed. D. O'Meara. Washington, D.C.: Catholic University of America Press, 1982: 79–106.

Mahdi, M. "Language and Logic in Classical Islam." *Logic in Classical Islamic Culture*. Ed. G. von Grunebaum. Wiesbaden: Harrasowitz, 1970: .

Makdisi, G. "The Scholastic Method in Medieval Education: An Inquiry into its Origins in Law and Theology." *Speculum* 49 (1974): 640–661.

________. "Dialectic and Disputation. The relation between the texts of Qirqisānī and Ibn 'Aqīl." *Mélanges d'Islamologie, Volume dédié à la mémoire de Armand Abel par ses collègues, ses élèves et ses amis*. ed. P. Salmon. Leiden: E. J. Brill, 1974a: 201–6.

———. "The Tanbīh of Ibn Taimīya on Dialectic." *Medieval and Middle Eastern Studies in Honor of A. S. Atiya*. Ed. S. Hanna. Leiden: E. J. Brill, 1972b: 288–96.

Moraux, P. "La joute dialectique d'après le huitième livre des Topiques." *Aristotle on Dialectic*. Ed. G. Owen. Oxford: Clarendon Press, 1968: 277–311.

Roueche, M. "Byzantine philosophical texts of the seventh centruy." *Jahrbuch der Österreichischen Byzantistik* 23 (1974): 61–76.

Spade, P. "Obligations." *The Cambridge History of Later Medieval Philosophy*. Ed. N. Kretzmann, J. Pinborg, and A. Kenny. Cambridge, England: Cambridge University Press, 1982: 335–41.

Strump, E. "Obligations." *The Cambridge History of Later Medieval Philosophy*. Ed. N. Kretzmann, J. Pinborg, and A. Kenny. Cambridge, England: Cambridge University Press, 1982: 315–334.

Vajda, G. "Autour de la theorie de la connaissance chez Saadia." *Revue des Études Juives* 126 (1967): 135–189; 375–397.

________. "Études sur Qirqisani V." *Revue des Études Juives* 122 (1963c): 7–74.

van Ess, J. "Disputationspraxis in der islamischen Theologie. Eine vorläufige Skizze." *Revue des Études Islamiques* 44 (1976): 23–60.

________. "Ibn al-Rēwandī or the making of an image." *al-Abḥāth* 27 (1978b): 5–26.

———. Review of *Kitāb ikhtilāf al-fuqahā'*, by Al-Qāḍī al-Nu'mān. Ed. S. Lokhandwalla. *Der Islam* 51 (1974b): 300–1.

———. Review of *Kitāb ikhtilāf al-fuqahā'*, . "The Beginnings of Islamic theology." *The Cultural Context of Medieval Learning*. Ed. J. Murdoch and E. Sylla. Dordrecht: J. Reidel, 1975: 87–111.

———. Review of *Kitāb ikhtilāf al-fuqahā'*, . "The Logical Structure of Islamic Theology." *Logic in Classical Islamic Culture*. Ed. G. von Grunebaum. Wiesbaden: Harrasowitz, 1970b: 21–50.

D. Other Sources Consulted in Revision

Allen, Benjamin. "Zeno, Aristotle, the Racetrack and Achilles: A Historical Philosophical Investigation." Ph.D. diss., Rutgers, The State University of New Jersey, 2008.

Pehlivan, Necmettin and Hadi Ensar Ceylan. "Ādābu'l-Baḥs Devrimine Doğru Son Evrim: Burhānuddīn en-Nesefī'nin el-Fuṣūl'ü." *Ankara Üniversitesi İlahiyat Fakültesi Dergisi,* 56:2 (2015): 1–75 (includes an edition of Nasafī's *Fuṣūl*).

Raynaud, Dominique. "Scientific Controversies: A Socio-Historical Perspective on the Advancement of Science [Chapter 5]." Somerset, NJ: Transaction Publishers 2015. Translation of Raynaud, Dominique. « Al-Samarqandī: Un précurseur de l'analyse des controverse scientifiques." *Al- Mukhatabat* 7 (2013): 8–25.

Sharḥ al-qusṭās. Landberg 1035, Ahlwardt 5166 [Digitalisierte Sammlungen der Staatsbibliothek zu Berlin (Preußischer Kulturbesizt): Werkansicht – PPN741370395] http://digital.staatsbibliothek-berlin.de.

Wisnovsky, R. "The nature and scope of Arabic philosophical commentary in post-classical (ca. 1100–1900 AD) Islamic intellectual history: Some preliminary observations." *Philosophy, Science and Exegesis in Greek, Arabic and Latin Commentaries*, ed. P. Adamson, H. Baltussen and M.W.F. Stone. London: 2004, 169–70.

Name Index

A
A'asam, A, 3
'Abd al-Jabbār, b. Aḥmad, al Qāḍī, 9, 17, 23, 54
Abū Ḥaiyān al-Tauḥīdī, 16, 29, 34
Abū l-Hudhayl, 23
Abū l-Ḥusain Muḥammad al-Baṣrī, 54
Abū l-Qāsim al-Balkhī, 3
Ahlwardt, W., 105
Aḥmadnagarī, 'Abd al Nabī, 97
Alexander of Aphrodisias, 14, 15, 22, 23, 30, 35–37, 45
Alexy, R., 119
Allen, B., 113
Altmann, A., 16
Ammonius, 15, 36
Āmulī, Shams al-Dīn, 125
Anawati, G., 79, 92, 104, 106, 108
Arberry, J., 104
Aristotle, 6, 7, 10, 14–16, 22, 23, 25, 26, 29–31, 33–38, 40–44, 52, 74, 91, 94, 99, 101, 103, 106, 109, 112, 115, 117, 118, 125
Ash'arī, Abū l-Ḥasan, 11
'Askarī, Abū Hilāl, 8, 20
Averroes, 29, 31, 34–37, 42, 43, 106
Avicenna, 29–32, 34–37, 40–44, 86, 89, 92, 94, 106, 116, 117
Avicenna, al-Safsaṭa, 43

B
Badawi, A., 7, 8, 16, 22, 26, 30–35, 42, 72, 107
Baghdādī, 'Abd al Qāhir, 2, 6, 11, 24, 51, 52, 107, 114
Baghdatli, I., 3, 104
Bājī, Abū l-Walīd, 1, 2, 48–70, 75, 78, 93, 113
Bāqillānī, 8, 9, 21, 22, 24
Barawī, 72, 73, 85–89, 92, 93
Bardy, J., 5, 23
Barnes, J., 11, 12
Becker, C., 22
Bihishtī al-Isfarā'īnī, 104, 109, 120
Boethius, 37
Boh, I., 80
Brockelmann, C., 48, 73, 76, 84, 89, 94
Brunschvig, R., 53, 55

D
de Rijk, L., 31
Diogenes Laertius, 44

E
Encyclopedia Iranica, 47
Encyclopedia of Men of Science, 104
Eustratius, 101

F
Fārābī, 4, 14, 15, 17, 29–34, 36–44, 106
Frank, R., 11, 112

G
Gerber, U., 29, 31, 33
Gethmann, C., 119
Ghazzālī, 72, 73, 79, 90, 106
Gimaret, D., 4
Goichon, A., 116

L. B. Miller, *Islamic Disputation Theory*, Logic, Argumentation & Reasoning 21,
https://doi.org/10.1007/978-3-030-45012-0

Goldziher, I., 18
Grabmann, M., 29
Gräf, E., 63

H
Ḥājjī Khalīfa, 104
Ḥārith al-Muḥāsibī, 26
Heidegger, 30

I
Ibn ʿAbd al Barr, 2
Ibn al Ḥājib, 73
Ibn al Nadīm, 29
Ibn al-Muqaffaʿ, 7, 14
Ibn al-Rīwandī, 1–5, 10, 11, 13, 16, 18, 26
Ibn ʿAqīl, 48, 50, 54, 56, 60–62, 68, 74, 75, 77
Ibn Fūrak, 4–15, 17–19, 21, 23–26, 48
Ibn Ḥazm, 4–6, 48, 75, 107
Ibn Khaldūn, 1, 75, 108
Ibn Miʿmār, 89–94
Isaac Israeli, 16
ʿĪsawī, A. and M. al Malih, 48, 82

J
Jabre, F., 90
Jacobs, L., 78
Jāhiẓ, 25
Jaunpūrī, ʿAbd al-Rashīd, 126
Jehamy, G., 35, 37
John of Damascus, 14
John Philoponus, 16, 101
Jurjānī, ʿAlī b., 101, 114, 125, 126
Juwaynī, Imām al-Ḥaramain Abū Maʿāli ʿAbd al Malik, 2, 6, 8, 19, 25, 48–75, 88, 93, 110

K
Kaʿbī, 3, 10, 17, 19
Kaḥḥāla, ʿU., 94, 104
Karkhī, 48, 51, 52
Kātib, Isḥāq b. Ibrāhīm, 2, 4–6, 8, 13, 16, 18, 21, 23–26, 35, 51
Kenny, A., 79, 126
Khaṭīb al-Baghdādī, 2, 5, 54, 58, 74, 75, 107
Kholeif, F., 6, 89
Khwārizmī, 29, 80, 81, 97, 98, 101
Kīlānī, 121
Kindī, Yaʿqūb b. Isḥāq, 7, 14, 29
Kneale, W., 79
Kretzmann, N., 79

L
Lane, E., 107
Lausberg, H., 14
Le Blond, J., 35, 38
Long, A., 7
Lorenz, 119
Lorenz, K., 119

M
Mach, R., 109
Mahdi, M., 32, 92
Makdisi, G., 2, 3, 48, 75, 77, 78, 94, 107, 126
Maqdisī, Muṭahhar b. Ṭāhir, 4–13, 17–21, 23, 24
Marwazī, 76, 77
Māturīdī, 3, 6, 16
Migne, J., 22
Mill, J., 78
Moraux, P., 41, 44
Muḥāsibī, al Ḥārith, 26
Muḥyī al-Dīn Jamāl al Islām a. Muḥammad, 92, 93

N
Nasafī, 79–84, 94–101, 103–105, 108, 111–114, 119–122, 126
Nashshār, ʿA., 78
Naṣīr al-Dīn al-Ṭūsī, 43, 101, 106
Naẓẓām, 50, 54
Nuʿmān al-Khwārizmī, 80

P
Pazdawī, Abū al-Yusr Muhammad, 75
Philodemus, 12
Pohlenz, M., 22

Q
Qirqisānī, Yaʿqūb b. Isḥāq, 3, 5, 7, 8, 11–14, 16–21, 23–26, 52, 77
Quintilian, 26

R
Rāzī, Fakhr al-Dīn, 2, 72, 73, 87, 89–91, 93, 101, 106, 117
Rescher, N., 17
Rosenthal, F., 1, 75
Rukn al-Dīn al-ʿAmīdī, 76, 78, 97
Ryun, G., 30

S

Sachau, E., 23
Saiyid, F., 23, 72, 75, 84, 89, 94, 104, 125
Samarqandī, Shams al-Dīn Muḥammad b. Ashraf., 80–83, 95, 98–100, 103–123, 125, 126
Sāwī, ʿUmar b. Sahlān, 104
Schacht, J., 50
Schofield, M., 11, 12, 22
Sellheim, R., 94, 104
Sezgin, F., 3, 4, 20, 52, 54, 55, 77, 104
Shehaby, N., 86
Sheshen, R., 89, 103, 106
Shīrāzī, Abū Isḥāq al, 47, 48, 53, 54, 56, 61, 63–70, 77
Shirwānī al-Rūmī, 120
Spade, P., 126
Strump, E., 126

T

Ṭabarī, Muḥammad b. Jarīr, 21, 48, 55, 56, 65
Taran, L., 15
Tauḥīdī, Abū Ḥaiyān, 16, 29, 34
Themistius, 16, 117
Throm, H., 30, 33, 36, 39
Toulmin, S., 118
Turki, A., 1, 48, 53, 75
Ṭūsī, Naṣīr al-Dīn, 43, 101

U

Urmawī, Sirāj al-Dīn, 94, 106

V

Vajda, G., 3–5, 12–14, 17, 18, 21, 33, 92
van Ess, J., 3–6, 9, 11–13, 15, 18, 20, 21, 25, 26, 35, 37, 50, 53–55, 57, 61, 66, 67, 69, 73, 78, 81, 85, 88, 107, 109, 112
Volkmann, 20, 63
von Grunebaum G., 6, 35, 66, 92
Voss, 5

W

Walzer, R., 31, 39, 106
Wansbrough, J., 22
Wisnovsky, R., 105

Z

Zimmermann, F., 15, 108

Subject Index

A
ādāb, x, 2, 24, 71, 85, 89, 95, 97, 103–105, 107, 114, 117, 119, 123, 125, 126
ādāb al-baḥth, x, 2, 71, 85, 95, 97, 103–105, 107, 109, 114, 119, 123, 125, 126
ādāb al-baḥth wal-munāẓara, 97
adab al-munāẓara, 126
addaba, 5
aḥāla, 23
ʿajz, 21, 23, 115
akhdh al-mūjib bi-ijrā' ʿillatihī, 12
akolouthia, 11
ʿalā al-ḥaqīqa, 7
ʿalā mujarrad al-manʿ, 111
al-ʿamal al-mushtarak, 34
al-muṭālaba bi-wajh al-dalāla, 9
al-nuṭq al-dākhilī, 92
al-sharṭī al-munfaṣil, 87
al-sibr wal-taqsīm, 87
al-sabab al-mūjib, 9
altercatio, 26
altercationis praecepta, 26
amāra, 54, 92, 119–121
amr mushtarak, 34
an yuʿallila wa-lā yujrī, 24
an yuṭāliba bil-dalāla ʿalayhī, 8
antiphaseōs, 15
apodeixis, 101
ʿaql, 6, 20, 22, 120
ʿaqlīya, 117, 119
ʿaqlīyāt, 117
ars obligatoria, 126
aṣḥāb al-manṭiq, 14
aṣl, 5, 53, 58, 60–63, 69, 70, 72, 73, 75
athar, 9, 78, 83, 86
ausāṭ, 115

B
baḥth, 6, 21, 60, 78, 103–105, 107, 109, 110, 112, 114, 123, 126
baiyina, 8
baṣīra, 99, 120
bāṭil, 90, 98
buht, 21
burhān, 4, 12, 31, 33, 35, 49, 51, 78, 87
burhān al khulf, 87

D
dafʿ, 21, 116
dākhil, 121
dalāla, 9, 53, 56, 58, 60, 65–67, 70
dalīl, 8–12, 18, 19, 52–54, 57, 59, 74, 76, 77, 82, 85, 92, 93, 95, 97, 100, 101, 109, 110, 112, 113, 115–117, 119–122
dalīl/madlūl, 100
ḍarūrī, 80
daʿwā, 9, 19
dawarān, 78, 79, 83, 85, 122
dhabb, 44
dhanab, 87
dhauq, 92
dhihnī, 81
duskolainein, 8, 112
duskolia, 22, 112

E
endoxa, 26, 29, 31, 33, 35, 41, 45, 125
enstasis, 32
enteuxeis, 33, 35

L. B. Miller, *Islamic Disputation Theory*, Logic, Argumentation & Reasoning 21,
https://doi.org/10.1007/978-3-030-45012-0

F
faḥṣ, 21, 33–35, 60
fakhwā al-khiṭāb, 53
fann, 86, 126
farʿ, 119
farq, 60, 69, 70
farq (afriq baynahumā), 13
faṣl, 17, 19, 24, 71, 89
fawwaḍa, 37
fīhī baḥth, 107
fīhī naẓar, 107
fikr, 107

G
game (theory), 36
ghair muṭṭarid, 72
ghalaba, 34, 35, 44
ghalabat al-ẓann, 117
ghaṣaba, 95
ghaṣb, 97, 112
gumnasia, 33

H
ḥadd, 4, 11, 74, 107, 109
ḥadd tāmm, 109
ḥādhiq al-mujādil, 25
ḥajr, 14, 37, 51
hastīya, 16
ḥifẓ, 41
ḥikma, 106
ḥīla, 34
ḥissan wa, 22
hoi epistēmonikoi sullogismoi [al-qiyāsāt al-ʿilmīya], 32
ḥukm maqṣūḍ, 67

I
ibṭāl, 44, 90
iḍṭirār, 22
iḍṭirāran, 22
ifḥām, 111
ifsād, 59
iḥkām, 5
iḥrām, 68
ījāb, 34
ijāra, 61
ʿilla tāmma, 121
ʿilm, 2, 9, 21
ʿilm al, 21
iltizām, 92
ilzām, 34, 49, 58, 68, 71, 111
ilzām bil, 49, 58
ilzāmīya, 117
imitiḥān, 32
ʿinād, 112
intahā al-muṭālaba, 7
intiqāl, 20, 23, 56, 74, 96, 97
iqnāʿī, 119
irtibāṭ, 86
istidlāl, 5, 6, 100, 101, 107
istifsār, 73, 116
istikhbār, 8, 12, 18
iṣṭilāḥ ahl al-naẓar wal-uṣuliyīn, 121
istiṣḥāb al-ḥāl, 53
istishhād, 10
iṭbāq, 18
ithbāt, 44, 122, 126
iʿtilāl, 20

J
jadal, vii, ix, 1–6, 8, 10, 14, 16, 17, 19, 24, 26, 27, 29, 30, 33–38, 40, 41, 43–45, 47, 48, 50, 52, 54–58, 60–63, 66, 68, 70, 73–75, 77, 78, 81–94, 96, 101, 106, 110, 113, 115, 117, 118, 125, 126
jadalīyāt, 117
jadalīyūn, 14, 60
jaḥd, 21, 22
jauhar, 38
jawāb, 77
jidāl, 26, 60

K
kalām, 10, 17, 21, 40, 77, 78, 84, 99, 108, 112
kasr, 68, 78
khabaṭ wa-takhlīṭ, 9
khabṭ, 110, 112
khārijī, 81
khaṣm, 65, 70, 95, 116
khilāf, 69, 76, 77, 106, 107, 125
khulf, 87
koinai ennoiai, 22
koinon ergon, 34

L
lāzim, 79, 80
limmīya, 40
luzūm, 81, 100, 117

M
mā al-madhhab, 13
mā yunāfīhī, 113
mā'īya, 16, 40
mā'īyat al madhhab, 8, 12, 49
ma'ānī, 9
mabāḥith, 95, 110
madār, 52, 83
madlūl, 9, 57, 95, 100, 111, 114, 115, 119
maḥkūm bihī, 99
ma'lūl, 118
malzūm, 79, 80
man', 111
ma'nā, 18
ma'nan (pl. ma'ānin), 108
māni', 112, 121
manṭiq, 4, 82, 86, 104
marāsim al-jadal, 60, 91, 107
marātib, 8, 87
martaba, 75
mashhūr, 100, 109
mashrūṭ, 100
maṭlūb, 112, 117
maujūd, 81
mawāḍi', 13
mē dous ta phainomena, 22
metabasis, 23
metalēpsis, 23
methodos kata peritropēn, 20, 63, 65–67
mithl, 113
modus tollens, 79, 86
mu'ānada, 32
mu'āraḍa, 4, 17–20, 24, 113, 121
mubāḥatha, 34
mudāfa'a, 21, 121
mudākhala, 87
mudhdhanib, 87
mufākara, 99
mufakkir, 5
mufarra', 13
mufāwaḍa, 35, 91
mughālaṭa, 15, 17, 94
mughālaṭa wal-inṣāf, 94
mughālaṭāt, 31
muḥāl, 100
muḥaṣṣilūn, 114
muḥāwara, 35, 91
muḥāwarāt irtiyāḍīya, 35
muḥiqq, 34
mujādala, 60, 90, 99, 125
mujārāt, 32
mujīb, 18, 37, 43
mujmal, 51, 66
mukābara, 21, 22, 84, 91, 112
mukābir, 6
mulāzama, 122
mumārī, 31
mumtaḥin, 32
munāqaḍa, 23, 50, 68, 70, 72, 74, 95–97, 101, 112, 121
munāẓara, 16, 21, 33–35, 60, 80, 86–91, 94–99, 105, 107, 120, 125, 126
munāẓarat al jumhūr, 35
Münchausen trilemma, 119
muqābala, 18, 49, 58, 59, 65, 70
musallamāt, 108
mushāghib, 32
mushāghibī, 31
mushāhada, 21, 22
mushārik, 33
mustanad, 111
muṭābaqa, 92
muṭālaba, 9, 12, 58, 59, 61, 64, 72, 109, 110
muṭālaba bi-wajh dalālat al-burhān, 12

N
naqḍ, 23, 44, 60, 67, 68, 72–74, 84, 92, 97, 109, 112, 113, 122
naqḍ ijmālī, 112
naql, 98
naqlīya, 119
naṣṣ, 96, 97
naẓar, 4, 5, 7, 8, 21, 22, 34, 42, 50, 53, 54, 57, 82, 88–90, 99, 100, 104, 107, 121, 125, 126
nihāyat fuṣūl al-naẓar, 9
nuṭq al-dākhilī, 92

P
parapan anaiskhuntein, 22
physikoi, 22
problēma/mas'ala, 31
protologic, 119
pusma, 14
pusmatikē, 15
pusmatikos, 14

Q
qabīḥ/mustadrak, 97
qalb, 50, 60, 63, 65–67, 72, 84, 93, 97, 113
qalb al tafriqa, 66

qalb al-ṣarīḥ, 67
qalb li, 67
qānūn, 86, 91, 94, 106
qānūn al-dīn wal-adab, 94
qānūn al-jadal, 86
qarīna, 67
qaul, 32
qiyās, 7, 10, 17, 31, 53–56, 58, 59, 79, 86, 93
quaesita, 16, 31, 41
quaesitum, 9, 31, 52, 112, 114, 116
quaestiones, 55

R
radduhū ilā naẓīrihī, 7
rasm, 109
ratio legis, 51, 53, 57, 58, 62–65, 67–70, 72, 73, 83, 86
riyāḍa, 33
rukn, 121

S
sabab, 9, 16, 86, 89
sabab al-mūjib, 9
saḥīḥ al-naẓar, 53, 104
sanad, 111
shaghab, 113
sharṭ, 86, 100, 121
shubah, 78
sibr, 87
ṣifa, 10, 51
ṣiḥḥa, 11, 91
ṣiḥḥat al-taʿlīl, 122
ṣināʿat al-jadal, 30
sipūr, 107
sukūt lil, 21
sunodoi/al-mufāwaḍāt al-jadalīya, 34
ṣūrat al-nizāʿ, 110

T
taʿassuf, 8
tabkīt, 41
tabyīn, 90, 122
taḍammun, 92
tadbīr, 114
tadhākur, 107
tafhīm, 38
tafrīʿ, 17
tafṣīl, 114
tafwīḍ, 14, 37
taḥaqquq, 79, 100
taḥrīr, 104, 108, 110
taḥrīr al-mabāḥith, 110
takhāluf, 67, 113
takhyīr, 15, 37
ṭalab al-ʿilla, 13
talāzum, 79–81, 104
taʿlīl, 112, 122
taʿlīq, 86
tamassuk bi, 94
ṭaʿn, 12
tanāfin, 79
tanāquḍ, 99
tanbīh, 113
taqdīr, 52
taqrīb, 4, 114
taqrīr, 37, 108, 110
taqsīm, 65
ṭaraf, 72
tarattub, 122
ṭard, 11, 13, 58, 72, 73
ṭard al-ʿilla, 11, 13
ṭard al-ʿilla fi al-maʿlūl, 11
ṭarīq, 30, 51
ṭarīq al-ḥukm, 51
ṭarīqa, 47, 75, 76, 78, 85, 97, 123
tarkīb, 87
tartīb, 1, 12, 48, 122
tasalsul, 115, 118
taṣḥīḥ, 9, 49, 58, 60, 64, 109, 110
taṣḥīḥ al-burhān, 49
taṣḥīḥ al-ʿilla, 9
taṣḥīḥ al-naql, 98, 109
taslīm, 112
taṣwīr, 38
taswīya, 18, 66
thubūt, 85, 122

U
ʿulūm, 115
ʿulūm al-ẓannīya, 115
umūr mashhūra, 98
uṣūl, 7, 47, 53–55, 60, 67, 69, 73, 78, 84, 85, 90, 92, 108, 120, 121
uṣūl al-fiqh, 47, 48, 53–56, 60, 67, 69, 73, 78, 84, 85, 90, 92, 108, 120, 121

W
wajh, 9, 57
wajh al-taʿalluq, 9
wajh dalālatihī, 9
whatness, 12, 40, 49

wujūd, 24, 100
wujūh, 2, 4, 35, 50, 51, 84

Y
yaḥjuru ʿalā, 14
yaqīn, 32, 54
yuʿāriḍ, 24

Z
zannīyāt, 117

MIX
Papier aus verantwortungsvollen Quellen
Paper from responsible sources
FSC® C105338

If you have any concerns about our products,
you can contact us on
ProductSafety@springernature.com

In case Publisher is established outside the EU,
the EU authorized representative is:
Springer Nature Customer Service Center GmbH
Europaplatz 3, 69115 Heidelberg, Germany

Printed by Libri Plureos GmbH
in Hamburg, Germany